COOKING
with MONA

COOKING
with MONA

THE ORIGINAL *Woodward's* COOKBOOK

MONA BRUN

whitecap

Special thanks to Sheila Peacock for providing a copy of the original 1977 edition of
Cooking with Mona and inspiring this revised edition.

Edited by Elaine Jones
Proofread by Marial Shea
Cover and interior design by Tanya Lloyd Kyi/Spotlight Designs
Cover and interior illustrations by Tom Huntley
Photographs of memorabilia by Regan Paynter
Woodward's memorabilia kindly provided by: Christine Dahlo (breakfast with Santa photo),
Harry Smith (wedding cake photos), Tom Farrell (Australia cake), Wendy Sotvedt (cottage cheese
container, honey container, Bea Wright recipe sheets), Vancouver Museum Collection (pp. 12, 13,
18, 29, 40, 46, 69, 119, 120, 127, 137, 143, 149, 154), City of Vancouver Archives (pp. 88
CVA 99–2063, Stuart Thomson photographer, p. 110 M–11–51, Broadbridge photographer).
All other photographs provided by Mona Brun

Printed and bound in Canda

NATIONAL LIBRARY OF CANADA CATALOGUING IN PUBLICATION DATA
Brun, Mona
    Cooking with Mona : the original Woodward's cookbook / Mona Brun. — Rev. ed.

    Includes index.
    ISBN 1-55285-449-3

    1. Cookery, Canadian. I. Woodward Stores Limited. II. Title.
TX715.6.B79 2003   641.5   C2003-911060-5

The publisher acknowledges the support of the Canada Council and the Cultural Services
Branch of the Government of British Columbia in making this publication possible.
We acknowledge the financial support of the Government of Canada through the Book
Publishing Industry Development Program for our publishing activities.

contents

SOUPS

MEATS

COOKIES, BARS AND SQUARES

PASTRIES AND DESSERTS

LIQUID REFRESHMENTS YOU'VE ALWAYS WANTED TO MAKE

SANDWICHES FOR ALL OCCASIONS

foreword

This cookbook is a revised edition of Mona's first printing, which was a huge success. It was well received because it contained a mix of standard "family-friendly" basics and recipes with a flourish to tantalize the reader.

Mona was doing a weekly show, *Culinary Capers,* when she was booked to appear on my BCTV morning program to promote a special event for Woodward's, which sponsored her. We were sitting on stools behind a desk when Mona said on air, "Jean, where's my tea towel?" I replied, "Mona, you're sitting on it!" That was the first of countless times I would drawl the name Mona out. She was capable of slipping in a comment that had a double meaning! Woodward's liked us together and so did the viewers. She was booked three times a week for Woodward's and once a week for B.C. Foods, for many years.

From the very first we bonded and today we are still the closest of friends. We had the same work ethics: I tried very hard to make sure my segments were as well prepared as possible, and Mona did the same with every recipe. Of course, with a "live" hour, sometimes things didn't go as planned! Mona never talked down to her viewers. She'd say, "I have found this to work for me—if you have another idea, please let me know." Recipes were crew tested, and "Prayer 39" (don't know where that came from) was invoked when unmoulding a jellied salad or upside-down cake!

Our shows together worked for so long because we were believably just two good friends viewers welcomed into their homes. They confirmed this many times in our volumes of mail.

This book will be as welcome as the first edition. What a great honour to write about a good friend's newest endeavour.

—JEAN CANNEM CARLSON, Kelowna, B.C.

It was a Christmas show and Jean and I were the carollers. Guess which one is tone deaf? You're right—me. Jean was so patient!

A FEW OF OUR GROCERY SPECIALS

FOR ONE WEEK commencing THURSDAY, OCTOBER 26th, ending WEDNESDAY, NOVEMBER 1st.

Bread Flour, Robin Hood
49 lb. cotton sack - **$1.29**

Peas, Sieve 5, Sweet Tender
Large tins, 2s, tall - **8½c.**

Mince Meat, for Hallowe'en
Argood, largest tin 4s, tin **32c.**

Tomato Soup
Clark's, tin **6½c.**

**Sugar Crisp Corn
Flakes,** large pkg. **5½c.**

Prepared Mustard
CROSSE AND BLACKWELL'S large jar 9 oz. net **9c.**

Carbolic Soap
Jumbo size, 3 cakes - **10c.**

Corned Beef
Armour's, 1s, tin **10c.**

An early Woodward's grocery ad.

introduction

It has been 15 years since Woodward's Food Floors closed its doors to legions of devoted loyal customers and 25 years since the first publication of *Cooking with Mona*. During this time there have been many changes to food and grocery shopping, meal preparation, ideas of health and nutrition—not to mention us!

When Mona was approached to republish her cookbook, she initially thought there would be little interest in such a project. But as she began mentioning the idea to the many and various individuals, marketing boards, food processors, restaurateurs, gourmands and gourmets who were originally involved in developing some of the recipes with her, she was overwhelmed by their enthusiasm and support. Indeed, even casual references to the reissuing of the cookbook generated numerous memories of Woodward's Food Floors, Bea Wright's kitchen and Mona's TV show *Culinary Capers* (which later became *Creative Cooking*). It would seem that every recipe had, if not its own "story," certainly a unique circumstance that warranted its inclusion in the cookbook.

This new edition will rekindle the Golden Era of the Woodward's Food Floors and transmit a little of that time to those generations not fortunate enough to experience it. The recipes are altered little and include a few new entries from Mona's great-grandson, Alex, and new grandson, Alexander. (At the ages of 6 and 3, respectively, they are already seasoned cooks—we're not sure if it's the genes or Mona's early tutelage that is responsible for this!) May you enjoy the new and improved *Cooking with Mona* as much as Mona, her family, friends and colleagues enjoyed this labour of love.

—SANDY BRUN

An original shopping bag from the Vancouver Museum.

the Woodward's era

Woodward's memories . . .

As a small child, Mona Brun and her mother would take the No. 2 or 3 ferry from their home in North Vancouver, cross Burrard Inlet to downtown Vancouver, then catch a streetcar to Woodward's department store.

As they walked downstairs to the store's basement, Mona would delight in the aroma of peanuts being ground for peanut butter, the sight of doughnuts being cooked and iced and the seemingly endless aisles containing brightly labelled tins of vegetables, fruits, jams and jellies. Little did she know then, in the 1930s, that one day she would become Woodward's famous TV food host and the face of good cooking across the West.

Mona is among generations of British Columbians and Albertans with fond memories of Woodward's.

In 1891 Charles Woodward, a merchant whose Ontario store had burned to the ground, headed west to start a new life for himself and his family. He arrived in Vancouver with his eight children and opened his store in 1892. By 1903 he moved the store into a new building at the corner of Hastings and Abbott streets. That downtown Vancouver store eventually grew to 600,000 square feet and was the first in what would become a 26-store Woodward's empire, the largest retail establishment in Western Canada.

Western families have never quite forgotten what they lost when the Woodward's chain finally went bankrupt in 1993 and all Woodward's stores closed.

Woodward's had been there since Vancouver was just a town with a population of 13,800, and a reel of Coates' thread sold for five cents. It was there through the first worldwide depression of 1913, the First World War, the stock market crash of 1929, the Great Depression of the 1930s, the Second World War and the growing prosperity that characterized the 50s, 60s and 70s.

This commemorative tile was produced for Woodward's 100th anniversary in 1992.

A most successful Woodward's innovation was the monthly one-price sale day. It began in 1910 in the horse-and-buggy days with a 25-cent Day. By 1919 it became a 95-cent Day. By then Woodward's had started selling food in the basement of its downtown Vancouver store. This "groceteria" offered meat, three-pound blocks of butter and other provisions—but not produce. In those days most people grew their own vegetables.

Woodward's introduced another new concept at the end of the First World War—a self-service food floor where customers were allowed for the first time to walk with a cart through aisles to make their own selections.

Despite the stock market crash of 1929 and the ensuing financial disaster to households and businesses across Canada, Woodward's survived. During the Depression, Vancouver customers would bring in their own containers and fill them with Woodward's famous peanut butter for ten cents per pound.

In 1930 Woodward's brought welcome joy to youngsters and their parents with its first Christmas window display—a magical array of mechanized teddy bears, dolls, reindeer and, of course, Santa Claus. The annual display has delighted youngsters and their parents for generations and is still shown at Vancouver's Canada Place each Christmas.

When Charles Woodward died at age 85 in 1937, his son W.C. (Billy) Woodward was appointed president of the company.

The Second World War brought shortages of merchandise. The one-price days had to be discontinued but were revived after the war. Few western Canadians will forget the jingle "$1.49 Day... Tuesday, $1.49 Day...Woodward's," advertised on radio and TV. Mona Brun remembers buying her kids' running shoes and underwear on $1.49 Days.

Postwar, Canadians enjoyed an economic boom. Woodward's downtown bakery department added ovens and produced 25,000 loaves of bread a day. In 1950, Park Royal, Canada's first shopping centre, opened in West Vancouver with Woodward's as an anchor tenant.

Woodward's became known for its fabulous selection and exotic treats. It offered 160 varieties of cheese from 13 different countries, 30 varieties

Mona on the set at ITV with her daughter, Maureen.

of bread, specialties such as snails from France, rattlesnake meat from Florida and pappadams from India. It would fill the special requests of customers, even blending tea to individual customers' tastes.

In 1957, the founder's grandson Charles (Chunky) became president and chief executive officer. During his 32 years at the helm, Chunky accelerated the expansion, adding 21 more department stores in B.C. and Alberta.

Meanwhile, Mona Brun was doing a little expanding of her own. She married in 1945, raised four children and at age 40 returned to working outside the home. She began by doing food demonstrations for Dairyland. That led to a regular segment on CBC Radio's *Food Facts* program in 1960.

Never camera-shy, Mona moved to CBC-TV's *Cuisine 30 Show,* where she made a name for herself, apparently unfazed by having to perform before a live TV audience. Easily able to cook and talk at the same time, Mona entertained viewers with her natural sense of humour. Mona says she gained a lot of her inspiration from "Mère," her French mother-in-law.

By 1963 Woodward's asked Mona to audition for its *Culinary Capers* TV show, which later became the *Jean Cannem Show.* When that show ended in the late 1970s, Woodward's sent Mona to Edmonton to do her own CTV show—*Creative Home Cooking,* which later became the *Dining Inn* show.

Woodward's cooking shows lasted in various forms for 23 years. Mona Brun became the familiar face of good cooking to thousands of western Canadian women who cooked and raised kids during the 60s, 70s and 80s.

Woodward's continued to expand, adding an in-house homemaking centre to its downtown store. The Bea Wright kitchen offered recipes, contests and culinary advice to customers in all Woodward's stores. (Bea Wright, by the way, was a take-off on—what else—Be Right!) In 1974 net sales of Woodward's topped $500 million.

In response to viewers' and customers' requests, in 1977 Mona came out with the first *Cooking with Mona* cookbook. She made sure that her recipes and menus were tasty, nourishing, economical and easy to make. And they've stood the test of time with

"Over 500 Recipes before metrics"

The original *Cooking with Mona* cookbook, published in 1977.

today's busy families. Mona's Hungarian Goulash is one of her most popular, as is Hale and Hearty Hamburger Soup.

In 1981, Mona Brun was a judge in the Woodward's Royal Wedding Cake Classic in which Woodward's bakers competed to send their own special cake to England for presentation at Buckingham Palace. (See page 135 for photos.) Bakers Harry Smith and Bob Miller won the contest. Their 69-pound cake, complete with nine royal crests sketched in icing, had a seat of its own on Air Canada and highlighted the Royal Wedding Breakfast Reception for Prince Charles and Lady Diana Spencer.

But the 1980s were characterized by major economic turmoil in the Canadian retail industry. In 1987 Woodward's reported its first annual loss since it became a public company in the 1950s.

Chunky Woodward tried to stem the flow by selling off the department store's popular and lucrative Food Floor operations to competitor Canada

Safeway Ltd. That may have been the wrong move: 1990 saw Woodward's suffer a loss of $59 million. Chunky Woodward died that year, and three years later the chain was bankrupt.

The days of Woodward's will never be forgotten. Today, when some supermarkets appear to consider customers mere necessary nuisances, it's easy to see why so much nostalgia surrounds Woodward's.

Those were the days of real food and superb customer service. And of Mona Brun, who was, and still is, an icon for many Canadian families.

—KATHY TAIT

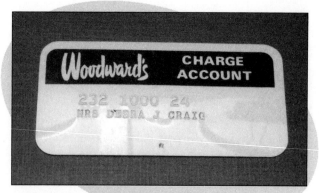

A Woodward's charge card, now in the Vancouver Museum Collection.

appetizers, snacks and dips

mona says . . .

- Before-dinner appetizers, whether delicate or hearty, are meant to whet the appetite, not to satisfy it. Plan them to complement the meal ahead—casual for casual dinners, elegant for formal dinners. When making appetizers, do not use the same ingredients you will be serving at dinner.

- At cocktail parties people usually eat a great many appetizers, tending to treat them as a light supper. Plan, therefore, not only on more appetizers, but also on more substantial ones.

- Always serve hot appetizers piping hot and cold ones icy cold. It's preferable to have fewer varieties, being careful not to duplicate flavours. Whenever possible use edible garnishes. Use plenty of attractively cut vegetables to set off the hors d'oeuvre. Provide small plates with forks if food cannot easily be eaten with the fingers. Replenishing several small platters is much easier than replenishing one large one.

TRY OUT ONE OF THESE IDEAS

- **Vegetable tray:** Select your vegetables and arrange them on platters near a bowl of your favourite dip. Use cauliflower florets, strips of green or red or orange peppers, onion rings, carrot sticks, whole mushrooms, tomato wedges, celery sticks, green onion sticks or cucumber sticks.

- **Prickly cabbage:** Select a good-sized head of cabbage and stud it with toothpicks. Place it on a bed of parsley on a platter and gently push a variety of foods onto the toothpicks. Use several varieties of cubed cheeses; cubed meats such as salami, summer sausage, beer sausage or garlic sausage; whole cherry tomatoes; black olives or pimiento-stuffed green olives; chunks of dill pickle; tinned water chestnuts. Do not choose food that dries out quickly or food with juices that drip.

Here are a few ideas for appetizers served well-chilled on skewers.

- pieces of ham or bacon with gherkins
- squares of cheese with green onions
- cubes of turkey with radish slices and squares of green peppers
- sour onions with cocktail sausages and gherkins
- dill pickle chunks with corned beef cubes
- cubes of tongue or ham with thin slices of carrot
- cucumber slices with shrimp and halved cherry tomatoes
- drained tinned smoked oysters with water chestnuts and green onion pieces

CRAB ASPARAGUS ROLLUPS

6 to 8 oz. crabmeat (fresh or canned)
1 Tbsp. lemon juice
$\frac{1}{2}$ cup diced celery
2 green onions, finely chopped
$\frac{1}{4}$ tsp. salt
$\frac{1}{8}$ tsp. pepper
$\frac{1}{8}$ tsp. dried tarragon
$\frac{1}{4}$ tsp. Worcestershire sauce
$\frac{1}{2}$ cup sharp Cheddar cheese, grated
2 Tbsp. mayonnaise
24 stalks asparagus (frozen, canned or fresh)
1 $\frac{1}{2}$ packages refrigerated crescent
   dinner rolls

Preheat oven to 375°F. Break up crabmeat. Drain if canned. Combine crab, lemon juice, celery, green onions, salt, pepper, tarragon, Worcestershire sauce, cheese and mayonnaise. If frozen or fresh asparagus is used, cook until just tender. Drain well if canned asparagus is used. Place a spoonful of crab mixture and 2 stalks of asparagus on each individual triangle of dough. Roll from shortest side of triangle into crescent shape and place with point down on ungreased cookie sheet. Bake for 10 to 12 minutes, or until golden brown. An excellent dish for bridge parties, luncheons, showers, etc. *Makes 12 rollups.*

APPETIZER MEATBALLS

2 lbs. lean ground pork
1 egg, well beaten
$\frac{1}{4}$ cup tomato paste
2 cups dry bread crumbs
1 tsp. salt
$\frac{1}{2}$ tsp. pepper
$\frac{1}{2}$ tsp. dried oregano
1 tsp. dried basil
1 recipe Barbecue Sauce

Combine pork, egg, tomato paste, bread crumbs and seasonings. Shape into bite-size balls. Brown in hot skillet. Pour off drippings and add barbecue sauce to skillet. Simmer until meatballs are tender and sauce is thickened, about 1 hour. *Makes 50 appetizers.*

Barbecue Sauce
1 Tbsp. salad oil
$\frac{3}{4}$ cup finely minced onion
1 beef bouillon cube
1 cup boiling water
$\frac{2}{3}$ cup ketchup
$\frac{2}{3}$ cup vinegar
$\frac{1}{2}$ cup brown sugar
2 Tbsp. cornstarch
2 tsp. dry mustard
$\frac{1}{2}$ tsp. garlic salt

Heat oil in skillet and sauté onion until transparent. Dissolve bouillon cube in boiling water; stir into skillet. Add remaining ingredients. Cover and simmer for 20 minutes. Will keep in the refrigerator for up to 1 week. *Makes 2$\frac{1}{2}$ cups.*

SALMON PANCAKE APPETIZERS

FOR THE FILLING:
1 can (7$\frac{1}{2}$ oz.) salmon
4 tsp. butter
4 tsp. all-purpose flour
$\frac{1}{4}$ tsp. curry powder, or to taste
$\frac{1}{4}$ tsp. salt
$\frac{1}{2}$ cup milk
2 Tbsp. butter
$\frac{1}{2}$ lb. fresh mushrooms, chopped
1 large onion, chopped
salt and pepper to taste

Drain and mash salmon (reserving juice for use in fish stock, soups, etc.). Melt the 4 tsp. butter; add flour, curry powder and salt. Blend. Add milk gradually. Cook and stir until sauce becomes bubbly. Remove from heat; set aside.

Melt the 2 Tbsp. butter in skillet. Add mushrooms and onion; cook until onions are tender and mushroom juices evaporated. Add sauce and salmon. Cook for 2 to 3 minutes longer. Season with salt and pepper.

FOR THE PANCAKE WRAPPERS:

1 cup packaged pancake mix

1/2 cup milk (extra)

2 Tbsp. butter

Preheat oven to 350°F. Prepare pancakes according to package directions for 1 cup mix, using 1/2 cup extra milk. Cook over medium-high heat in lightly oiled skillet, using 1 Tbsp. of batter for each tiny pancake and cooking both sides.

Place approximately 1 tsp. of salmon filling in middle of each cooked pancake; roll up and place seam side down in buttered casserole dish. Melt the 2 Tbsp. butter and drizzle over top of pancake rolls. Bake, uncovered, for 15 minutes. *Makes approximately 40 tiny pancakes.*

Note: Pancakes may be prepared and filled ahead and refrigerated for several hours. Increase baking time to 25 minutes.

SALMON CHEESE PÂTÉ

1 can (7 1/2 oz.) salmon, well drained

1 package (8 oz.) cream cheese, softened

1/4 cup blue cheese, crumbled

2 Tbsp. grated Parmesan cheese

2 Tbsp. grated onion

1 Tbsp. chopped fresh parsley

1 1/2 Tbsp. finely chopped celery

1 Tbsp. lemon juice

1 tsp. Worcestershire sauce

1/2 small clove garlic, crushed (optional)

pinch freshly ground black pepper

fresh parsley sprigs, for garnish

Drain salmon thoroughly. Set aside. Blend cream cheese, blue cheese and Parmesan cheese together until smooth. Stir in drained salmon, onion, parsley, celery, lemon juice and Worcestershire sauce. Add garlic, if desired, and sprinkle with pepper. Stir until all ingredients are well combined. Line a small bowl with plastic wrap. Place mixture in bowl and pat down. Chill for several hours. Unmould. To serve, garnish with parsley sprigs. Serve with melba toast, crackers,

toast rounds or thin slices of rye bread. *Serves 10 to 12.*

Note: Salmon Cheese Pâté is a delicious stuffing for celery sticks or hollowed cherry tomatoes. You can also use it to stuff mushrooms; broil until bubbly.

DANISH CAMEMBERT LAYER

1 round Camembert cheese

4 oz. cream cheese

1 Tbsp. dry sherry

2 Tbsp. sliced almonds

2 Tbsp. pitted sliced grapes

With sharp knife, cut cheese in half horizontally, forming 2 round layers. In small bowl, blend cream cheese with sherry to soften; add almonds and grapes. Reserve 1 Tbsp. cream cheese mixture for garnish and spread remainder on bottom layer of cheese. Carefully place top layer on filling. Garnish with reserved cream cheese mixture in centre on top. Add a few more almond and grape slices, if desired, as garnish. A great hors d'oeuvre! *Serves 6 to 8.*

SMOKED OYSTER SPREAD

1 can (3 2/3 oz.) smoked oysters, drained and finely chopped

1 tsp. lemon juice

1 green onion, finely chopped

1 Tbsp. mayonnaise

2 tsp. chili sauce

1 Tbsp. chopped fresh parsley

1/4 tsp. dry mustard

pinch pepper

dash Worcestershire sauce

chopped fresh parsley or halved pimiento-stuffed green olives (optional)

In small bowl, thoroughly combine oysters, lemon juice, green onion, mayonnaise, chili sauce, parsley, mustard, pepper and Worcestershire sauce. Cover; chill for several hours. Spread over crackers. Garnish with parsley or olive halves, if desired. *Serves 6.*

CHEESE PORCUPINE

A delicious, eye-catching addition to any party.

4 oz. blue cheese
1 package (8 oz.) cream cheese
1 lb. sharp Cheddar cheese, shredded
1 Tbsp. minced onion
1 tsp. Worcestershire sauce
$1/2$ cup finely chopped walnuts
1 Tbsp. finely chopped fresh parsley
pepper to taste
paprika
pimiento-stuffed green olives, for garnish

Soften cheeses at room temperature. Cream well. Add onion, Worcestershire sauce, walnuts, parsley and pepper. Combine thoroughly. On waxed paper form mixture into oval shape. Refrigerate for several hours. Roll in paprika. Allow to stand at room temperature for $1/2$ hour before serving. To garnish, spear olives on toothpicks and stick on porcupine for "quills." Serve with variety of crisp crackers. *Serves 6 to 8.*

OLIVE CHEESE BALLS

1 cup finely grated Cheddar cheese
$1/4$ cup softened butter or margarine
$1/2$ cup all-purpose flour
pinch salt
$1/2$ tsp. paprika
24 pimiento-stuffed green olives

Preheat oven to 400°F. Blend cheese with butter. Add flour, salt and paprika. Mix well. Mould about 1 tsp. of dough around each olive, covering it completely. Bake for approximately 10 minutes or until golden brown. Either serve immediately or cool and reheat in preheated 300°F oven for 7 to 8 minutes. *Makes 24 cheese balls.*

CHEDDAR PUFFS

$1/2$ cup butter
1 cup grated sharp Cheddar cheese
$1 1/4$ cups sifted all-purpose flour
$1/4$ tsp. salt

Preheat oven to 400°F. In a medium-sized bowl, cream butter with cheese until smooth. Blend in flour and salt. Knead lightly with hands to form soft dough. Roll 1 tsp. at a time into small balls. Place on greased cookie sheet. Bake for 12 minutes or until golden. Serve hot. *Makes approximately 3 dozen.*

MOON ROCKS

A zippy, dippy appetizer that is addictive. This recipe comes to us from Lois Cutler, host of the Kamloops television show Let's Visit Awhile. *I was regularly invited as a special guest on her show, and helped introduce the Woodward's Food Floor to her viewers.*

1 generous cup hot Italian sausage squeezed out
   of casing
$1/2$ lb. sharp Cheddar cheese, grated
$1 1/2$ cups buttermilk baking mix (such as Bisquick)

Preheat the oven to 350°F. Using your hands, mix the sausage, cheese and baking mix together. Roll into bite-size balls. Bake for 12 to 15 minutes until golden brown.

Serve with Mustard Dipping Sauce.

Mustard Dipping Sauce

$1/4$ cup white vinegar
$1/2$ cup dry mustard
$1/4$ cup sugar
1 egg
$1/4$ cup mayonnaise

Mix the vinegar and mustard well. Let rest for 30 minutes. Beat the sugar and egg into the mixture. Cook over medium heat until thick. Cool. Whisk in the mayonnaise. *Makes 5 dozen small servings.*

I first met Mona in the 1960s while hosting a daily television show, *Let's Visit Awhile*. She introduced "the Food Floor" to my audience and because Woodward's was the show sponsor it was appropriate we work together often. As the years passed and *Carefree Cooking* was created, Mona's regular appearances were highlights of each year. She is a great cook but a better friend.

—Lois Cutler

SCANDINAVIAN STUFFED EGGS
A great smorgasbord dish.

6 hard-cooked eggs
4 oz. fresh or canned smoked salmon, finely chopped
$1/4$ cup mayonnaise
2 tsp. prepared mustard
2 tsp. chopped fresh parsley
$1/4$ tsp. salt, or to taste
pinch pepper
pitted black olives, drained
1 pimiento, cut into thin strips

Halve eggs lengthwise with a sharp knife. Carefully remove yolks and place in a small bowl. Set egg whites aside. Mash yolks. Add salmon, mayonnaise, mustard, parsley, salt and pepper. Combine well. Fill whites with yolk mixture, mounding it high (or use a decorator bag). Garnish with pieces of olive and pimiento strips. Refrigerate, covered, for at least 2 hours before serving. *Makes 12 stuffed eggs.*

ROSY PICKLED EGGS

1 cup juice from canned pickled beets
1 cup vinegar
4 cups water
1 clove garlic
1 medium bay leaf
2 tsp. mixed pickling spice
$1/2$ tsp. salt
12 hard-cooked eggs, shelled
1 small onion, sliced and separated into rings

Combine beet juice, vinegar, water, garlic, bay leaf, pickling spices and salt in a large bowl or jar. Mix well. Add eggs and onion rings. Cover and refrigerate for several days. *Makes 12 eggs.*

ANTIPASTO SALAD
A tasty, colourful dish for holiday entertaining.

1 head romaine lettuce
1 can (14 oz.) garbanzo beans
1 recipe Zippy Parmesan Dressing (page 38)
1 small cantaloupe
$1/4$ cup pitted ripe olives, halved
1 green pepper, halved, seeded and sliced into rings
1 red pepper, halved, seeded and sliced into rings
$1/2$ cup fresh sliced mushrooms
Parmesan cheese (optional)

Several hours before serving, wash lettuce and dry well. Tear into bite-sized pieces and refrigerate in plastic bag. Drain beans and place in small bowl. Combine with $1/3$ cup Zippy Parmesan Dressing; cover and refrigerate for at least 1 hour.

Just before serving, line long, shallow platter that has curved sides with romaine lettuce. Halve, seed and peel cantaloupe. Cut into thin slices and halve slices. Arrange beans, cantaloupe, olives, green and red pepper and mushrooms attractively over romaine lettuce. Sprinkle with Parmesan cheese, if desired. Serve remaining dressing separately. *Serves 12.*

Note: For a smaller group, this recipe can easily be halved.

A Woodward's recipe sheet from the 1950s offers helpful hints on hosting a fondue party.

CRISPY FRENCH-FRIED ONION RINGS

A favourite of James Beard.

> 4 to 5 large onions
> ice water
> 1 ½ to 1 ¾ cups all-purpose flour
> 1 tsp. salt
> ¾ tsp. baking soda
> 2 eggs
> 1 ½ to 2 cups buttermilk
> oil for deep frying, heated to 375 °F

Slice onions ¼ inch thick. Soak in ice water for 1 hour (this is essential for crisp results). Sift together flour, salt and baking soda. Combine with eggs and buttermilk to make a batter.

Dry onions thoroughly; dip in batter. Deep-fry several at a time in preheated oil until crisp and brown. Drain on absorbent paper. Keep onions hot by placing in preheated 275 °F oven while cooking remaining onions. Serve hot and crisp. *Serves 4.*

Note: Batter is excellent for cheese or poultry fondues.

CHEESE FONDUE

The memories of Erwin Doebeli, his charming wife, Josette, and the William Tell Restaurant are very special to me. Erwin was a strong supporter of Woodward's adventure in foods and I was very fortunate to have the opportunity to work with him. Just recently I enjoyed an evening at the restaurant and was able to introduce the third generation of my family to fondue. They were sold—hook, line and sinker. Erwin very kindly permitted me to pass his recipe on to you.

> 1 clove garlic, cut in half
> 1 clove garlic, finely minced
> ⅞ cup dry white wine
> ½ lb. grated Swiss Gruyère
> ⅓ lb. grated Swiss Emmentaler
> pinch ground black pepper
> pinch ground nutmeg
> 1 tsp. cornstarch
> 2 tsp. Kirsch
> approximately 1 lb. cubed crusty French bread

Rub pan with garlic halves. On medium heat combine finely chopped garlic with wine. Stir in grated cheese gradually until completely melted. Mix pepper, nutmeg and cornstarch together. Combine with Kirsch, add to fondue and continue stirring until smooth and bubbly.

Use fondue forks to dip crusty bread into melted cheese mixture. *Serves 2.*

Erwin Doebeli doing a television show with Laurier LaPierre. The young boy is Erwin's son and is now the manager of the Bistro at the William Tell Restaurant.

BEER-CHEDDAR FONDUE

1 lb. shredded sharp Cheddar cheese
1/2 cup beer
1 clove garlic, crushed
2 tsp. Worcestershire sauce
1/2 tsp. dry mustard
dash hot pepper sauce (such as Tabasco)
1 Tbsp. cornstarch
2 Tbsp. water
French bread, cubed

Have cheese at room temperature. With electric mixer, beat cheese at low speed until blended; gradually add beer, mixing at medium speed until mixture is light and fluffy. Add garlic, Worcestershire sauce, mustard and hot sauce. Beat thoroughly to distribute seasonings. Place mixture in fondue pot and place on stovetop to melt. Blend cornstarch and water; add to fondue. Cook, stirring constantly, until mixture is thickened and bubbly. Transfer fondue pot from stove to fondue burner. Spear bread cubes with fondue forks and dip into melted cheese. *Serves 4 to 6.*

ZIPPY TOMATO-CUCUMBER JUICE

2 cups tomato juice
1 cucumber, peeled, seeded and grated
1 Tbsp. vinegar
2 Tbsp. salad oil
pinch paprika
1/2 tsp. salt
1/4 tsp. dried basil
dash Worcestershire sauce
pinch freshly ground black pepper
1/2 cup cracked ice
chopped fresh parsley and lemon slices, for garnish
  (optional)

Combine juice, cucumber, vinegar, salad oil, paprika, salt, basil and Worcestershire sauce in shaker. Sprinkle with pepper. Shake well. Allow to chill. Just before serving add cracked ice. Pour into glasses and garnish with parsley and lemon slices, if desired. *Serves 4.*

  Note: This recipe can easily be doubled.

CRÊPES WITH CREAMED SEAFOOD

FOR THE BATTER:
1/2 cup cold water
3 eggs
1/2 tsp. salt
1 1/2 cups sifted all-purpose flour
3 Tbsp. melted butter or margarine
oil for frying crêpes

Combine all batter ingredients in blender; whirl for about 1 minute. Refrigerate for at least 1 hour.

  Coat a 7- to 8-inch skillet with oil. Heat over medium-high heat just until it begins to smoke. Pour 3 Tbsp. of batter into pan. Quickly tilt pan to cover bottom with thin layer of batter. Cook crêpe for about 1 minute until brown; turn over and cook other side for about 1/2 minute. Remove to plate. Continue same method for remaining crêpes; stack crêpes with sheet of waxed paper between each. *Makes about 12 crêpes.*

FOR THE FILLING:
2 cups hot medium cream sauce*
2 Tbsp. dry sherry or Sauternes
1/2 cup grated Swiss cheese
2 cups shellfish meat, fresh or canned
3 Tbsp. chopped green onions
salt and pepper to taste
additional grated Swiss cheese, for topping

Preheat oven to 425°F. Combine cream sauce, sherry or Sauternes and cheese. Blend half of the sauce with seafood and scallions; add salt and pepper. Place a large spoonful on each crêpe. Roll up and place in baking dish. Pour remaining sauce over top. Sprinkle with additional grated cheese. Bake for about 15 minutes, until hot and browned. *Serves 6.*

  *Make your own favourite medium cream sauce.

BROILED OYSTERS ON THE HALF SHELL

36 oysters, shucked and drained
1/2 tsp. salt
1/8 tsp. pepper
1/2 cup bread crumbs
2 Tbsp. melted butter

Place oysters on deep half of shells. Sprinkle with salt and pepper. Combine bread crumbs with melted butter and sprinkle over oysters. Place oysters on broiler pan about 3 inches from heat and broil 5 minutes, or until brown. *Serves 6.*

MUSHROOM LOGS

2 Tbsp. butter
1 cup fresh mushrooms, finely chopped
1 green onion, minced
1/4 tsp. dried tarragon
1 tsp. cornstarch
1/2 tsp. salt
1/4 cup light cream
1/4 cup dry sherry
16 thin slices bread
butter for bread

Preheat oven to 400°F. In saucepan, melt butter; add mushrooms, green onion and tarragon. Cook over medium heat for 3 minutes, stirring frequently. Remove pan from heat. Add cornstarch and salt; stir until well mixed. Add cream and sherry; cook, stirring constantly, until thick and creamy.

Remove crusts from bread slices; butter slices lightly. Spread with mushroom mixture. Roll bread slices, as tightly as possible, jelly roll fashion. Secure with toothpick and place logs side by side in cake pan. Bake for 15 to 20 minutes or until golden brown. These freeze very well uncooked. To serve, bake unthawed as above (will take longer than for fresh). *Makes 16 logs.*

MUSHROOMS AND OYSTERS

This recipe was given to me by a very dear friend, the late Muriel Downes, M.B.E., Co-director of the Cordon Bleu Cookery school in London, England.

FOR THE MORNAY SAUCE:
4 tbsp butter
3 Tbsp. all-purpose flour
2 cups milk
3/4 cup grated sharp Cheddar cheese, or for a special party, use 1/2 Gruyère and 1/2 Parmesan cheese

Melt butter. Blend in flour. Gradually add milk. Cook, stirring all the time until mixture thickens. Do not overcook. Fold in grated cheese.

FOR THE TOPPING:
2 Tbsp. grated Parmesan cheese
1 Tbsp. browned crumbs
2 Tbsp. melted butter

Combine well.

1 to 1 1/2 lbs. fresh mushrooms
6 Tbsp. fresh white bread crumbs
2 Tbsp. melted butter
2 egg yolks
3 Tbsp. light cream
1 Tbsp. chopped fresh parsley
1 Tbsp. snipped chives
1 clove garlic, crushed with 1/2 tsp. salt
6 to 12 fresh oysters (1 to 2 per shell, as desired)

Preheat oven to 425°F. Wash mushrooms, removing stems from 12 to 18 of them (2 to 3 caps per person). Chop remaining mushrooms and stalks. Add crumbs and then butter, egg yolks and cream. Mix in parsley, chives, garlic and salt. Fill mushroom caps with herb mixture. Arrange in buttered shells with oysters. Coat with Mornay Sauce; sprinkle with cheese-crumb topping. Bake for 12 to 15 minutes. *Serves 6.*

BLUE CHEESE STUFFED MUSHROOMS

12 to 15 large fresh mushrooms
¼ cup butter or margarine
¼ cup chopped green onions
2 Tbsp. crumbled blue cheese
4 Tbsp. fine dry bread crumbs
salt and pepper to taste

Preheat oven to 350°F. Wash mushrooms; dry well. Remove and chop stems. Melt butter in skillet and gently sauté chopped stems and green onions until tender, about 5 minutes. Add cheese, 3 Tbsp. of the bread crumbs, salt and pepper. Combine well. Fill mushroom caps with mixture; sprinkle with remaining 1 Tbsp. bread crumbs. Place on baking sheet and bake for 12 minutes or until piping hot. *Serves 4 to 6.*

MUSHROOMS A LA GRECQUE

1½ lbs. small fresh mushrooms
⅓ cup olive oil
2 Tbsp. wine vinegar
1 clove garlic, finely chopped
½ tsp. salt
½ tsp. pepper
2 sprigs fresh parsley
pinch dried thyme or dried oregano
1 cup water

Wash mushrooms quickly in cold water or wipe with damp cloth. Trim off tips of stems. In saucepan, blend together remaining ingredients. Cook to boiling point, about 3 minutes. Reduce heat and cook gently for 5 minutes. Add mushrooms and continue cooking over low heat for another 5 minutes. Chill mushrooms in the cooking liquid. Drain just before serving. Serve as a relish with meat or as an hors d'oeuvre. *Serves 6 to 8.*

GUACAMOLE

2 medium ripe avocados
1 Tbsp. lemon juice
2 medium tomatoes, peeled and finely chopped
1 cup finely chopped onion
1½ tsp. seasoning salt
½ tsp. seasoning pepper

Peel avocados; add lemon juice and mash well with a fork or process in blender. Add remaining ingredients. Combine thoroughly. Serve with warm broken taco shells or corn chips. *Makes about 3 cups.*

  Note: If a creamier consistency is desired, add mayonnaise or sour cream.

Shown here conjuring Mona, this bear was a familiar symbol on the Woodward's recipe sheets.

Woodward's offered its own line of products, including cottage cheese.

WHIPPED CHEESE DIP

$\frac{1}{2}$ cup shredded sharp Cheddar cheese
$\frac{1}{2}$ cup crumbled blue cheese
2 Tbsp. grated Parmesan cheese
$\frac{1}{2}$ cup cottage cheese
$\frac{1}{4}$ cup sour cream
2 tsp. grated onion
$\frac{1}{2}$ to 1 tsp. Worcestershire sauce

Combine all the cheeses. Allow to come to room temperature. Beat with electric mixer until mixture is smooth and creamy. Add sour cream, onion and Worcestershire sauce. Beat until fluffy. Chill thoroughly. Serve with crackers, chips or raw fresh vegetables. *Makes about 1 $\frac{1}{3}$ cups.*

FLUFFY DANISH BLUE DIP

2 cups Danish blue cheese, crumbled and firmly packed
$\frac{3}{4}$ cup whipping cream
3 Tbsp. sherry

In mixing bowl, blend together blue cheese, $\frac{1}{4}$ cup of the whipping cream and sherry. Beat until light and creamy. Whip remaining $\frac{1}{2}$ cup whipping cream until soft peaks form; gently fold into blue cheese mixture. Chill for at least 1 hour to let flavours blend. Serve with chips. Also delicious as a dip with favourite fruits. *Makes about 3 cups.*

SEASONED AVOCADO-TOMATO DIP

2 cups sour cream
1 package dehydrated onion soup mix
$\frac{1}{2}$ tsp. ground cumin (optional)
1 avocado, peeled, pitted and finely chopped
1 tomato, peeled, finely chopped and drained

In bowl, combine all ingredients. Cover and chill thoroughly. Serve with corn chips, potato chips or raw vegetable dippers. *Makes about 3 cups.*

Note: To vary this dip, omit the chopped tomato.

FROSTED FRUIT

Try frosting fruit to garnish appetizer trays, to decorate fruitcakes or steamed puddings, to garnish turkey, ham or game, or as a table centrepiece. It's easily done and yields eye-catching results. Use lemons, limes, seedless green grapes, Concord or Tokay grapes—the fruit of your choice. Wash the fruit well and pat it thoroughly dry. The number of egg whites and the amount of sugar will vary with the amount of fruit to be frosted. Use 2 lightly beaten egg whites for 3 lemons, 3 limes, $\frac{1}{2}$ lb. each of green and Concord grapes. Dip the fruit into the egg whites, or brush fruit with egg whites, and then sprinkle with superfine granulated sugar. Allow the fruit to dry on wire racks until the coating is firm.

salads and dressings

- All ingredients should be fresh, clean, dry and well chilled ahead of time. Chill your salad plates and bowls as well.
- Aim for variety in greens. Combine different types of lettuce: romaine, Boston, bibb, leaf or endive in addition to iceberg.
- Tear lettuce; do not cut it.
- When making dressing, choose a good salad oil or olive oil.
- Prepare salad ingredients in generous portions, with attention to variety in colour, shape and texture.
- A chef's flavour trick is to sprinkle salt lightly into a wooden salad bowl and rub the inside of the bowl thoroughly with a cut clove of garlic.
- Toss ingredients. Never stir.
- Before storing salad greens, discard any wilted or discoloured leaves. Shower the greens with cold water but don't soak; drain well and dry very carefully. Store in a plastic bag in the crisper.
- To prevent dressing from becoming diluted, add cut-up tomatoes just before serving.
- The terms chop, dice and mince have different meanings. To chop is to cut food into pieces about the size of peas. To dice is to cut into small cubes of uniform size and shape. To mince means to chop very finely.
- To peel potatoes for a hot salad, use the point of a knife to score raw potatoes around their middles and then cook them in boiling, salted water until tender. Spear the potatoes with a fork in the score mark and peel.

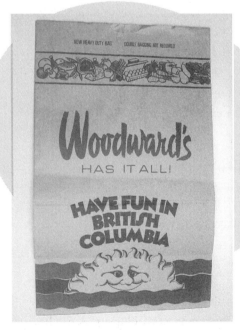

A Woodward's grocery bag promoting British Columbia.

TURKEY MUSHROOM SALAD

2 cups cooked, cubed turkey

1 cup sliced fresh mushrooms

¾ cup chopped celery

¼ cup diced green pepper

¼ cup thinly sliced radishes

2 Tbsp. sliced pimiento

¼ cup stuffed green olives, sliced (optional)

⅓ cup mayonnaise or salad dressing

1 Tbsp. lemon juice

2 tsp. very finely chopped onion

romaine lettuce leaves

freshly cracked black pepper to taste

chopped fresh parsley

1 medium tomato, cut into thin wedges

In bowl, lightly combine turkey, mushrooms, celery, green pepper, radishes, pimiento and olives. In separate small bowl, combine mayonnaise or salad dressing, lemon juice and onion. Add to turkey mixture. Toss lightly to coat evenly. Cover and chill thoroughly.

To serve, line bottom and sides of salad bowl with lettuce leaves. Spoon turkey mixture on leaves. Sprinkle pepper and parsley over top. Place tomato wedges decoratively at outer edge of salad. Serve with crusty rolls. *Serves 4 to 6.*

MOULDED SALMON SALAD

This was the recipe I used for my audition at BCTV, which won me the honour of presenting the Woodward's cooking show for the next 25 years!

1 Tbsp. gelatin

½ cup cold water

½ cup boiling water

2 cups fresh or canned sockeye salmon

½ cup finely chopped celery

2 Tbsp. sweet pickle, finely chopped

⅓ cup vinegar

½ cup mayonnaise

½ cup ketchup

salt and pepper to taste

lettuce leaves

olives, devilled eggs and tomato slices (optional)

Soften gelatin in cold water; add boiling water and stir until gelatin is dissolved. Add the remaining ingredients, seasoning to taste with salt and pepper, and mix well. Turn into individual moulds (or large mould) that have been rinsed with cold water. Chill until firm. To serve, unmould on bed of crisp lettuce and garnish with ripe olives, devilled eggs and tomato slices, if desired. *Serves 4 to 6.*

WINTER MOULDED GARDEN LOAF

2 packages (3 oz. each) lemon jelly powder

3½ cups hot water

2 Tbsp. vinegar

1 Tbsp. lemon juice

½ tsp. salt

12 whole green beans or asparagus spears, very well drained (or use whole frozen beans or asparagus spears, cooked and well drained)

4 long thin strips canned pimiento

¾ cup cooked cauliflower florets

½ cup cooked sliced carrots

¼ cup chopped green pepper

¼ cup chopped celery

¼ cup chopped green onions

¼ cup finely sliced radishes

lettuce leaves

tomato wedges and fresh parsley sprigs, for garnish (optional)

Place jelly powder in bowl, add hot water and stir to dissolve. Add vinegar, lemon juice and salt. Pour about ½ inch of mixture into 8½ x 4½ x 2 ½-inch loaf pan (or similar size). Chill until set.

Divide beans or asparagus into 4 bundles; wrap each with pimiento strip around centre. Arrange on gelatin in pan. Chill remaining gelatin until partially set. Pour enough gelatin over bean or asparagus bundles to cover; chill until firm. Meanwhile combine remaining gelatin with cauliflower, carrots, green pepper, celery, green onions and radishes (do not chill). Pour over firm gelatin in pan, then chill until set. To serve, unmould salad loaf on bed of lettuce and garnish with tomato wedges and parsley sprigs, if desired. *Serves 8.*

JELLIED SPANISH SALAD

I like this recipe because it can be prepared ahead of time and serves as both appetizer and salad—a great time saver!

1 package (3 oz.) lemon jelly powder
3/4 cup boiling water
1/3 cup chopped canned pimientos, drained
3/4 cup chopped English cucumber, unpeeled
1/3 cup chopped green pepper
1 can (7 1/2 oz.) tomato sauce
1/3 cup chopped green onions
1 clove garlic, crushed
3 Tbsp. vinegar
1 to 1 1/2 tsp. salt
1/4 tsp. pepper

Place jelly powder in bowl and disolve in boiling water. Stir in remaining ingredients. Chill until slightly thickened. Pour into 1-quart mould or 6 individual serving glasses. Chill until firm. *Serves 4 to 6.*

Variation: I often top this with shrimp mixed with a little mayonnaise. Season with salt and pepper to taste. Sprinkle paprika and chives over top and serve with a slice of lemon.

HOT POTATO SALAD—VERY TASTY

1/2 lb. bacon
1/3 cup bacon drippings
1/3 cup vinegar
2 1/2 Tbsp. water
1 egg, slightly beaten
1 tsp. sugar
1 tsp. salt
pinch pepper
2 tsp. chopped fresh parsley
5 cups diced, cooked potatoes
1/3 cup chopped onion
1/3 cup finely chopped celery

Cook bacon until crisp; crumble. Combine bacon drippings, vinegar, water, egg, sugar, salt, pepper and parsley. Stir and heat until thickened. Add potatoes, onion, celery and bacon; toss and heat through. *Serves 6.*

MOULDED POTATO SALAD

10 medium potatoes, cooked, peeled and diced
5 radishes, diced
3 green onions, chopped
3 stalks celery, finely chopped
1/2 green pepper, chopped
2 Tbsp. chopped fresh parsley
3 hard-cooked eggs, chopped
1 cup mayonnaise
1/4 cup vinegar
1/8 tsp. pepper
1 tsp. dry mustard
1/2 tsp. fresh basil, minced
1 1/2 tsp. salt
1/8 tsp. paprika

Toss potatoes with radishes, green onions, celery, green pepper, parsley and eggs. Mix mayonnaise with vinegar, pepper, mustard, basil and salt. Pour mayonnaise over potato mixture and mix well. Lightly oil angel cake pan and spoon in potato salad. Press down lightly to pack and make top even. Cover and chill for at least 2 hours. When thoroughly chilled, place plate over top of pan and invert. Sprinkle with paprika. *Serves 10 to 12.*

BUFFET SALAD

1 small package seashell pasta, cooked, drained and chilled
1/2 cup finely diced green pepper
1 cup finely chopped celery
3 green onions, finely snipped
1 cup canned or fresh shrimp, drained
3/4 cup mayonnaise
1/2 cup chili sauce
salt and pepper to taste

Mix pasta, green pepper, celery, onions and shrimp. In a bowl, combine mayonnaise and chili sauce. Add vegetable-shrimp mixture; toss lightly. Season to taste. *Makes 4 to 6 small servings.*

GIBRALTAR LAYERED SALAD

This is a perfect salad for dinner parties, as you can make it the day before. It is very attractive and tasty.

1 cup quick-cooking rice

2 Tbsp. butter

2 cups chopped mushrooms

1/4 cup snipped fresh chives

1/2 cup scant prepared Ranch-style dressing

2 green onions, chopped

2 large tomatoes, seeded and chopped

2 cups broccoli florets (small pieces), blanched and drained

2 red peppers, chopped

1 to 1 1/2 cups shredded mild Cheddar cheese

1 package (12 oz.) frozen green peas, thawed

1/2 cup salad dressing

1/2 cup prepared Ranch-style dressing

Prepare rice as directed on package. Let stand for 5 minutes to cool. In non-stick skillet, melt butter and add mushrooms. Sauté, stirring frequently, until mushrooms are browned and all liquid has evaporated. Combine rice with mushrooms and chives. Gently but thoroughly mix the scant 1/2 cup Ranch-style dressing with rice-mushroom mixture. Place in bottom of large glass serving bowl. (A "trifle-type" bowl is ideal.)

Layer green onions, tomatoes, broccoli, red peppers, cheese and peas in the bowl. Mix salad dressing with remaining 1/2 cup Ranch-style dressing. Carefully spread mixture over top layer. Prepare early in the day or the day before for best results. Garnish as desired. *Serves 10 to 12.*

TANGY COLE SLAW

1 cup wine vinegar

1 cup mild-flavoured honey

1 small onion, finely chopped

1 tsp. celery seed

1 tsp. salt, or to taste

4 cups shredded cabbage

1 cup chopped celery

1 cup chopped green pepper

In small saucepan, combine vinegar, honey, onion, celery seed and salt. Bring mixture to a boil, reduce heat and simmer for 5 minutes. Cool completely.

In large bowl, place cabbage, celery and green pepper. Toss vegetables with enough of prepared dressing to coat lightly and evenly. Cover; chill for several hours or overnight to blend flavours. Great with ham or chicken. *Serves 10 to 12.*

CREAMY WALDORF COLE SLAW

2 cups red cabbage, grated or finely chopped

4 cups green cabbage, grated or finely chopped

1/4 cup chopped green pepper

1/2 cup chopped walnuts

2 medium apples, unpeeled and diced

2 tsp. lemon juice

1/2 cup mayonnaise

1/4 cup sour cream

1 Tbsp. lemon juice

freshly ground black pepper to taste

2 tsp. sugar

chopped fresh parsley, for garnish

In large bowl combine red cabbage, green cabbage, green pepper and walnuts. In small bowl toss diced apple with the 2 tsp. lemon juice. Add to cabbage mixture. Combine mayonnaise, sour cream, the 1 Tbsp. lemon juice, pepper and sugar. Toss with cabbage and apple mixture until all ingredients are evenly coated. Garnish with parsley. *Serves 8.*

CELERY SALAD

3 cups thinly sliced celery

1/2 cup grated carrot

1/3 cup salad oil

2 Tbsp. red wine vinegar

1 Tbsp. sugar

1 tsp. salt

pinch pepper

pinch paprika

1/2 cup sour cream

Place celery and carrot in salad bowl. In small bowl beat together oil, vinegar, sugar, salt, pepper and paprika; beat in sour cream a little at a time. Pour over vegetables and toss lightly. *Serves 6.*

ORIENTAL CELERY

2 or 3 small celery hearts
1 medium onion, sliced
2½ cups water
¼ cup soy sauce
½ cup salad oil
¼ cup rice wine vinegar
1 clove garlic, crushed
½ tsp. sugar
½ tsp. salt
½ tsp. chopped fresh dill
shredded lettuce

Thoroughly wash celery hearts. Trim root ends and remove all but smallest leaves. Place onion and celery hearts in shallow saucepan or frying pan with cover. Add water and soy sauce. Cover pan. Bring to a boil, reduce heat and simmer for about 15 minutes or until celery is tender. Remove from heat and cool vegetables in sauce.

Blend oil, vinegar, garlic, sugar, salt and dill. Remove celery from sauce, cut in half lengthwise and place in shallow dish. Pour dressing over celery. Cover and chill for several hours. To serve, drain off most of dressing and place celery on shredded lettuce. *Serves 4 to 6.*

JAPANESE CUCUMBER SALAD

2 medium cucumbers, peeled and seeded
2 tsp. salt
⅓ cup seasoned gourmet vinegar
1 tsp. soy sauce
¼ tsp. grated fresh ginger or ⅛ tsp. ground ginger

Cut cucumbers into thin slices; sprinkle with salt. Let stand at room temperature for 1 to 2 hours. Drain and squeeze out excess liquid. Combine vinegar, soy sauce and ginger in bowl; stir in cucumber and mix well. Chill thoroughly before serving. *Serves 4.*

Variation: Marinate well-drained canned shrimp, canned salmon (flaked), fresh mushrooms (whole or sliced), thinly sliced abalone or clams in 2 or 3 Tbsp. seasoned gourmet vinegar for about 2 hours. Drain and add to cucumber mixture.

COBB SALAD WITH FRENCH DRESSING

1 head romaine lettuce, torn in fine pieces
1 head iceberg lettuce, torn in fine pieces
6 strips bacon, crisp-cooked, drained and crumbled
¼ lb. Roquefort cheese, crumbled
3 hard-cooked eggs, finely chopped
2 tomatoes, peeled, seeded and chopped
2 avocados, peeled, pitted and chopped
¼ lb. Gruyère cheese, chopped
½ cup chopped fresh parsley
1 recipe French Dressing

Arrange romaine and iceberg lettuce in bottom of salad bowl. Arrange remaining ingredients, except parsley and dressing, in rows across top of greens. Sprinkle parsley over all. At the table, just before serving, add approximately ½ cup French dressing and toss. *Serves 8.*

French Dressing
½ cup wine vinegar
1 Tbsp. water
1 tsp. salt
1 tsp. Worcestershire sauce
½ tsp. cracked pepper
¼ tsp. dry mustard
⅔ cup olive oil

Combine all ingredients except oil in screw-top jar. Add oil and shake well. Prepare dressing several hours before serving to blend flavours. *Makes approximately 1½ cups.*

SALAD OF THE GODS

This recipe comes from my good friend Joyce Pearson.

FOR THE DRESSING:
1/2 cup vinegar
1/4 cup oil
1 Tbsp. fresh lemon juice
1/2 tsp. fresh tarragon
1/4 tsp. fresh marjoram
pinch salt, sugar and pepper

Combine all ingredients and blend or shake thoroughly. Prepare up to 24 hours in advance—more than that will affect the delicate flavour of tarragon.

FOR THE SALAD:
1 large head romaine lettuce
1 can (14 oz.) pineapple chunks
1 can (20 oz.) lychees in syrup
1 red apple, unpeeled
1 large orange
1/2 lb. seedless red or green grapes

Wash and dry lettuce thoroughly. Wrap tightly in paper towels. Place in plastic bag. This will produce very crisp lettuce in 12 to 24 hours. (It really needs the time to obtain maximum crispness.)

Drain pineapple and lychees thoroughly. Coarsely chop apple and toss with a small amount of pineapple juice to prevent browning. Peel and slice orange and halve grapes. Toss fruit with small amount of dressing.

Along with many of my high-school classmates, I became a part-time employee of the Woodward's store in New Westminster. We were staunch Woodward's supporters, as we now had money for movies and treats at White Spot. But most importantly, with Woodward's strong support, many of us went on to graduate from the University of British Columbia. I received my Home Economics degree there in 1960.
    —Joyce Pearson

To serve, toss fruit with lettuce leaves torn into large pieces. Add additional dressing and serve immediately. The colours of this salad look beautiful when served in a glass bowl. Serves 6 to 8.

CHEF'S SALAD WITH RUSSIAN DRESSING

1 clove garlic
1 large head romaine lettuce or 1 bunch leaf lettuce
2 cups cooked ham strips
1/2 lb. sharp Cheddar cheese, cut into strips
1 large tomato, cut into thin wedges
3 hard-cooked eggs, quartered lengthwise
1 bunch radishes, thinly sliced
1 bunch green onions, sliced
chopped fresh chives, chopped fresh parsley or sliced ripe olives, for garnish (optional)
salt and pepper to taste
1 recipe Russian Dressing

Rub salad bowl with cut clove of garlic. Wash and dry lettuce leaves. Arrange in bowl, lining sides and bottom. Attractively arrange ham, cheese, tomato, eggs, radishes and green onions over lettuce. Garnish with chives, parsley or olives, if desired. Sprinkle with salt and pepper. Serve with Russian dressing on the side. *Serves 4 to 6.*

Russian Dressing
1/4 cup sugar
3 Tbsp. water
1 1/2 tsp. celery seed
1/2 tsp. salt
1/2 tsp. paprika
2 1/2 Tbsp. lemon juice
1 Tbsp. Worcestershire sauce
1 Tbsp. vinegar
1 cup salad oil
1/2 cup ketchup
1/4 cup grated onion

Cook sugar and water until mixture spins a thread (232°F). Cool. Mix remaining ingredients and beat into syrup. Chill. *Makes 2 cups.*

MARINATED CUCUMBERS

1/3 cup water
1/4 cup vinegar
1 Tbsp. salad oil
1/2 tsp. sugar
1/2 tsp. salt
freshly ground black pepper to taste
1/8 tsp. garlic powder
1 tsp. chopped fresh parsley
1 large cucumber
finely chopped green onions, for garnish (optional)

Beat water, vinegar, salad oil, sugar, salt, pepper, garlic powder and parsley in medium bowl until very well blended. Score cucumber skin lengthwise with tines of fork. Slice thinly. Toss cucumber slices gently in marinade. Cover and refrigerate. To serve, drain marinade. Sprinkle with chopped green onions, if desired. *Serves 4 to 6.*

CUCUMBER-ORANGE SALAD

This is a refreshing addition to a rich meal or a buffet salad.

1 large cucumber, peeled and thinly sliced
3/4 tsp. salt, or to taste
pinch pepper
2 oranges, peeled, halved and thinly sliced
2/3 cup coarsely chopped green pepper
1 Tbsp. chopped fresh parsley
1 cup plain yogurt or sour cream
1/2 tsp. crushed thyme (optional)
lettuce leaves
walnuts, for garnish (optional)

Place cucumber in large bowl; sprinkle with salt and pepper. Add oranges, green pepper, parsley and yogurt or sour cream mixed with thyme, if desired. Toss gently to mix dressing evenly. Refrigerate, covered, for 1 hour to blend flavours. Serve on a bed of crisp lettuce leaves and garnish with walnuts, if desired.

MAXINE'S BUFFET SALAD

Maxine Wilson is known as the "hostess with the mostest"!

4 cucumbers, cut into 1/2-inch-thick slices, then quartered
4 green peppers, cut into 1/2-inch-thick slices, then quartered
3 tomatoes, cut into wedges
1 onion, sliced and separated into rings
1/3 to 1/2 cup oil
salt and pepper to taste
pinch dried oregano
1/4 to 1/3 cup black olives, halved
3/4 lb. feta cheese

Combine cucumbers, green peppers, tomatoes and onion in bowl. Season oil with salt, pepper and oregano. Pour oil over vegetables (amount used depends on personal preference) and toss gently. Cover and refrigerate for 2 hours. To serve, toss vegetables and sprinkle olives and feta cheese over all. *Serves 8.*

HARVEST APPLE-ZUCCHINI TOSS

3 Tbsp. salad oil
2 Tbsp. vinegar
1 1/2 tsp. sugar
1/2 tsp. salt, or to taste
pepper to taste
6 cups torn leaf lettuce
2 cups unpeeled diced red apple
1 cup unpeeled thinly sliced zucchini
1 small green pepper, cut into thin julienne strips
2 Tbsp. chopped walnuts (optional)

Combine oil, vinegar, sugar, salt and pepper and whisk or shake vigorously. Chill. Have all vegetables washed, dried and well chilled. Place lettuce, apple, zucchini and green pepper in bowl. Shake prepared dressing and toss salad with just enough dressing to coat vegetables lightly. Sprinkle chopped walnuts over top, if desired. Serve immediately. *Serves 6.*

NIÇOISE SALAD

4 large potatoes, cooked, drained and cooled

1 lb. green beans, cooked, drained and cooled

²⁄₃ cup olive or salad oil

¹⁄₃ cup tarragon or wine vinegar

2 cloves garlic, crushed

2 to 3 tsp. Dijon mustard

salt and freshly ground black pepper to taste

1 small head Boston lettuce

1 medium head romaine lettuce

1 red onion, coarsely chopped

1 green pepper, halved and cut into thin strips

4 hard-cooked eggs, quartered lengthwise

8 pitted ripe olives

1 Tbsp. chopped fresh parsley

2 large tomatoes, cut into wedges

2 cans (7 oz. each) chunk tuna, drained and broken
    into pieces

2 tsp. lemon juice

1 can (2 oz.) rolled anchovy fillets*, drained
    (optional)

Cut potatoes into slices and place in shallow dish. Place beans in separate shallow dish. Combine oil, vinegar, garlic, mustard, salt and pepper and whisk or shake vigorously. Drizzle ¹⁄₂ cup over potatoes and 2 Tbsp. over beans. Allow to marinate for 1 hour. Line a large salad bowl with Boston and romaine lettuce. Layer potatoes, beans, onion, and green pepper in a mound. Arrange quartered eggs and olives around edge of mound. Sprinkle parsley over top. Place tomato wedges in petal pattern around centre of mound. Sprinkle drained tuna with lemon juice. Mound tuna on top in centre of salad. Garnish with anchovy fillets, if desired. Pass remaining dressing separately. Do not toss. *Makes 8 meal-size servings.*

*Soak in milk to counteract excessive saltiness.

TOMATOES A LA FRANÇAISE

4 medium-ripe firm tomatoes, cut into slices

1 cup salad oil

¹⁄₂ cup vinegar

1 clove garlic, crushed

2 Tbsp. sugar

1 tsp. salt

1 tsp. paprika

1 tsp. dry mustard

³⁄₄ tsp. celery salt

1 tsp. minced onion

¹⁄₄ tsp. pepper

lettuce leaves

bottled French dressing

Place tomato slices in bowl. Combine oil, vinegar, garlic, sugar, salt, paprika, dry mustard, celery salt, minced onion and pepper in a jar or bowl. Whisk or shake vigorously. Pour over tomatoes. Allow to marinate for several hours. Line small individual salad bowls with lettuce. Serve drained tomatoes on lettuce cups and sprinkle each with 1 Tbsp. bottled French dressing. *Serves 4 to 6.*

The sheets featuring Bea Wright Recipes were available only on the Woodward's Food Floors.

Woodward's brand honey was a household favourite.

FRENCH SPINACH SALAD

FOR THE DRESSING:

2 Tbsp. lemon juice

2 Tbsp. white wine vinegar

$1/2$ cup salad oil

1 tsp. salt

1 tsp. sugar

pinch pepper

1 clove garlic

$1/4$ tsp. dry mustard

In jar or bowl, combine all dressing ingredients. Shake or whisk vigorously. Refrigerate for several hours. Remove garlic clove just before using dressing.

FOR THE SALAD:

$3/4$ lb. tender young spinach leaves

$1/3$ cup sliced radishes

$1/3$ cup thinly sliced green onions

1 small cucumber, peeled and thinly sliced

$1/2$ cup halved cherry tomatoes

Have all vegetables for salad washed, well dried and thoroughly chilled. Remove spinach stems; tear into bite-size pieces and place in salad bowl. Add radishes, green onions and cucumber. Cover and refrigerate until just before serving. Add tomatoes to salad just before serving. Toss with enough dressing to coat spinach well and serve. *Serves 4 to 6.*

COLD BEAN SALAD

1 can (14 oz.) yellow wax beans

1 can (14 oz.) green string beans

1 can (14 oz.) kidney beans

1 can (14 oz.) garbanzo beans

1 thinly sliced onion

1 chopped green pepper

$1/2$ cup salad oil

$1/2$ cup vinegar

$1/2$ cup honey or sugar

Drain liquid from yellow and green beans. Rinse and drain kidney beans and garbanzo beans. Combine. Add onion and green pepper. Combine oil, vinegar and honey or sugar and pour over bean salad. Cover and refrigerate 2 hours or more before serving. *Serves 6 to 8.*

SUMMER FRUIT SALAD

2 large bananas, peeled and cut on the bias

1 red-skinned apple, unpeeled, cored and thinly sliced

3 medium oranges, peeled, halved and thinly sliced

1 cup strawberries, washed, hulled and sliced in half lengthwise

$2/3$ cup seedless green grapes, halved lengthwise

1 recipe Honey-Sour Cream dressing

Place bananas and apple in bowl. Cover completely with oranges, strawberries and grapes. Cover bowl and chill. Just before serving, pour dressing over fruit; toss gently until fruit is well coated. Serve immediately. *Serves 8.*

Honey-Sour Cream Dressing

$1/2$ cup sour cream

1 Tbsp. orange juice

1 Tbsp. honey

Blend all ingredients well. *Makes $1/2$ cup.*

The recipe sheet mascot serves up a bowl of salad fixings.

WINTER ORANGE SALAD BOWL

1 small head lettuce
$^1/_2$ head endive
2 oranges, peeled and sliced
$^1/_2$ mild white onion, sliced and separated into rings
1 recipe Walnut Croutons
bottled Italian dressing

Have all vegetables well chilled. Tear lettuce and endive into bite-size pieces. Place in salad bowl. Add prepared orange slices, onion rings and hot walnut croutons. Toss with enough Italian dressing to coat greens. *Serves 6 to 8.*

Walnut Croutons
1 $^1/_2$ tsp. butter or margarine
$^1/_4$ tsp. salt
$^1/_3$ cup walnut halves

Melt butter or margarine in skillet; add salt. Add walnut halves; brown mixture over medium heat, stirring constantly. *Makes $^1/_3$ cup.*

JEAN'S FAVOURITE GOLD COIN CARROT SALAD
Great with any dish.

2 to 3 lbs. carrots, steamed until almost tender
1 small to medium onion, sliced or chopped
$^1/_2$ large green pepper, seeded and thinly sliced
1 can (10 oz.) tomato soup
$^1/_3$ to $^1/_2$ cup sugar
$^1/_4$ cup salad oil
$^1/_3$ to $^1/_2$ cup cider vinegar
salt and pepper to taste

Combine carrots with onion and green pepper. Combine remaining ingredients in a saucepan and bring to a boil. Pour hot marinade over salad. Chill for approximately 24 hours before serving. Stir occasionally. *Serves 6.*

ZIPPY PARMESAN DRESSING

$^2/_3$ cup salad oil
$^1/_2$ cup vinegar
1 tsp. salt
1 tsp. mixed Italian herbs, crumbled
pepper to taste
2 Tbsp. Parmesan cheese

Combine all ingredients in bowl or screw-top jar. Whisk or shake well. Chill. Serve with Antipasto Salad, page 23.

BLENDER MAYONNAISE

1 egg
1 tsp. salt
1 tsp. sugar
1 tsp. mustard
$^1/_2$ tsp. paprika
3 Tbsp. vinegar or lemon juice
$1^1/_2$ cups salad oil

Place egg, salt, sugar, mustard, paprika and vinegar or lemon juice in blender. Cover and blend for a few seconds. Gradually add salad oil with the motor running. Blend until very thick and smooth. Refrigerate and use immediately. *Makes approximately 2 cups.*

Variations

- **Cucumber Mayonnaise:** Into 1 cup mayonnaise, fold $^1/_2$ cup peeled, chopped and drained cucumber (good with fish).
- **Thousand Island Dressing:** Into $^2/_3$ cup mayonnaise, blend $^1/_3$ cup chili sauce, $1^1/_2$ Tbsp. chopped green pepper, 2 Tbsp. chopped pimiento, 1 Tbsp. chopped fresh chives and 2 tsp. chopped fresh parsley.
- **Fruit Dressing:** Into 1 cup mayonnaise, blend 2 Tbsp. pineapple juice, 2 Tbsp. orange juice and 2 Tbsp. honey.
- **Russian Dressing:** Into $^2/_3$ cup mayonnaise, fold 3 Tbsp. chopped olives, 2 Tbsp. chopped sweet pickles, $^1/_3$ cup chili sauce, 1 finely chopped hard-cooked egg and 2 tsp. finely chopped fresh parsley.
- **Cheesy Mayonnaise:** In bowl, stir together $^1/_2$ cup mayonnaise and $^1/_2$ cup cream. Add 4 oz. softened and creamed cream cheese, $^1/_4$ to $^1/_2$ cup crumbled blue cheese and 1 Tbsp. lemon juice. Blend thoroughly. Serve with vegetables, salad greens or fruits.
- **Whipped Cream Dressing:** Whip $^1/_2$ cup whipping cream; fold into 1 cup mayonnaise.
- **Berry Whipped Cream Dressing:** Into Whipped Cream Dressing (above), fold 1 cup crushed strawberries or raspberries and sweeten with 1 to 2 Tbsp. icing sugar.

SIMPLY SCRUMPTIOUS DRESSING

$^1/_2$ cup oil
$^1/_4$ cup wine vinegar or rice vinegar (such as Marukan)
1 Tbsp. fresh lemon juice
2 Tbsp. grated onion
1 Tbsp. grated Parmesan cheese
1 tsp. salt
$^3/_4$ tsp. Worcestershire sauce
$^3/_4$ tsp. dry mustard
$^3/_4$ tsp. dried basil
$^3/_4$ tsp. dried oregano
$^3/_4$ tsp. sugar
$^3/_4$ tsp. black pepper

Combine ingredients in a blender and whirl for 30 seconds. This dressing may be refrigerated for up to 5 days. Serve with an interesting selection of salad greens. *Makes approximately 1 cup.*

A masthead from one of Mona's Creative Home Cooking! recipe sheets.

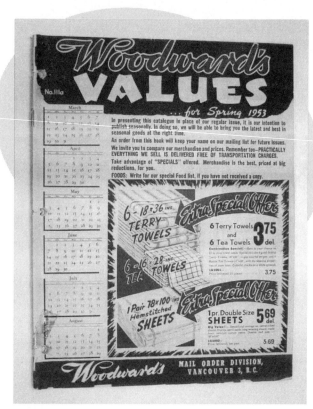

This Woodward's Values catalogue dates from 1953.

COTTAGE CHEESE DRESSING

1 cup salad oil
$1/4$ cup vinegar
$1/2$ tsp. salt
3 Tbsp. cottage cheese
pinch cayenne pepper
$1/4$ tsp. white pepper
2 Tbsp. chopped fresh parsley
1 Tbsp. chopped fresh chives

Combine all ingredients in a jar and shake thoroughly. Serve with crisp, tossed greens. *Makes 1 1/2 cups.*

OIL-VINEGAR-GARLIC DRESSING

$1/4$ tsp. salt
1 clove garlic, cut in half
$1/8$ tsp. dry mustard
$1/2$ tsp. salt
$1/4$ tsp. pepper
$1/2$ tsp. sugar
1 Tbsp. vinegar
3 Tbsp. salad oil

Rub salt over garlic; rub garlic over salad bowl. Mix together mustard, salt, pepper, sugar, vinegar and salad oil. Blend well. A quick tangy dressing for a tossed green salad. *Makes 1/4 cup.*

mona says . . .

- Flavour too bland? To a meat soup, add a dash of Worcestershire sauce, hot pepper sauce, bottled meat sauce, or perhaps fried onions. To cream soup, try adding extra salt. To almost anything, add salt and/or pepper.

- Flavour too salty? When food is too salty or too spicy, the ideal solution is to make a second batch, omitting the offensive seasoning. Combine the two batches and freeze half for later use.

- Flavour too sharp? The second-batch trick works with food that tastes too sharp or too acidic, but you can also soften the taste by adding a teaspoon or two of sugar.

- Flavour too sweet? Add a teaspoon of vinegar.

FREEZING STOCK
Leftover soup or soup stock can be frozen in ice-cube trays. Frozen cubes can then be stored in resealable plastic bags and used in small amounts or for another meal.

HALE AND HEARTY HAMBURGER SOUP

This is my daughter Maureen's recipe. It has become a family favourite over the years.

1 Tbsp. butter or margarine
1 lb. ground beef
4 small onions, sliced and separated into rings
1 clove garlic, crushed
1 can (19 oz.) tomatoes
3 Tbsp. lemon juice
3 Tbsp. Worcestershire sauce
salt and pepper to taste
5 cups water
3 large carrots, thinly sliced on the bias
3 celery stalks, thinly sliced on the bias
3 medium potatoes, diced
1 can (10 oz.) corn niblets, undrained
¾ cup elbow macaroni

In large Dutch oven, melt butter or margarine; add beef and cook slightly, stirring with fork. Add onions and garlic. Cook until tender. Add tomatoes, lemon juice, Worcestershire sauce, salt, pepper and water. Bring to a boil; cover and simmer for 1 hour. Add carrots, celery, potatoes and undrained corn. Simmer, covered, for 1 hour longer or until vegetables are tender. Stir in macaroni during last 20 minutes of cooking. Serve hot with crusty rolls. *Serves 6.*

CLAM AND CORN CHOWDER

4 slices bacon, diced
1 large onion, chopped
⅓ cup chopped green pepper
2 Tbsp. butter or margarine
2 Tbsp. all-purpose flour
3 cans (5 oz. each) clams (or equivalent amount)
1 can (12 oz.) whole kernel corn
1 medium tomato, peeled and chopped
2 cups diced peeled potato
1 tsp. salt, or to taste
⅛ tsp. pepper, or to taste
water

In Dutch oven, cook bacon until it is limp. Add onion, green pepper and butter or margarine. Continue cooking until bacon is crisp and onion is tender. Remove from heat. Add flour and stir until smooth. Drain clams and corn, reserving liquid. Add clams, corn, tomato, potato, salt and pepper to mixture in Dutch oven. Combine reserved clam and corn liquid. Add water to measure 4 cups. Add to mixture in Dutch oven. Bring to a boil, reduce heat and cover. Simmer for 25 to 30 minutes or until potatoes are tender, stirring occasionally. *Serves 6 to 8.*

WESTCOAST CLAM CHOWDER

6 medium peeled sliced potatoes
1 medium peeled sliced onion
3½ cups water
2 tsp. salt, or to taste
1 tsp. pepper, or to taste
½ tsp. garlic powder, or to taste
3 Tbsp. butter
2 cups whole milk, cream or evaporated milk
3 cans (5 oz. each) clams
2 Tbsp. chopped fresh parsley

Put potatoes and onion in 3-quart heavy saucepan. Add 2½ cups of the water, salt, pepper and garlic. Cover tightly. Bring mixture to a boil, then reduce heat and simmer for 10 minutes or until potatoes are tender. Process potatoes and onions in their liquid, using a beater or immersible blender. Add butter, milk or cream, remaining 1 cup water and clams (with their liquid). Heat to serving temperature. Garnish with parsley. *Serves 4 to 6.*

Note: If you desire a thicker soup, mix ¼ cup flour with ½ cup water. Add to soup mixture. Simmer for 3 to 4 minutes, stirring gently.

BERMUDA SALMON CHOWDER

1/4 cup butter
2 large onions, chopped
2 Tbsp. all-purpose flour
1 can (10 oz.) condensed beef consommé
2 cups clam juice
1 large green pepper, chopped
1 cup thinly sliced celery, cut on the bias
3 cups medium white sauce (use your favourite recipe)
2 cups canned salmon, undrained and broken into chunks
1 cup diced cooked potato
1/2 tsp. dried crumbled thyme
chopped fresh chives and sliced hard-cooked eggs, for garnish (optional)

In large saucepan, melt 2 Tbsp. of the butter; cook onions slowly until tender but not browned. Add flour and allow to brown. Add consommé and clam juice; cook and stir constantly until thickened.

In small saucepan, melt remaining 2 Tbsp. butter. Cook green pepper and celery until soft. Add to onion mixture. To white sauce, add salmon and salmon liquid, cooked potato and thyme; heat to serving temperature. Add hot clam juice mixture. Serve immediately. Garnish with chives and egg slices, if desired. *Serves 8.*

EGG DROP SOUP

4 chicken bouillon cubes
4 cups hot water
1 cup diced fresh tomato
1 egg, slightly beaten

In a pan, dissolve bouillon cubes in hot water. Add diced tomato; simmer for 5 minutes. Add slightly beaten egg to soup and stir constantly for 1 or 2 minutes, or until egg separates in shreds. Serve immediately. *Serves 4 to 6.*

BROCCOLI CREAM SOUP

1 1/4 lbs. fresh broccoli, cooked, drained and chopped
1/4 cup chopped onion
2 cups chicken stock
2 Tbsp. butter
1 Tbsp. all-purpose flour
2 tsp. salt
1/8 tsp. mace
pinch pepper
2 cups light cream

In medium saucepan, combine broccoli, onion and chicken stock; bring to a boil. Simmer for about 10 minutes, or until broccoli is tender. Whirl broccoli mixture in blender until very smooth, or press through wire strainer. Melt butter in pan; add flour, salt, mace and pepper, stirring until smooth. Slowly stir in cream, then add broccoli purée. Cook over medium heat, stirring frequently, until soup bubbles. Serve hot. *Serves 6 to 8.*

An illustration from the Woodward's recipe sheets.

CREAM OF MUSHROOM SOUP

1¼ cups fresh mushrooms, sliced through cap
  and stem
¼ cup chopped onion
2 Tbsp. butter or margarine
2 Tbsp. all-purpose flour
2 cups chicken, brown or beef stock
½ cup light cream
½ tsp. salt, or to taste
pinch pepper
¼ tsp. ground nutmeg
chopped fresh chives or snipped fresh parsley, for
  garnish (optional)

In large saucepan, gently sauté mushrooms and onion in butter or margarine until tender but not browned. Add flour and blend; add stock. Cook and stir until slightly thickened. Cool slightly; add cream, salt, pepper and nutmeg. Heat through but do not boil. Serve immediately, garnished with chives or parsley, if desired. *Serves 4 to 6.*

HUNGARIAN POTATO SOUP

3 Tbsp. butter or margarine
1 medium onion, chopped
4 medium potatoes, peeled and diced
1½ tsp. salt, or to taste
1 cup water
1 cup sour cream
¼ cup all-purpose flour (use 1 Tbsp. less flour for a
  thinner soup)
1 tsp. paprika
2½ cups milk
salt and pepper to taste
chopped fresh chives, for garnish

In saucepan, melt butter or margarine. Cook onion until tender but not browned. Add potatoes, salt and water. Cover and cook until potatoes are tender, approximately 15 minutes. In bowl, blend sour cream, flour and paprika until smooth. Stir into potato mixture. Add milk. Heat, stirring constantly,

until mixture is piping hot but not boiling. Cook for 1 minute. Season with salt and pepper. Sprinkle chives over top and serve immediately. *Serves 6.*

SUPER GAZPACHO

1 cup peeled and finely chopped tomato
½ cup finely chopped cucumber
½ green pepper, finely chopped
1 stalk celery, finely chopped
1 small onion, finely chopped
1 Tbsp. chopped fresh parsley
1 clove garlic, crushed
2 tsp. chopped fresh chives
2 Tbsp. vinegar
2 Tbsp. salad oil
salt and pepper to taste
1 tsp. Worcestershire sauce
1 Tbsp. lemon juice
2½ cups tomato juice
croutons (optional)

Combine all ingredients except croutons in large bowl, mixing well. Cover and chill for several hours. Serve in chilled cups. Top with croutons, if desired. *Serves 6.*

VICHYSSOISE

4 leeks (white part only), thinly sliced
1 medium onion, thinly sliced
¼ cup butter
5 medium potatoes, thinly sliced (about 4 cups)
4 cups chicken stock (or 4 chicken bouillon cubes
  dissolved in 4 cups boiling water)
1 Tbsp. salt
2 cups milk
2 cups light cream
1 cup whipping cream
salt and pepper to taste
chopped fresh chives, for garnish

Cook leeks and onion in butter until tender but not brown; add potatoes, stock and salt. Cook for 35 to 40 minutes. Rub through fine sieve and return to heat; add milk and light cream. Season to taste. Bring to a boil. Cool, then rub through very fine sieve. Chill. Add whipping cream just before serving. Garnish with chives. *Serves 8.*

BLENDER CUCUMBER SOUP

2 cans (10 oz. each) condensed cream of celery soup
1 small cucumber, peeled and chopped
2 Tbsp. finely chopped green onions
1 Tbsp. chopped fresh parsley
pepper to taste
2 sprigs watercress, chopped (optional)
2 cups milk
$1/2$ cup sour cream
chopped fresh chives, for garnish (optional)

In blender, whirl 1 can of soup at a time. Then add cucumber, green onions, parsley, pepper and watercress, if desired. Blend until mixture turns pale green. Stir in milk. Chill until serving time. Serve in mugs or soup bowls. Top each with a spoonful of sour cream and sprinkle of chives, if desired. *Serves 6.*

Our class at San Miguel.

Note: This recipe can be made with an electric mixer. Ensure all vegetables are finely chopped before adding to condensed soup, Proceed as directed for blender.

AVOCADO TORTILLA SOUP

This recipe comes from a course in Mexican cuisine given by the Imle Institution in San Miguel, Mexico. I took the course with four other "foodies" from Canada. This soup and the Margarita Pie (page 166) were our absolute favourites.

$1/4$ cup butter
2 Tbsp. all-purpose flour
2 quarts well-seasoned beef or chicken stock
salt and pepper to taste
hot pepper sauce to taste
2 tortillas
2 Tbsp. salad oil
5 good-sized avocados
lemon juice
$1/2$ cup light cream
$1/2$ tsp. onion powder

Melt butter in large, heavy saucepan. Blend in flour. Gradually add stock. Stir constantly over medium heat until mixture thickens slightly and comes to a boil. Remove from heat and add salt, pepper and hot pepper sauce. The amount of salt and pepper used will vary according to seasoning of beef or chicken broth. Set broth mixture aside.

Cut tortillas into small squares or triangles. Heat salad oil in skillet and sauté tortilla pieces. Drain on paper towels. Set aside and keep warm.

Mash avocados and sprinkle with lemon juice to prevent discolouration. Blend in cream and onion powder.

To serve, bring broth mixture back to a boil. Place generous spoonful of avocado-cream mixture in bottom of each soup bowl. Pour in hot broth mixture. Add warmed tortilla squares or triangles and serve immediately. *Serves 6 to 8.*

Woodward's really did sell everything, from watering cans to walnuts.

mona says . . .

- Make use of all the meat you buy. Save bones for soups and stocks, melt down fat trimmings for drippings, simmer lean trimmings for soup stock or gravy.
- Buy meat in terms of meals. A small amount left over—too skimpy for a second meal—can be expensive, but planned leftovers can provide delicious meals without any leftover look or taste.
- Use leftover cooked ham, chicken or beef to stuff a cabbage. Mix the meat with rice or bread crumbs, herbs, onions and 1 egg for every 2 cups of stuffing mixture. Steam the cabbage or cook it in stock. Serve with tomato sauce.
- Leftover beef, pork, lamb or turkey makes a delicious meat loaf. Grind the meat, add onions, and use bread crumbs that have been soaked in bouillon or mixed with a small amount of milk as a binder. Squeeze the crumbs dry and add 1 egg for every 2 cups of mixture. Add leftover vegetables, such as cooked and chopped broccoli or spinach. For spices, choose sage, thyme or garlic. Parmesan cheese makes a delicious addition. Cook in a loaf pan in a preheated 350°F oven for approximately 1 hour or until done.
- Curry can transform leftover lamb, beef, veal or chicken into an exotic dish.

- For budget steaks, buy chuck or bottom round. Marinate or tenderize the meat, then broil to medium-rare for maximum tenderness.
- Calculate costs on price per cooked serving rather than price per pound. As a general rule, 1 lb. of bony meat, like spareribs, equals 1 serving; 1 lb. of small bone meat, like roasts, 2 servings; 1 lb. of boneless meat, 3 to 4 servings.
- Less tender cuts are usually cheaper than the more tender cuts, yet when cooked properly, they can be juicy, tender and still provide the same high-quality protein.
- Dry heat (roast, broil, pan-fry) and moist heat (braise, stew) are the two basic methods of cooking beef. Use dry heat for the more tender cuts and moist heat for the less tender cuts.
- Broiling: Place steak on rack of broiler pan approximately 3 inches from source of heat. When top surface is browned, turn steak and season. Cook to desired degree of doneness. Good for sirloin, porterhouse, club, rib, T-bone and for marinated or tenderized flank or top round steaks. Beef patties may also be broiled.
- Pan-Broiling: Place steaks or patties—the same as those for broiling—in a hot heavy skillet. Add a small amount of oil or butter if meat is very lean.

Turn steaks only once for best results and turn with tongs to avoid piercing the meat.

- Braising: Use a deep pan like a Dutch oven with a lid. Season meat with salt and pepper or as directed in recipe. Brown in its own fat or, if meat is very lean, brown it in a small amount of salad oil or butter, or in a combination of both. Add a small amount of liquid, cover and allow to simmer. Pot roasts, Swiss steak and short ribs are commonly cooked by this method.
- Stewing: Stewing meat is seasoned and sometimes browned, then covered with liquid and simmered gently until tender.
- Gravy too thick? Stir in a little more liquid.
- Gravy too thin? Mix some water and flour or cornstarch to a smooth paste. Stir into the gravy and bring to a boil, stirring constantly. If a gravy thickened with cornstarch becomes too thin, you have probably overcooked it. Add more cornstarch and cook just until thickened again, then remove from the heat.

BEEF WELLINGTON

1 lb. beef tenderloin
salt and pepper to taste
1 to 2 Tbsp. chopped shallots
clarified butter
$^1/_2$ to $^2/_3$ cup finely chopped fresh mushrooms
$^1/_2$ can (2 oz.) goose liver pâté
dash cognac
finely chopped fresh parsley
1 egg yolk
dried rosemary to taste
salt and pepper to taste
puff pastry
1 egg, slightly beaten

Preheat oven to 350°F. Season beef tenderloin with salt and pepper (do not use head or tail of tenderloin). Sear on all sides in hot skillet until brown. Set aside.

Fry shallots in a little clarified butter until golden brown; add mushrooms. Simmer until all moisture is evaporated. Cool.

Mix vegetables with goose liver pâté, cognac, parsley and egg yolk. Season with rosemary, salt and pepper. Spread this mixture over tenderloin. Roll out puff pastry to approximately $^1/_3$ inch thick, large enough to cover the tenderloin completely. Brush with beaten egg.

Place meat on pastry and brush surface towards the meat. Fold pastry around meat so ends and sides are tucked underneath. Brush top with beaten egg. Bake until crust is golden brown (meat will be medium-rare). With a sharp knife, cut slices across the grain of the meat. *Serves 3.*

TOURNEDOS WITH EGGPLANT

4 Tbsp. olive oil or salad oil
4 small eggplant rings
12 cherry tomatoes (skinned, if desired), stems removed
3$^1/_2$ Tbsp. butter
4 tournedos (small filet mignons), each cut approximately 1 $^1/_2$ inches thick
freshly ground black pepper to taste
2 Tbsp. chopped shallots or green onions
$^1/_3$ cup Madeira
1 cup brown sauce or beef gravy
$^1/_3$ cup water
salt and pepper to taste
fresh parsley sprigs or watercress, for garnish (optional)

Heat 3 Tbsp. of the oil in skillet. Sauté eggplant slices on both sides until tender and lightly browned. Remove from skillet; keep warm. Add remaining 1 Tbsp. oil to skillet. Cook tomatoes for 2 minutes; remove from skillet, keep warm.

In large skillet, heat 1$^1/_2$ Tbsp. of the butter until golden brown. Sprinkle meat with pepper. Cook meat on both sides until browned and to desired degree of doneness (about 5 minutes each side for rare). Remove steaks from skillet to warm serving platter. Add shallots or green onions to drippings in skillet. Cook briefly, then pour in wine. Add brown sauce or gravy and water. Season with salt and pepper. Remove skillet from heat. Swirl in remaining 2 Tbsp. butter. Top each tournedo with a sautéed eggplant slice and 3 tomatoes. Pour some of the sauce over meat. Pass remaining sauce separately. If desired, garnish with parsley sprigs or watercress. *Serves 4.*

BEEF POT ROAST WITH VEGETABLES

3½ lbs. beef pot roast
2 Tbsp. all-purpose flour
salt and pepper to taste
2 Tbsp. salad oil (add more if necessary)
1½ cups sliced onion
1 cup beef stock (or 1 beef bouillon cube dissolved
    in 1 cup boiling water)
1 bay leaf
1 can (7½ oz.) tomato sauce
6 medium potatoes, peeled and halved lengthwise
6 carrots, peeled and halved crosswise
6 small white turnips, peeled and halved crosswise
¼ cup all-purpose flour
½ cup water
salt and pepper to taste

Wipe roast well. In small bowl, place the 2 Tbsp. flour. Season with salt and pepper. Sprinkle mixture over roast and rub into surface. In large Dutch oven, heat salad oil. Add roast and brown well on all sides (this takes about 15 to 20 minutes). When meat is partially browned, add sliced onion and brown well (this gives good colour and flavour). Add beef stock and bay leaf. Reduce heat; cover and simmer for 1½ hours.

Turn roast. Add tomato sauce and potatoes, carrots and turnips. Vegetables should be covered with liquid. Cover and simmer for 1½ hours longer or until meat and vegetables are tender. Arrange roast and vegetables on warm serving platter and keep warm.

To make gravy, strain pan liquid. Skim off all fat. Measure; add water if necessary to yield 2½ cups. Return liquid to Dutch oven. In small bowl, thoroughly blend the ¼ cup flour and water. Slowly stir into liquid in Dutch oven. Season with salt and pep-

per. Bring mixture to a boil, stirring constantly. Reduce heat and simmer for 5 minutes. Serve gravy with meat and vegetables. *Serves 6.*

FREEZER-TO-TABLE STEAK WITH PISTOU

Here's a rush-hour meal for unexpected company. Spread frozen steak with a wonderful herb-cheese combination and pop it straight under the broiler. This recipe was a great success at the PNE cooking shows. Recipe courtesy of the B.C. Beef Information Centre.

4 frozen strip loin, sirloin or rib-eye steaks
½ cup Pistou

Brush steaks on both sides with pistou. Broil or grill over hot coals or at high setting on a gas barbecue for 4 to 5 minutes on each side for rare, 5 to 7 minutes per side for medium.

Serve with linguini or boiled new potatoes and steamed green beans. *Serves 4.*

Note: Fresh or thawed steaks can be used. Adjust cooking times accordingly.

Pistou
5 cloves garlic, finely chopped
1 cup fresh basil
1 cup freshly grated Parmesan cheese
3 Tbsp. tomato paste
½ cup olive oil

In bowl, pound garlic and basil into a paste. Work in Parmesan cheese and tomato paste. Beat in olive oil, 1 Tbsp. at a time. The pistou will keep indefinitely in a jar in the refrigerator. *Makes 1½ cups.*

Woodward's Food Floor was one of the first grocery stores to run ads without featuring a specific special. A tempting picture and a catchy tagline pulled in customers.

MINUTE STEAK SCRAMBLE

Serve with hot rice. Very easy, fast and colourful.

4 cube (or minute) steaks, 4 oz. each, cut
   into julienne strips

1 tsp. ground ginger

¼ tsp. salt

¼ tsp. garlic salt

¼ cup salad oil

2 medium green peppers, cut into julienne strips

1 cup celery, cut on the bias

½ cup green onions, cut on the bias

2 Tbsp. cornstarch

⅓ cup soy sauce

1 cup hot water

2 medium tomatoes, peeled and cut into eighths

Season meat with ginger, salt and garlic salt. Heat half the oil in skillet over medium heat; add meat and brown quickly on all sides. Remove meat. Heat remaining oil and add peppers, celery and green onion; cook just until tender, about 5 minutes. Combine cornstarch and soy sauce; stir in water. Add mixture to skillet. Cook and stir over low heat until mixture thickens and boils. Add meat and tomatoes; heat through for approximately 5 minutes. *Serves 4.*

DANISH STEAK DELUXE

Elizabeth, my Danish hairdresser, recommends this recipe highly. Samsoe cheese is difficult to find these days. It was always my favourite of the superb Danish cheeses. Tybo is still available and extremely good.

4 lean beef sirloin steaks, about ⅓ lb. each

1 tsp. Dijon-style mustard

4 thin slices cooked ham

4 thin slices Samsoe or Tybo cheese

⅓ cup all-purpose flour

1 tsp. salt

½ tsp. pepper

1 egg, slightly beaten

⅔ cup bread crumbs

⅓ cup butter

sliced lemon, sliced tomato and fresh parsley sprigs,
   for garnish

Pound each steak to about 4 x 7 inches and ⅓ inch thick. Spread with mustard. Top each steak with slice of ham and slice of cheese (be sure to cut ham and cheese slices smaller than steak). Fold steak over to enclose ham and cheese; secure with skewers. Season flour with salt and pepper. Place flour, beaten egg and bread crumbs in three shallow dishes. Dip each steak on both sides, first in flour, then in egg and finally in bread crumbs. Heat butter in large frying pan until light brown. Sauté steaks for about 4 minutes on each side or until golden brown. Remove skewers. Garnish with lemon, tomato slices and parsley sprigs before serving. *Serves 4.*

Tony Wilson was a frequent guest over the years. He represented Danish cheese and was a great favourite with the viewers. Danish Steak Deluxe was just one of his delicious recipes using Danish cheese.

SENSATIONAL PEPPER STEAK

1/4 cup salad oil

salt and pepper to taste

1 clove garlic

1 1/2 lbs. round steak, 1/2 inch thick, cut diagonally
  into thin slices

1 medium onion, finely chopped

3 green peppers, cut into 1-inch chunks

2 stalks celery, thinly sliced on the bias

1 cup hot beef stock (or 1 beef bouillon cube
  dissolved in 1 cup boiling water)

2 Tbsp. cornstarch

3 Tbsp. water

2 tsp. soy sauce

tomato wedges and lemon slices, for garnish (optional)

Heat oil in skillet. Add salt, pepper and garlic clove. Brown meat to desired doneness over high heat, stirring frequently. Remove meat from skillet. Keep warm. Discard garlic.

In same oil cook onion until transparent; add green peppers, celery and stock. Cook, covered, until vegetables are tender-crisp. Blend cornstarch, water and soy sauce to smooth paste. Slowly add to vegetable mixture. Stir until thickened. Return meat to skillet. Heat through. Serve immediately. Garnish with tomato and lemon, if desired. *Serves 4.*

FLANK STEAK MARINADE

1 1/2 lbs. flank steak

2/3 cup oil

1/3 cup soy sauce

1/4 cup red wine

2 Tbsp. lemon juice

2 Tbsp. Worcestershire sauce

2 Tbsp. minced dried onion

1 Tbsp. dry mustard

2 cloves garlic, crushed (or 1/4 tsp. garlic powder)

1 1/2 tsp. salt

1/2 tsp. pepper

1 1/2 tsp. chopped fresh parsley

Place steak in shallow dish. Thoroughly combine remaining ingredients. Pour marinade over steak. Marinate overnight in refrigerator (or at room temperature for several hours). Remove steak from marinade; pat dry with paper towels. Broil meat to medium-rare. To serve, cut meat in thin slices diagonally across grain. *Serves 6 to 8.*

Note: This marinade is also great for barbecued flank steaks.

ROASTED BARBECUE STEAK

1 round steak (2 to 2 1/2 lbs.), 1 to 1 1/2 inches thick

1/2 cup butter

1 small onion, cut into rings

1/4 cup chili sauce

1 Tbsp. vinegar

1 tsp. prepared mustard

1 Tbsp. Worcestershire sauce

1 tsp. salt

1 medium green pepper, cut into strips

2 medium carrots, cut into sticks

1 large tomato, cut into wedges

Preheat barbecue to hot. Place steak on barbecue rack 4 to 6 inches above heat; brown for 4 to 5 minutes on each side. Reduce heat to low. While steak is browning, combine butter, onion, chili sauce, vinegar, mustard, Worcestershire sauce and salt in small saucepan. Stir over low heat until butter is melted.

Tear off about a 4-foot length of aluminum foil; fold in half lengthwise. Centre steak on foil and cover with green pepper, carrots and tomato. Pour sauce over steak. Bring up sides of foil and fold down in tight double folds. Fold ends to seal in meat. Place over low heat for about 1 hour, or until tender. *Serves 4.*

Note: To bake in oven, place meat under broiler 2 to 3 inches from heat; broil each side for 4 to 5 minutes to brown. Preheat oven to 350°F. Prepare steak as directed and bake in preheated oven for about 1 hour, or until tender.

NO-PEEK STEW

This recipe is from Doris Guest, who called it her lifesaver. She should know—she brought up nine children and still had time to work as one of our best models in Park Royal.

1 1/2 to 2 lbs. stewing beef
1/2 package dehydrated onion soup mix
1 can (10 oz.) cream of mushroom soup
1 can (10 oz.) mushrooms, undrained
1/2 cup Burgundy

Preheat oven to 250°F. Place meat in casserole; sprinkle with dry onion soup; cover with mushroom soup and mushrooms. Pour wine over all. Cover. Bake for 3 to 4 hours or until done. Do not peek during cooking time. *Serves 4 to 6.*

JAMES BEARD'S MARVELLOUS BEEF STEW

Oh so good—worth the extra work. I use this recipe for special occasions.

FOR THE MUSHROOMS:
1/4 cup butter
1 lb. fresh mushrooms (whole if small, sliced if large)

Melt butter over medium heat in 8- to 10-inch skillet of enamel or stainless steel. (Enamel or stainless steel pans keep the mushrooms light-coloured.) When butter is frothy, toss mushrooms lightly for 2 to 3 minutes or until slightly soft. Set aside.

FOR THE ONIONS:
1 Tbsp. butter
1/2 lb. side bacon, cut into strips, about 1 1/2 inches long, 1/4 inch diameter
6 medium onions, cut into 1/4-inch slices

Melt butter in heavy skillet over medium heat and brown bacon strips, stirring constantly, until crisp and golden. Remove bacon from pan with slotted spoon; drain on paper towels. Brown onions slightly in bacon drippings over medium-high heat, shaking pan to rotate onions and colour as evenly as possible. Transfer onions to dish and add mushrooms; set aside.

FOR THE BEEF:
4 sprigs fresh parsley
1 bay leaf
3 lbs. lean boneless beef (chuck or rump, cut into 1 1/2-inch chunks)
1/4 cup green onions, finely chopped
1/2 cup finely chopped carrots
1/4 cup all-purpose flour
1 cup hot beef stock, fresh or canned (or 1 beef bouillon cube dissolved in 1 cup boiling water)
2 cups dry red wine
1 Tbsp. ketchup
1 clove garlic, finely chopped
1 tsp. ground oregano
3/4 to 1 tsp. salt
freshly ground black pepper to taste
3 Tbsp. finely chopped fresh parsley

Tie parsley sprigs and bay leaf together with a piece of cotton thread to make a bouquet garni.

Preheat oven to 350°F. Use skillet with bacon drippings; fat should be approximately 1/16 inch deep over surface of pan. Add a little oil or butter, if necessary. Over medium-high heat, bring fat almost to smoking point. Dry beef with paper towels, then brown in fat. Brown only 5 to 6 chunks at a time. Add more drippings or oil if necessary. When chunks are evenly browned on all sides, remove with tongs to a heavy ovenproof 5- to 6-quart casserole dish. Bury bouquet garni in the meat.

After meat is browned, add green onions and carrots to remaining drippings in pan. Cook over low heat, stirring constantly until lightly coloured. Stir in flour. If mixture looks dry, add a little more oil. Stir constantly, until flour begins to brown lightly, being careful not to burn. Remove from heat, cool for 1 minute, then add hot beef stock and blend quickly with wire whisk. Blend in wine and ketchup. Bring to a boil, whisking constantly as sauce thickens. Mix in garlic, oregano, sautéed bacon strips, salt and pepper. Pour sauce over beef, stirring gently to coat each beef cube with sauce. Sauce should almost, but not quite, cover beef in pan. If desired, add more wine. Bring to a boil on top of stove; cover tightly. Place casserole in lower third of oven and simmer gently for 1 1/2 to 2 hours. Regulate oven temperature to guarantee continuous low simmering.

Cook beef until tender when pierced by sharp knife tip. Gently stir in browned onions and mushrooms, adding any juices that might have accumulated. Continue baking for another 15 to 20 minutes. To serve, remove bouquet garni and skim off any excess fat. Taste sauce and correct seasonings. Sprinkle with parsley and serve directly from casserole. *Serves approximately 6.*

Note: Cooking the mushrooms, onions and beef separately before finally combining them guarantees that no one ingredient is overdone.

HUNGARIAN GOULASH

My favourite goulash. It freezes well.

2 Tbsp. salad oil (add more if necessary)
1 1/2 lbs. round steak, cut into 1/2-inch cubes
1 medium onion, chopped
1 large clove garlic, crushed
2 Tbsp. all-purpose flour
3/4 tsp. paprika
3/4 tsp. salt, or to taste
1/8 tsp. pepper
1/8 tsp. dried thyme
1 3/4 cups canned tomatoes and liquid
1 bay leaf
1/2 cup sour cream
hot cooked noodles
chopped fresh parsley, for garnish (optional)

Heat salad oil in skillet and brown meat in hot oil. Reduce heat. Add onion and garlic. Cook until onion is tender but not browned. Blend in flour. Stir in paprika, salt, pepper, thyme, tomatoes and bay leaf until seasonings are well distributed. Cover and simmer for approximately 1 hour, or until meat is tender, stirring occasionally. Stir fairly frequently during last part of cooking time. Just before serving,

blend in sour cream. Do not boil. Serve over noodles, garnished with parsley, if desired. *Serves 4.*

GROUND BEEF RING

1 1/2 lbs. ground lean beef
1 cup shredded carrot
1 1/2 Tbsp. prepared horseradish
1 package (1 1/2 oz.) dehydrated onion soup mix
1 1/4 cups quick-cooking rolled oats
1 egg, slightly beaten
2/3 cup evaporated milk
3/4 tsp. salt
1/8 tsp. pepper
mixed steamed vegetables for serving

Butter 4 1/2-cup ring mould. Preheat oven to 350°F.

Turn meat into bowl and break up with fork. Mix in carrot, horseradish, onion soup mix, rolled oats, egg, evaporated milk, salt and pepper. Turn into prepared mould and pack lightly. Bake for 40 to 45 minutes. To serve, unmould and fill centre with mixed steamed vegetables. *Serves 6.*

EASTERN-STYLE MEATBALLS

1 lb. ground beef
1 small onion, finely chopped
1/4 cup uncooked long-grain rice
1 egg
2 slices bread, torn in pieces
4 Tbsp. soy sauce
1 can (10 oz.) condensed tomato soup
1 cup water
1 Tbsp. soy sauce

Blend beef, onion, rice, egg, bread and the 4 Tbsp. soy sauce. Shape into 20 meatballs. In large frying pan blend tomato soup, water and the 1 Tbsp. soy sauce. Arrange meatballs, side by side, in mixture. Cover and simmer for 1 hour, or until rice is cooked. *Serves 4.*

BETTY'S FAVOURITE CABBAGE ROLLS WITH SWEET AND SOUR SAUCE

Betty Dexall is a special friend and fabulous cook. Many people attended the Royal City Hadassah Bazaar each year just to sample Betty's cabbage rolls.

1 medium head cabbage
1 lb. lean ground beef
$3/4$ cup bread crumbs
1 clove garlic, crushed
1 egg, beaten
1 Tbsp. chopped fresh parsley
salt and pepper to taste
1 recipe Sweet and Sour Sauce

Core cabbage. Place in boiling salted water and simmer, covered, for 10 to 15 minutes. Lift out cabbage and drain well. Separate leaves and lay out on paper towels to dry.

Thoroughly combine remaining ingredients except for sauce, handling meat as lightly as possible. Add just enough water to make a soft consistency. Shape meat mixture into balls and place one ball in middle of each cabbage leaf. Roll up leaves. Place seam-side down in casserole dish.

Preheat oven to 275°F. Pour sweet and sour sauce over cabbage rolls. Bake, uncovered, for 3 hours. Cover during last part of cooking time if cabbage leaves begin to brown.

This dish has much more flavour if refrigerated overnight and reheated. *Serves 5.*

Sweet and Sour Sauce

2 cans ($7^{1}/_{2}$ oz. each) tomato sauce
$1/2$ cup chopped onion
2 Tbsp. ketchup
2 bay leaves
salt and pepper to taste
1 cup brown sugar
3 Tbsp. vinegar or lemon juice

Thoroughly combine all ingredients. *Makes approximately 3 cups.*

BASIC BURGER MIX

1 lb. ground beef
$1/4$ cup fine bread crumbs
$1/4$ cup minced onion,
$1/2$ tsp. salt
$1/8$ tsp. pepper
$1/4$ cup tomato sauce

Combine beef, bread crumbs, onion, salt, pepper and $1/4$ cup of the tomato sauce; mix well. Form into 4 patties. In frying pan, brown both sides of meat; drain off excess fat. Simmer in any of the following sauces for 15 minutes. *Serves 4.*

Sauce Variations

• **Western:** To $3/4$ cup tomato sauce, add $1/4$ tsp. salt, $1/4$ cup water, 1 tsp. Worcestershire sauce and 1 can (4 oz.) sliced ripe olives. Pour sauce over burgers; let simmer for 15 minutes.

• **Mexican:** To $3/4$ cup tomato sauce, add $1/4$ cup chopped onion, 1 tsp. chili powder and 1 can (14 oz.) kidney beans. Pour sauce over burgers; let simmer for 15 minutes. Top with a sprinkling of grated Cheddar cheese just before serving.

• **German:** To $3/4$ cup tomato sauce, add $1/4$ cup vinegar, $1/3$ cup water, 5 whole cloves and 5 crumbled gingersnap cookies. Pour sauce over burgers; let simmer for 15 minutes.

• **Swedish:** To $3/4$ cup tomato sauce, add $1/2$ cup white wine, 1 Tbsp. sugar and $1/4$ tsp. nutmeg. Pour sauce over burgers; let simmer for 20 minutes.

• **Italian:** To $3/4$ cup tomato sauce, add $1/4$ cup water, $1/4$ tsp. dried basil and $1/4$ tsp. ground oregano. Pour sauce over burgers; let simmer for 15 minutes.

Burger Variations

• **Mushroom Pizza Burger:** Shape meat into 4 patties; broil several minutes on each side or until almost done. Remove from oven. Season meat lightly with salt and freshly ground black pepper. Top each patty with 1 to 2 Tbsp. prepared bottled pizza, spaghetti or barbecue sauce, 1 thin slice mozzarella cheese, pinch crushed oregano and several mushroom slices. Return to oven and broil just until bubbly.

- **Bacon Onion Burgers:** Mix ground beef with $1/3$ cup finely chopped sautéed onions and $1/3$ cup crisp-cooked, crumbled bacon. Season to taste with salt, pepper and Worcestershire sauce. Shape into patties. Pan-fry, broil or barbecue until done.

- **Herbed Burgers:** Mix ground beef with 1 Tbsp. chopped fresh chives, 1 Tbsp. fresh dill, 1 Tbsp. sour cream and 1 Tbsp. capers (optional). Shape into patties. Season with salt and cracked black pepper to taste. Pan-fry, broil or barbecue until done.

- **Stuffed Blue Cheese Burgers:** Shape meat into 6 thin patties. Mash 1 to $1 1/2$ Tbsp. crumbled blue cheese with just enough milk or cream to make an easy spreading consistency. Spread mixture over top of 3 patties. Top with remaining 3 patties and pinch edges to seal. Broil, pan-fry or barbecue patties until done.

- **Burgers Diane:** Shape very lean ground beef into 4 patties. In skillet, melt 2 Tbsp. unsalted butter; cook patties on both sides to desired degree of doneness. Remove to a warmed serving platter. Season with salt and pepper to taste. Keep warm. Into pan drippings, add 3 Tbsp. dry sherry, 1 Tbsp. unsalted butter, 1 Tbsp. chopped fresh parsley, 1 Tbsp. chopped fresh chives, 1 Tbsp. cognac (optional), 1 tsp. Dijon-style mustard and 1 tsp. Worcestershire sauce. Heat, stirring in any crusty brown bits until bubbly. Pour sauce over cooked meat patties. Serve immediately.

PARISIAN GROUND STEAK

$2 1/2$ lbs. lean ground beef
salt and pepper to taste
$2/3$ cup crumbled Roquefort or other blue cheese
1 Tbsp. finely chopped green onion
$1/4$ cup butter
$1/2$ lb. fresh mushrooms, sliced
1 Tbsp. chopped fresh parsley
$1/4$ cup dry red wine

Season ground beef lightly with salt and pepper. Mix, handling lightly. Divide mixture into 12 balls and flatten balls. Combine cheese and green onion. Spread mixture evenly over 6 patties. Place remaining 6 patties over cheese-topped patties; seal edges. In skillet, melt 2 Tbsp. of the butter. Add mushrooms and sauté until tender. Remove mushrooms with slotted spoon, leaving juices in skillet. Add remaining 2 Tbsp. butter to skillet. Brown stuffed meat patties well on both sides. Return mushrooms to skillet. Add parsley and wine. Simmer, uncovered, for 5 minutes or until done, basting constantly. Serve immediately. *Serves 6.*

MEATBALL TIP

For even-sized meatballs, press meat mixture into a square or rectanglar pan, then cut into squares of equal size, according to the size of meatballs desired. Roll each square into a ball.

MEATZZA PIE

The evaporated milk lends a very smooth flavour.

1 lb. ground beef
$2/3$ cup evaporated milk
$1/4$ cup fine dry bread crumbs
$1/2$ cup chopped onion
1 clove garlic, crushed
salt and pepper to taste
1 cup canned tomatoes, crushed and very well drained
$1 1/3$ cups shredded sharp Cheddar cheese
1 tsp. ground oregano
anchovy fillets, soaked in milk to remove excess
    saltiness (optional)

Preheat oven to 400°F. In bowl, combine beef, milk, bread crumbs, onion, garlic, salt and pepper. Mix well, handling lightly. Press mixture evenly along sides and on bottom of 9 inch pie plate to form a "shell." Crimp edges (flour fingers). Spread tomatoes over meat. Sprinkle with cheese and oregano. Garnish with anchovy fillets, if desired. Bake for 25 to 30 minutes or until done. *Serves 6.*

FIVE STAR CHILI

My daughter Maureen won a prize for this chili. Serve it with cole slaw and hot buttered buns.

1 lb. ground beef
1 clove garlic, crushed
1 1/2 cups sliced onions, separated into rings
1 cup celery cut on the bias
1 green pepper, cut into 1-inch dice
1 can (28 oz.) tomatoes, crushed
1 can (7 1/2 oz.) tomato sauce
1 tsp. salt, or to taste
1/4 tsp. finely ground black pepper
1 to 3 Tbsp. chili powder (according to preference)
1 1/2 Tbsp. vinegar
2 tsp. Worcestershire sauce
2 cans (14 oz. each) red kidney beans, well-drained

Heat large skillet; add ground beef (if beef is very lean, add small amount of oil when cooking to avoid sticking), garlic, onions, celery and green pepper. Crumble beef with fork or potato masher. Cook until meat is no longer pink and vegetables are tender but not browned. Reduce heat to simmer; add tomatoes with juice, tomato sauce, salt, pepper, chili powder, vinegar and Worcestershire sauce. Stir to combine seasonings well. Allow mixture to simmer for approximately 1 1/2 hours.

Stir in kidney beans and simmer for 30 minutes longer. Serve piping hot. *Serves 6.*

Note: This freezes well and leftovers make a tasty meal.

POOR MAN'S BEEF WELLINGTON

8 slices bacon
1 lb. ground beef
1 medium onion, finely chopped
3 Tbsp. minced fresh parsley
1 whole egg
1 egg, separated
1/3 cup chili sauce
salt and pepper to taste
pinch garlic powder
dash Worcestershire sauce
1/4 lb. sharp Cheddar cheese, grated
Sour Cream Pastry (page 162)
1 Tbsp. milk

Fry bacon in skillet until crisp. Drain, crumble and set aside. Pour off bacon fat. In same skillet cook ground beef, onion and parsley until meat is no longer pink and onion is transparent. Transfer meat to a medium-size mixing bowl, draining off as much liquid as possible. Allow to cool for 15 minutes. In a small mixing bowl beat together egg and egg white until combined; add bacon, chili sauce, salt, pepper, garlic powder, Worcestershire sauce and cheese; stir thoroughly into cooled meat mixture.

Preheat oven to 375°F. Roll pastry into a 14- to 15-inch circle. Place on a foil-lined 15 x 10-inch (approximately) baking sheet. Pile meat mixture on half the pastry. Gently fold other half over and pinch edges together, using a little water to seal edges. In small bowl beat egg yolk and milk; brush

Bea Wright's kitchen was located at the main Woodward's store in downtown Vancouver.

over pastry. Prick top of loaf with fork in several places to allow steam to escape. Bake for about 40 minutes or until golden brown. Cut into wedges and serve. *Serves 6.*

MEATBALL VEGETABLE STEW

1 lb. lean ground beef

salt and pepper to taste

1 clove garlic, crushed

1 egg

1 small onion, finely chopped

1/2 cup fine dry bread crumbs

1 Tbsp. salad oil

3 Tbsp. all-purpose flour

1 can (28 oz.) tomatoes, undrained and broken up

1/2 tsp. salt, or to taste

pepper to taste

1 Tbsp. sugar

1 Tbsp. Worcestershire sauce

1/2 tsp. crushed dried basil

3 medium potatoes, peeled and finely diced

4 small carrots, peeled and thinly sliced on the bias

1 onion, peeled and coarsely chopped

2 stalks celery, thinly sliced on the bias

2 Tbsp. chopped fresh parsley

In bowl, lightly combine beef, salt, pepper, garlic, egg, onion and bread crumbs. Form mixture into meatballs. Heat oil in skillet. Brown meatballs on all sides. Remove meatballs from skillet and set aside. Blend flour into drippings in skillet (add more salad oil if necessary to make about 3 Tbsp.). When mixture is smooth, add remaining ingredients. Stir well to distribute seasonings. Pour mixture into slow cooker or crockpot. Add meatballs. Cover. Set on medium heat and cook for 8 to 10 hours or until vegetables are tender. *Serves 4 to 6.*

Note: Cooking times may vary according to type of slow cooker used.

MARINATED BEEF TERIYAKI

2/3 cup soy sauce

1/4 cup dry sherry

2 Tbsp. sugar

1/2 to 1 tsp. ground ginger

1 clove garlic, crushed

2 lbs. beef sirloin, 1/2 inch thick, cut into serving-size portions

Combine soy sauce, sherry, sugar, ginger and garlic. Whisk or shake vigorously. Place steak in shallow dish and cover with marinade. Marinate at room temperature for approximately 30 minutes, turning meat several times.

Drain meat well, reserving marinade. Broil 3 inches from heat for 5 to 7 minutes on each side; baste with marinade several times while cooking. *Serves 6 to 8.*

TERIYAKI BEEF KABOBS

1 top round steak, approximately 2 lbs., cut about 1 inch thick

1/4 cup brown sugar

2 Tbsp. lemon juice

1 Tbsp. salad oil

3 Tbsp. soy sauce

1 clove garlic, minced

1/8 tsp. ground ginger

1 small pineapple, cut into 1-inch chunks

Trim excess fat from meat; cut into 1-inch chunks. In medium bowl, combine brown sugar, lemon juice, oil, soy sauce, garlic and ginger. Add meat cubes. Cover and refrigerate for at least 4 hours, stirring meat frequently.

Just before cooking, thread meat and pineapple chunks alternately on 12-inch metal skewers. Broil kabobs for 12 to 18 minutes, or until desired degree of doneness, basting occasionally with marinade and turning once. Serve with hot cooked rice and a crisp green salad. *Serves 6.*

SUKIYAKI

1 lb. sirloin steak
2 Tbsp. salad oil
1/2 cup beef broth
1/3 cup soy sauce
2 Tbsp. sugar
1 bunch green onions, washed, trimmed and cut into
   1-inch pieces
1/2 lb. fresh mushrooms, thinly sliced
3 stalks celery, sliced on the bias
2 large onions, thinly sliced and separated into rings
1 can (10 oz.) bamboo shoots, drained
3 cups spinach, washed and trimmed

Cut steak into 1/4-inch-thick slices across the grain; cut into approximately 2-inch-long pieces. In large skillet or wok, brown prepared steak quickly in oil. Push meat to one section of skillet. Stir broth, soy sauce and sugar together and pour into skillet. In separate sections of the pan, place green onions, mushrooms, celery, onion rings and bamboo shoots. Leave a good-sized section for spinach. Do not stir. Cover skillet. Simmer for 8 to 10 minutes. Turn vegetables in each section to cook evenly. Add spinach in reserved section; simmer for 5 minutes longer or until spinach is cooked. Serve over hot cooked rice. Pass extra soy sauce, if desired. This dish looks very attractive served at the table in its cooking utensil. *Serves 4.*

These Woodward's brand spices and herbs were a staple in households across Western Canada.

ORIENTAL DINNER

2 Tbsp. oil
2 cups beef (or chicken breasts), cut into 1/4-inch
   julienne strips
10–12 cups salted water
2 cups turnips, cut into 1/4-inch julienne strips
2 cups celery, cut on the bias
1 large onion, cut into 1/4-inch slices, separated
   into rings
2 cups carrots, cut on the bias into 1/4-inch-thick
   slices
1 beef bouillon cube
1 tsp. ground ginger (optional)
1 1/2 Tbsp. cornstarch
1 Tbsp. soy sauce

In skillet or wok, heat oil to almost smoking. (If using inexpensive cuts of beef, sprinkle with tenderizer according to manufacturer's directions.) Stir-fry meat until almost cooked. Remove to warm platter. Keep warm.

In large kettle or Dutch oven, heat water to boiling point. Blanch turnips, celery, onion and carrots for 2 to 4 minutes (depending on age and size of vegetables) or until almost tender. Remove vegetables with sieve or slotted spoon; shake well to remove moisture. Reserve vegetable water. Add a little more oil to drippings in pan if necessary. Stir-fry vegetables until each vegetable is lightly coated with drippings and vegetables are a vibrant colour. Dissolve beef bouillon cube in 1/2 cup of hot vegetable water. Mix well with vegetables in skillet. Sprinkle meat with ginger, if desired. Return meat to skillet; toss with vegetables. Cover and steam for 4 to 5 minutes or until vegetables are tender-crisp (add a little more vegetable water if necessary).

Mix cornstarch with 1/4 cup cooled vegetable water; add soy sauce. When vegetables are cooked, stir cornstarch mixture into meat-vegetable mixture; stir until liquid is thickened and sauce is bubbly. Correct seasoning by adding more soy sauce if desired. Serve with bowls of hot steaming rice and extra soy sauce. *Serves 4 to 6.*

ROUND STEAK ITALIANO

1½ to 2 lbs. round steak, cut 1 inch thick
2 Tbsp. all-purpose flour
⅛ tsp. garlic powder
2 tsp. salt, or to taste
¼ tsp. pepper
3 Tbsp. salad oil (more if necessary)
12 thin slices salami
6 slices onion
1 jar (16 oz.) spaghetti sauce
½ cup water
½ tsp. sugar
½ tsp. crushed oregano
2 tsp. chopped fresh parsley

Preheat oven to 350°F. Cut meat into 6 serving-size portions. In small bowl, combine flour, garlic powder, salt and pepper. Pound mixture into both sides of steak. Heat oil in skillet; brown meat well on both sides, then place meat in single layer in shallow baking dish. Place 2 pieces salami (overlapping slightly) and one slice onion on each piece of meat.

Combine spaghetti sauce, water, sugar, oregano and parsley. Pour sauce carefully over and around meat. Cover and bake for 1 hour. Remove cover and continue cooking for 20 to 30 minutes longer or until meat is tender. Delicious served with fluffy mashed potatoes or spaghetti and a crisp green salad. *Serves 6.*

KIDNEY WITH WINE SAUCE

2 lbs. beef kidneys
1 can (10 oz.) condensed beef broth
½ cup chopped onion
1 clove garlic, minced
½ tsp. salt
1 cup coarsely chopped carrot
1 cup coarsely chopped celery
2 Tbsp. dry red wine
2 Tbsp. cold water
2 Tbsp. all-purpose flour

Remove membranes and hard parts from kidneys; cut meat into 1-inch pieces. In a saucepan, mix together kidney, beef broth, onion, garlic and salt. Cover tightly; cook slowly for 1½ hours. Add carrots and celery; cook until tender, about 25 minutes longer. Blend wine, water and flour until smooth. Stir into kidney mixture. Cook, stirring, until thickened and bubbly. Serve over hot cooked rice. *Serves 4 to 6.*

MÈRE'S BURGUNDY OXTAILS AND GLAZED ONIONS
My mother-in-law's great recipe. Try it and give your family a treat.

2 large oxtails, cut into 2-inch sections
¼ cup oil
4 medium onions, finely chopped
½ cup Burgundy
1 cup well-seasoned beef broth
1 can (5½ oz.) tomato paste
bouquet garni composed of 1 bay leaf and several
   sprigs fresh parsley, tied with string
pinch dried thyme
salt and pepper to taste
18 small onions, peeled and partially cooked
6 Tbsp. butter
2 tsp. sugar

In large skillet or Dutch oven, brown oxtails on all sides in oil; pour off excess fat. Add finely chopped onions, wine, beef broth, tomato paste, bouquet garni, thyme, salt and pepper. Cook mixture for 3 to 3½ hours at low temperature.

Just before serving, glaze small onions in separate skillet. Melt butter, stir in sugar, add onions and cook, turning frequently, until nicely glazed. Serve oxtails and sauce surrounded with glazed onions. *Serves 4 to 6.*

ENGLISH MIXED GRILL

This dish will bring back many memories for those of us with British heritage. The servings are very large. If desired, the steaks can be omitted.

FOR THE KIDNEYS:
3 veal kidneys
3 cups water
1 Tbsp. vinegar
1 tsp. salt

Rinse kidneys. Place in medium saucepan with water, vinegar and salt; bring to a boil. Lower heat and simmer, covered, for 10 minutes; drain. Split kidneys lengthwise. Refrigerate, covered, until ready to use.

FOR THE BUTTER SAUCE:
$1/2$ cup butter or margarine
2 Tbsp. lemon juice
2 Tbsp. finely chopped fresh parsley
1 tsp. salt
$1/8$ tsp. pepper

In small saucepan, melt butter or margarine. Add lemon juice, parsley, salt and pepper. Set aside.

FOR THE CRUMB TOPPING:
2 Tbsp. butter or margarine, melted
$1/3$ cup soft bread crumbs
$1/4$ tsp. dried basil leaves
$1/4$ tsp. dried rosemary leaves

In small bowl, combine melted butter or margarine, bread crumbs, basil and rosemary. Set aside.

TO FINISH THE DISH:
12 slices bacon
6 link sausages
6 loin lamb chops, 1 inch thick (approximately $2^{1}/2$ lbs.)
3 medium tomatoes, halved
6 club steaks (approximately $2^{1}/2$ lbs.)
instant meat tenderizer (optional)
watercress or sprigs fresh parsley, for garnish

Pan-fry bacon in large skillet. Drain, one slice at a time, and immediately roll up and fasten with toothpick, to form curl.

Place sausages in large skillet. Cover with cold water and bring to a boil over medium heat. Drain, then sauté, turning sausages occasionally, until nicely browned.

Meanwhile, arrange lamb chops on rack in broiler pan. Brush well with some of the butter sauce. Broil 6 inches from heat for 12 minutes. Turn chops. Arrange tomatoes, cut side up, on broiler rack. Brush chops and tomatoes with butter sauce. Broil for 12 minutes longer or until chops are cooked.

Meanwhile sprinkle steaks with meat tenderizer, if using, according to package directions. When sausages are brown, remove and keep warm. Discard drippings in skillet. Heat skillet, add steaks and cook over high heat for 3 to 5 minutes. Brush with butter sauce; turn, brush again with sauce and cook for 3 to 5 minutes longer, or until done as desired. Keep warm.

When chops are cooked, remove to serving platter. Keep warm. Divide crumb topping evenly over tomatoes. Arrange kidneys, cut side up, on broiler rack. Brush with butter sauce and broil tomatoes and kidneys for 1 to 2 minutes longer, or just until crumbs are golden and kidneys heated through. Arrange bacon curls, sausages, steaks and tomatoes on platter with chops and kidneys. Garnish with watercress or parsley sprigs, if desired. *Makes 6 large servings.*

WAYS WITH LIVER

Remove membrane and veins from 1 lb. calf liver, $3/8$ to $1/2$ inch thick. Cook using any of the following methods. *Serves 4.*

- **Pan-fried:** Coat slices of liver with seasoned all-purpose flour; brown quickly on one side in $1/4$ cup hot oil (about 1 minute); turn over and cook other side for 2 to 3 minutes. Do not overcook.
- **Braised:** Coat liver slices in $1/4$ cup all-purpose flour seasoned with salt and pepper. Quickly brown on both sides in 3 to 4 Tbsp. hot oil. Reduce heat. Dissolve 1 beef bouillon cube in $1/2$ cup boiling

water; add to skillet with 1 thinly sliced medium onion. Cook over low heat for 15 to 20 minutes.

- **Broiled:** Cover liver slices in 2 Tbsp. melted butter or French salad dressing. Broil 3 inches from heat for 3 minutes. Turn and top with bacon slices; broil for 3 minutes longer; turn bacon once.
- **French Fried:** Cut liver in 1/2-inch-wide strips. Let stand in 1/2 cup French salad dressing for 30 minutes; drain. Dip in 1 beaten egg, then roll in 1 cup salted cracker crumbs. Cook in deep hot vegetable or salad oil (360°F) for about 2 minutes. Drain.

WIENER SCHNITZEL À LA HOLSTEIN

1 1/2 lbs. veal cutlets or round steak, cut 1/2 inch thick
1/4 cup all-purpose flour
salt and pepper to taste
1 egg, beaten
1 Tbsp. milk
1 cup fine dry bread crumbs
2 Tbsp. salad oil
2 Tbsp. butter
2 tsp. lemon juice
4 eggs
2 Tbsp. butter
1 Tbsp. water
lemon wedges and fresh parsley, for garnish (optional)

Cut meat into 4 pieces. Pound until 1/4 to 1/8 inch thick with meat mallet. Make small slashes around edge of meat to prevent curling. Coat meat on both sides with flour; season with salt and pepper. Combine beaten egg with milk. Dip floured cutlets into egg mixture; then into bread crumbs.

Heat oil, 2 Tbsp. butter and lemon juice in hot skillet. Cook meat for 2 to 3 minutes on each side or until tender and golden brown.

Meanwhile, in separate skillet, fry eggs in remaining 2 Tbsp. butter until whites are set. Add water. Cover and cook until eggs are done. Place 1 egg on each cooked veal cutlet. Garnish with lemon wedges and parsley, if desired. *Serves 4.*

VEAL PARMESAN
This dish is also delicious made with turkey scallops.

1 1/2 lbs. veal scallops
2 eggs
3/4 cup fine dry bread crumbs
1/2 cup grated Parmesan cheese
2 Tbsp. salad oil
1/2 lb. brick or mozzarella cheese, thinly sliced
1 recipe Tomato Sauce

Preheat oven to 350°F. Pound veal until fairly thin. Slightly beat eggs in small bowl. Combine bread crumbs and 1/4 cup of the Parmesan cheese. Dip veal in egg then in bread crumb mixture. Heat oil in large skillet and cook veal until browned slightly on both sides. Remove from skillet and place in 9 x 9 x 2-inch baking dish (or similar size). Cover with 2/3 of the tomato sauce. Cover this with sliced cheese. Top with remaining tomato sauce and sprinkle remaining 1/4 cup Parmesan cheese over all. Bake for approximately 30 minutes or until bubbly. *Serves 5 or 6.*

Tomato Sauce
1 Tbsp. salad oil
2 medium onions, finely diced
3 cloves garlic, crushed
1 can (14 oz.) tomatoes, broken up
1 can (7 1/2 oz.) tomato sauce
1 Tbsp. dried parsley
1/2 tsp. salt
1/2 tsp. ground oregano
1/4 tsp. ground thyme
pepper to taste

Heat oil in skillet. Sauté onion and garlic until tender but not browned. Add remaining ingredients and simmer for approximately 20 minutes. *Makes about 3 cups.*

VEAL CUTLETS SICILIAN STYLE

One of James Beard's favourites, this is also delicious using turkey cutlets.

3 large, very thin veal cutlets, cut across the leg

¼ lb. Hungarian or Italian salami

½ lb. mortadella cheese, sliced

¼ lb. prosciutto or ham, sliced

¼ cup fine bread crumbs

2 cloves garlic, minced (or ¼ tsp. garlic powder)

chopped fresh parsley to taste

1 tsp. dried basil

5 hard-cooked eggs

oil

salt and pepper to taste

5 slices bacon

2 cups tomato sauce

1 whole clove garlic

Preheat oven to 350°F. Leave veal slices whole, but remove bone. Pound until very thin. Arrange slices side by side (the long sides adjoining) so they overlap slightly. Pound overlapping areas thoroughly to press them together. On veal arrange rows of overlapping slices of salami. Top with rows of sliced cheese and finally the sliced prosciutto or ham.

Sprinkle surface with fine bread crumbs, garlic, parsley and basil. Down centre place row of peeled hard-cooked eggs. Sprinkle with oil, salt and pepper. Roll up very carefully as for jelly roll, making certain that eggs stay in place in centre. Place roll in baking dish and top with bacon. Over all pour tomato sauce with clove of garlic added. Bake for 1 hour. *Serves 8.*

Note: This dish is exceptionally good the next day, sliced and served cold. It looks great and is ideal for a buffet.

His plate loaded with savouries, this bear offered party-hosting tips to the readers of the Bea Wright sheets.

LIME TENDERLOIN BITS

1 1/2 lbs. pork tenderloin
1/3 cup lime marmalade
1/4 cup soy sauce
1/4 cup cider vinegar
3 Tbsp. brown sugar

Preheat oven to 450°F. Cut tenderloin into generous bite-size pieces. Place in foil-lined broiler pan or shallow roasting pan. Bake for approximately 30 to 40 minutes or until browned. Remove meat from oven and drain fat, if any, from pan. Reduce oven temperature to 350°F. Thoroughly combine marmalade, soy sauce, vinegar and brown sugar. Pour sauce over meat and return to oven. Bake for 30 minutes longer or until tender, basting occasionally. Serve over fluffy rice. *Serves 4.*

Note: This also works well with orange marmalade.

BAKED PORK CHOPS WITH BEANS

4 large loin or thin shoulder pork chops
salt and pepper to taste
1 medium onion, chopped
1/2 cup chopped green pepper
1 clove garlic, crushed
2 tsp. brown sugar
1/2 tsp. dry mustard
1 1/2 cups lima beans
1 can (14 oz.) red kidney beans, drained
1/3 cup chili sauce
1 Tbsp. vinegar

Preheat oven to 350°F. Trim excess fat from chops and melt fat in skillet. Brown chops on both sides; season with salt and pepper. Remove chops and drain.

To drippings in skillet, add onion, green pepper and garlic. Sauté until tender but not browned. Add brown sugar, mustard, lima beans, kidney beans, chili sauce and vinegar. Mix well.

Pour bean mixture into 2-quart casserole. Arrange chops on top. Cover and bake for 45 minutes or until beans are piping hot and chops are tender. *Serves 4.*

BAKED PORK CHOPS IN BARBECUE SAUCE

1 can (7 1/2 oz.) tomato sauce
1/2 cup water
1 tsp. mustard
1/2 tsp. hot pepper sauce, or to taste
1 tsp. Worcestershire sauce
2 Tbsp. brown sugar
3/4 cup diced celery
4 lean pork chops, well trimmed (use fat trimmings to brown chops, if you wish)

Preheat oven to 350°F. Combine tomato sauce, water, mustard, hot pepper sauce, Worcestershire sauce, brown sugar and celery in a saucepan over medium heat. In skillet, brown pork chops in trimmed fat. Place chops in casserole and cover with hot barbecue sauce. Cover and bake for 1 to 1 1/4 hours. Remove cover and bake 15 minutes longer. *Serves 4.*

ORIENTAL-STYLE PORK CHOPS

6 pork chops, 3/4 inch thick
1/2 cup water
1/4 cup soy sauce
3 Tbsp. honey
1 Tbsp. ketchup
1/2 cup finely chopped onion
1/8 to 1/2 tsp. ground ginger
1/8 tsp. pepper
1 1/2 Tbsp. toasted sesame seeds

Preheat oven to 350°F. Trim excess fat from chops. Place trimmings in skillet and melt (if necessary, add a small amount of salad oil). Brown pork chops on both sides. Place in a 13 x 9 x 2-inch baking dish. Combine water, soy sauce, honey, ketchup, onion, ginger and pepper. Stir well. Pour mixture over chops in baking dish. Sprinkle with sesame seeds. Cover and bake for approximately 45 minutes or until chops are tender. *Serves 6.*

PORK CHOPS DIJONNAISE

2 Tbsp. butter or margarine

4 loin or rib pork chops, approximately 1 inch thick

salt and black pepper to taste

2 Tbsp. chopped green onions

1 Tbsp. all-purpose flour

1 cup chicken broth (or 1 chicken bouillon cube dissolved in 1 cup boiling water)

2 Tbsp. brown sauce or beef gravy

2 to 3 tsp. Dijon mustard

2 Tbsp. chopped sweet pickle

Heat 1 Tbsp. of the butter or margarine in skillet. Brown chops on both sides. Season meat with salt and pepper. Reduce heat; cover and cook over low heat until chops are tender, turning occasionally. When chops are completely cooked, remove to a warm serving platter. Keep warm.

Pour off all but 1 Tbsp. drippings in skillet. Add green onions. Cook, stirring constantly, until green onions are wilted. Sprinkle with flour and continue to stir. Gradually add broth and brown sauce or beef gravy to flour mixture; stir constantly with a wire whisk until sauce is blended and smooth. Place chops in sauce and cook for about 5 minutes per side. Return chops to warm serving platter.

Add mustard, sweet pickle and remaining 1 Tbsp. butter to sauce. Stir to distribute ingredients. Do not boil. Spoon sauce over chops and serve piping hot. *Serves 4.*

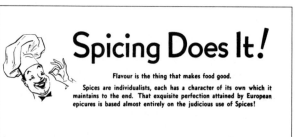

More cooking advice from the Bea Wright sheets.

ORANGE PORK CHOPS

6 pork chops, 3/4 inch thick

salt and pepper to taste

milk, for dipping

all-purpose flour, for dipping

3 Tbsp. salad oil

1/2 tsp. allspice

1 tsp. freshly squeezed lemon juice

1 tsp. grated orange peel

3/4 cup freshly squeezed orange juice

2 Tbsp. honey

2 oranges, each peeled and cut into 3 thick slices crosswise

Preheat oven to 350°F. Season chops well on both sides with salt and pepper. Dip chops in milk, then coat lightly with flour. Heat oil and brown chops well. Transfer chops to casserole.

Combine allspice, lemon juice, orange peel and orange juice. Pour mixture over chops. Cover and bake for 35 minutes. Remove cover and bake for 10 minutes longer. Remove chops to warm serving platter. Blend honey into pan drippings; add orange slices and glaze 1 or 2 moments on each side. Top each chop with orange slice and pour remaining sauce over top. Serve at once. *Serves 4 to 6.*

BARBECUE RIBS

1/4 cup oil

1 large onion, chopped

1 can (7 1/2 oz.) tomato sauce

1/4 cup brown sugar

1/4 cup water

1/4 cup chili sauce

1/4 cup lemon juice

1/4 cup bottled steak sauce

1 tsp. salt

4 lbs. meaty pork spareribs, sprinkled with seasoning salt

Heat oil in a medium saucepan; cook onion until tender but not brown. Add remaining ingredients, except for the ribs, and simmer, uncovered, for 20 to 25 minutes or until sauce is of a good basting consistency.

Preheat barbecue to high. Lace ribs accordion-style onto skewers approximately 14 to 16 inches long. Place skewered ribs on grill. Cook ribs for 15 to 20 minutes on each side. Brush ribs with sauce and cook for an additional 15 to 20 minutes on each side, brushing frequently with sauce. *Serves 4 to 5.*

SPICY SPARERIBS

2 lbs. country-style spareribs
1 clove garlic, crushed
1 Tbsp. lemon juice
pepper to taste
1 cup ketchup
3 Tbsp. Worcestershire sauce
salt to taste
dash hot pepper sauce
3 Tbsp. vinegar
$1/8$ tsp. dry mustard
pinch chili powder
1 cup water
1 lemon, thinly sliced

Preheat oven to 450°F. Place spareribs in single layer in large casserole dish. Top with garlic, lemon juice and pepper. Bake for 35 to 40 minutes or until nicely browned. Drain off fat.

Combine ketchup, Worcestershire sauce, salt, hot pepper sauce, vinegar, mustard, chili powder and water. Stir to blend well. Pour sauce over spareribs. Reduce oven temperature to 350°F and bake for 1 hour, basting occasionally. Remove spareribs from oven and top with lemon slices. Baste lemon slices with sauce, return to oven and bake for 15 minutes longer. Spareribs should be very tender. *Serves 4.*

PARTY HAM WITH ORANGE GLAZE

6- to 7-lb. rolled boneless ready-to-eat ham
$2/3$ cup frozen concentrated orange juice
$1/4$ cup firmly packed brown sugar
$1/2$ tsp. dry mustard
1 tsp. Worcestershire sauce

Preheat oven to 350°F. Slice ham into $1/4$-inch-thick slices, keeping ham together by running a long skewer through the centre. Place ham in large shallow baking pan. Bake in oven, allowing 15 minutes per pound (or about $1 1/2$ hours).

To make orange glaze, combine juice, sugar, mustard and Worcestershire sauce in small saucepan. Heat, stirring constantly, until sugar dissolves.

After 30 minutes, spread top of ham generously with orange glaze. Continue baking, basting every 10 minutes with additional orange glaze, for 1 hour longer, or until richly glazed. To serve, place ham with skewer still in place on serving tray or platter. *Serves 24 to 28.*

HAM GLAZES

- **Golden Glaze:** In small bowl, combine 1 cup light molasses and $1/4$ cup prepared mustard. Brush on prepared ham for final hour of baking time. Baste with glaze. *Makes $1 1/4$ cups.*

- **Honey-Orange Glaze:** In small bowl, combine 1 cup brown sugar, $1/2$ cup honey and $1/2$ cup orange juice. Brush on prepared ham during the last half hour of baking time. Baste with remaining glaze. *Makes approximately 2 cups.*

- **Tutti-Frutti Glaze:** In small bowl, combine 1 cup peach jam, $1/4$ cup frozen orange juice, $1/4$ cup brown sugar and 2 Tbsp. flour. Spread glaze on prepared ham during the last 35 to 40 minutes of cooking time. Baste with remaining glaze. *Makes approximately $1 1/2$ cups.*

WAYS WITH LEFTOVER HAM

There are many varied and delicious ways to use left-over ham.

- **Hot Appetizers:** Slice leftover ham paper-thin; heat and serve with thin raw onion rings in small hot biscuits. Great for a late night snack!
- **Chef's Salad:** Toss thin strips of ham with Swiss cheese and crisp salad greens. Top with your favourite dressing.
- **Ham Spread or Dip:** Blend ground ham with cream cheese. Season with garlic salt and Worcestershire sauce. Spread over crisp crackers and top with olives, cheese, hard-cooked egg slices or whatever is in your fridge that is suitable. Thin with pickle juice for a dip.
- **Ham and Melon:** Arrange thinly sliced pieces of ham on melon wedges or other fruit to serve with breakfast, lunch or as a first course at dinner.
- **Hearty Soups:** Use ham bone to make split pea, bean or lentil soup. Serve with crusty bread and carrot and celery sticks and you have a nourishing and hearty supper.
- **Omelet Filling:** Use finely chopped ham and minced green pepper or chopped green onion to fill an omelet.

BACON RAREBIT

6 slices bacon
$\frac{1}{2}$ cup chopped onion
$\frac{1}{2}$ cup chopped celery
$\frac{1}{4}$ cup all-purpose flour
1 cup milk
1 can ($7\frac{1}{2}$ oz.) tomato sauce
1 cup shredded Cheddar cheese
1 tsp. Worcestershire sauce
6 English muffins, toasted and split

Cook bacon until crisp; drain and set aside. Cook onion and celery until tender in about 5 or 6 Tbsp. of the bacon drippings. Blend in flour. Add milk and tomato sauce slowly, whisking until smooth. Cook, stirring, until thickened. Add cheese and Worcestershire sauce. Continue stirring until cheese melts.

Spoon mixture over muffin halves; top with a bacon strip. *Serves 6.*

SAUSAGE COMBO

8 slices bacon, diced in 1-inch pieces
1 lb. sausages, cut into 1-inch pieces
$\frac{2}{3}$ cup thinly sliced celery
1 large onion, chopped
1 small green pepper, chopped
1 can (28 oz.) baked beans
2 tsp. Worcestershire sauce
1 clove garlic, crushed
$\frac{1}{2}$ tsp. dry mustard
salt and pepper to taste
1 large tomato, coarsely chopped
$1\frac{1}{2}$ cups grated sharp Cheddar cheese

Preheat oven to 375°F. Sauté bacon and sausages in skillet until cooked. Remove and set aside. Drain all but $1\frac{1}{2}$ Tbsp. of drippings from pan. Add celery, onion and green pepper and sauté until tender but not browned. Combine beans, Worcestershire sauce, garlic, mustard, salt and pepper in large casserole dish. Add cooked bacon, sausages, celery, onion, green pepper and tomato. Stir well. Bake, covered, for 25 to 30 minutes. Remove from oven and sprinkle with cheese. Return to oven and bake, uncovered, for 10 to 15 minutes longer or until cheese is melted and beans are piping hot. *Serves 4.*

MY FAVOURITE LAMB CURRY

3 lbs. boneless lamb, cubed
seasoned all-purpose flour
$\frac{1}{4}$ cup salad oil or butter
2 Tbsp. curry powder
2 large onions, chopped
$\frac{1}{2}$ tsp. minced fresh ginger
2 large tart apples, peeled and diced
2 cups chicken broth
2 Tbsp. tomato paste
2 Tbsp. whipping cream

Dust lamb with flour. Heat oil or butter in Dutch oven, add curry powder and onions, and cook over medium heat for 3 to 4 minutes. Add meat and brown. Add ginger, apples, broth and tomato paste and simmer for about 1 hour, covered, until meat is tender. Add cream and reheat. Serve with rice and bowls of chutney, raisins, peanuts and cucumber. *Serves 12.*

SAVOURY LAMB STEAK AND VEGETABLE DINNER

4 lamb steaks, cut $^1/_2$ inch thick

$^1/_2$ tsp. dried rosemary, crushed

salt and pepper to taste

1 to 2 Tbsp. salad oil

1 medium onion, thinly sliced and separated into rings

1 clove garlic, crushed

$^1/_4$ cup chopped green pepper

$^1/_2$ cup sliced mushrooms

1 large tomato, cut into thin wedges

$^1/_3$ cup dry white wine

1 Tbsp. all-purpose flour

2 Tbsp. cold water

Remove and discard any excess fat from steaks; season with rosemary, salt and pepper. Heat oil in large skillet; brown steaks on both sides. Add onion, garlic and green pepper. Cook until tender, but not browned. Reduce heat to low. Add mushrooms, tomato wedges and wine. Cook, covered, for 35 minutes. Uncover and cook over low heat for 10 minutes longer or until meat is tender. Remove meat and vegetables to warmed serving platter, leaving juices in skillet. Keep warm.

Measure juices and add enough water to yield 1 cup liquid. Return juices to skillet. Blend flour and water and stir into meat juices. Cook, stirring constantly, until mixture thickens and bubbles. Serve gravy alongside lamb steaks and vegetables. *Serves 4.*

LAZY DAY LAMB PILAF

1 lb. boneless lamb stewing meat

1 Tbsp. butter or margarine

3 Tbsp. teriyaki sauce

2 Tbsp. dehydrated onion soup mix

2 cups boiling water

$^3/_4$ cup uncooked long-grain rice

4 Tbsp. teriyaki sauce

2 Tbsp. chopped pimiento

Preheat oven to 350°F. Cut lamb into $^3/_4$-inch cubes. Melt butter or margarine in frying pan with cover. Add lamb and brown. Stir in the 3 Tbsp. teriyaki sauce, cover and simmer for 50 to 60 minutes, or until lamb is tender (stir occasionally and, if necessary, add some water).

Meanwhile, combine soup mix, boiling water, rice, the 4 Tbsp. teriyaki sauce and pimiento in $1^1/_2$-quart baking dish. Cover and bake for 25 to 30 minutes, or until rice is tender. Remove lamb from sauce and add to hot rice. Toss gently to combine. *Serves 4.*

YORKSHIRE PUDDING

1 cup all-purpose flour

$^1/_3$ tsp. salt

1 cup milk

2 eggs, slightly beaten

Sift flour with salt into mixing bowl. Make a well in centre; gradually add milk to form smooth heavy batter; add eggs. Beat steadily for 2 minutes with beater.

Preheat oven to 400°F. Pour batter into roasting pan or muffin tins containing $^1/_4$ to $^1/_2$ inch of hot roast beef fat. Bake for 20 to 25 minutes, decrease the heat to 350°F and bake for 5 to 8 minutes longer. Cut into squares and serve with juice or gravy spooned over top. *Serves 6.*

MOUSSAKA

2 large eggplants
1 cup all-purpose flour
6 Tbsp. oil
2 large onions, chopped
6 Tbsp. butter or margarine
2 lbs. ground lamb (or beef)
$\frac{1}{2}$ cup dry red wine
$\frac{1}{4}$ cup finely chopped fresh parsley
3 Tbsp. tomato paste
2 tsp. salt, or to taste
pepper to taste
$\frac{1}{4}$ tsp. ground cinnamon
2 cups milk
$\frac{1}{2}$ tsp. salt
$\frac{1}{8}$ tsp. ground nutmeg
1 cup cottage cheese
2 eggs
$\frac{1}{4}$ cup dry bread crumbs
1 cup grated Parmesan cheese

Cut eggplant into $\frac{3}{4}$-inch slices. Coat slices lightly on both sides with about $\frac{2}{3}$ cup of the flour. Heat oil and sauté eggplant slices on both sides until golden brown. Drain on paper towels.

Sauté onions in 2 Tbsp. of the butter or margarine until soft but not browned. Add ground meat and cook for 10 minutes, or until meat is browned and crumbly. Add wine, parsley, tomato paste, the 2 tsp. salt, pepper and cinnamon. Cover and simmer for about 30 minutes or until sauce is very thick, stirring occasionally.

Melt remaining 4 Tbsp. butter in saucepan and blend in remaining $\frac{1}{3}$ cup flour, stirring constantly. Gradually stir in milk, $\frac{1}{2}$ tsp. salt and nutmeg. Continue cooking over low heat until smooth and thickened. Remove from heat and vigorously stir in cottage cheese and eggs.

Preheat oven to 350°F. Grease 13 x 9-inch baking pan. Sprinkle with bread crumbs. Cover with meat sauce and sprinkle with $\frac{1}{4}$ cup grated Parmesan cheese. Cover with prepared eggplant. Spoon white sauce over top and sprinkle with remaining $\frac{3}{4}$ cup grated cheese. Bake for 1 hour, or until set and lightly browned. Let stand for 10 minutes or longer before cutting into squares. *Serves 6 to 8.*

SPICY CARBONATED MARINADE FOR BEEF STEAKS

1 medium onion, chopped
1 clove garlic, crushed
1 Tbsp. soy sauce
2 tsp. pepper, or to taste
1 tsp. salt, or to taste
$\frac{1}{2}$ cup salad oil
1 cup carbonated lemon-lime beverage

This Woodward's ad appeared on the inside cover of a Vancouver tourism publication.

In bowl, stir onion and garlic with soy sauce, pepper and salt. Mix in oil, then lemon-lime beverage. Stir thoroughly before pouring over steaks and marinating for several hours. *Makes approximately 2 cups.*

MÈRE'S CURRY SAUCE

3 Tbsp. butter

2 Tbsp. arrowroot

1 Tbsp. onion powder

2 Tbsp. curry powder

$1/4$ tsp. salt

2 cups rich milk

Melt butter in saucepan. Stir in arrowroot, onion powder, curry powder and salt until well blended. Add milk. Stir constantly until mixture is thickened. *Makes $2^1/4$ cups.*

Note: Use amount of seasonings according to personal preference. This sauce is great served with seafood, chopped meat, hard-cooked eggs or sautéed mushrooms. Use to fill cooked small pastry shells or serve over hot cooked rice.

MAKE-YOUR-OWN CURRY POWDER

$1/2$ cup turmeric

2 Tbsp. ground coriander

4 Tbsp. black pepper

2 Tbsp. cardamom

1 Tbsp. cayenne pepper

1 Tbsp. ground ginger

1 Tbsp. ground cumin

This formula is for a fairly hot curry mix. It can be blended and stored in a screw-top jar. *Makes $1^1/4$ cups.*

This unopened jar of Woodward's brand curry powder is now in the Vancouver Museum Collection.

SPICY HORSERADISH SAUCE

4 oz. cream cheese

$1^1/2$ tsp. sugar

1 to $1^1/2$ Tbsp. prepared horseradish

$1/2$ tsp. Worcestershire sauce

2 tsp. lemon juice

$1/4$ cup whipping cream, whipped

Soften cream cheese; blend in sugar, horseradish, Worcestershire sauce and lemon juice. Fold in whipped cream. Serve with ham, corned beef, cold roast beef, or cold cuts. *Makes 1 cup.*

The mascot bear in his role as butcher.

WHIPPED ONION BUTTER

A great topping for piping hot steaks or hamburgers.

$1/4$ cup butter or margarine
1 tsp. Worcestershire sauce
$1/4$ tsp. seasoning pepper
$1/4$ tsp. dry mustard
2 Tbsp. minced onion
2 Tbsp. chopped fresh parsley

In small bowl, combine butter or margarine, Worcestershire sauce, seasoning pepper and mustard. Cream with wooden spoon until light and fluffy. Stir in onion and parsley. Spoon over piping hot steak or hamburgers. *Makes approximately $1/3$ cup.*

SPICY BARBECUE BUTTER

$1/2$ cup butter
3 Tbsp. vinegar
3 Tbsp. Worcestershire sauce
2 Tbsp. brown sugar
1 Tbsp. chili powder
2 tsp. salt
2 tsp. dry mustard
$1/4$ tsp. hot pepper sauce
$1/2$ cup ketchup

Cream together all ingredients. Refrigerate for several hours. Brush on hamburgers and steaks while cooking. *Makes $1 1/2$ cups.*

domestic poultry and other birds

mona says . . .

- To avoid having soggy stuffing, dry the cavity of the bird before stuffing it.
- Do not refreeze poultry that has been completely thawed. Refreeze only after once-frozen poultry has been thawed and cooked.
- After handling raw poultry on a cutting board or a work surface, always thoroughly wash the board or surface with cold water and then scrub again with hot water and soap.
- Chicken and turkey lend themselves to festive dining. When roasting the whole bird, try a different and glamorous stuffing. Add a touch of colour—a bouquet of parsley, nasturtium leaves, flowers, orange slices or another favourite garnish—just enough to accent the bird.
- Carve at the table so that everyone may fully enjoy the occasion.
- To estimate the roasting time of unstuffed turkeys, deduct 5 minutes per pound. If using a meat thermometer to know when the bird is cooked, insert it into the middle of a thick thigh muscle, being sure it does not touch bone. When the bird is cooked, the thermometer should read 180°F. If not using a thermometer, protect your fingers from heat by using a clean cloth or paper towel and pinch the thick muscle of a drumstick or the breast: it should feel soft. Or a leg should move easily when twisted.
- As a rough guide, allow approximately ³/₄ to 1 cup of stuffing per pound of ready-to-cook turkey. Pack stuffing lightly into turkey in order to permit dressing to expand. Bake any leftover dressing separately in a greased and covered casserole for approximately 30 to 60 minutes (time depending on the quantity) in order to cook through and blend the flavours. For additional taste, drizzle a spoonful or two of pan drippings over the stuffing before cooking it.

A handy two-page spice chart was one of the items featured in the Bea Wright sheets.

- Carving Hints: Cover turkey loosely and let stand for 15 minutes before carving. Pull leg away from body; cut through meat between thigh and backbone. With tip of knife remove leg bone from backbone. Holding leg vertically, large end down, slice meat parallel to bone and beneath some tendons, turning leg for even slices. Or, first separate thigh and drumstick; slice thigh meat by cutting parallel to bone. Before carving breast meat, make a deep horizontal cut into breast close to wing tips. (Fold wing tips behind back before roasting so that carving may be done without removing wings.) Cut thin slices from breast down to horizontal cut; follow curve of breast bone for final smaller slices.
- Turkey Chunks: Use in hot or cold salads, soufflés, casseroles, turkey tetrazzini or curried turkey. Spear cubes with toothpicks, and serve with a spicy dunking sauce as an appetizer.
- Small Turkey Pieces: Use in recipes for hashes, croquettes, turkey loaf or patties. Use in omelets and "à la king" recipes, or add to homemade or appropriate canned soups.
- Turkey Bones: Make turkey stock and use as a base for soup, a liquid or part of the liquid in gravies, sauces, creamed mixtures or casseroles, or for cooking vegetables.

ROCK CORNISH HENS

Cornish game hens roasted to perfection are a practical dinner choice of homemakers cooking for one or two. These small birds are available frozen at your food store.

1 cup finely chopped onion
1 1/2 cups finely chopped celery
1/2 cup finely chopped mushrooms
3 Tbsp. butter or margarine
1 1/2 cups rice cooked according to package
   directions
3/4 tsp. salt
3/4 cup white wine or apple juice
1 tsp. sage or poultry seasoning
6 Rock Cornish game hens
oil or melted butter

Preheat oven to 400°F. Sauté onion, celery and mushrooms in butter or margarine for 5 minutes, or until golden. Combine vegetables with rice; add salt, wine or apple juice and sage or poultry seasoning. Stuff hens and truss. Place in shallow baking pan. Brush with oil or butter. Roast, uncovered, for 1 hour. *Serves 6.*

Variation: Hens may be oiled and sprinkled with paprika and seasoning salt. Cook on rotisserie for about 1 hour or until tested done. Baste during the last 15 minutes with a mixture of 1/4 cup corn syrup and 1/4 cup consommé.

CHICKEN KIEV

3/4 cup softened butter
2 Tbsp. chopped fresh parsley
1 Tbsp. chopped fresh chives
1/2 tsp. dried tarragon
1 clove garlic, crushed
salt and pepper to taste
3 whole large boneless chicken breasts, split
1/3 cup all-purpose flour
2 eggs, well beaten
1 1/4 cups fine dry bread crumbs
salad oil or shortening, for deep-frying
lemon wedges and fresh parsley sprigs, for garnish
   (optional)

To make herb butter, thoroughly mix butter, parsley, chives, tarragon and garlic in small bowl. Season with salt and pepper and refrigerate until firm.

To flatten chicken, place each piece, smooth side down, on sheet of waxed paper; cover with second sheet of waxed paper. Using a mallet or other heavy object, pound chicken to approximately 1/4 inch thick, being careful not to break the meat.

Divide hardened butter into 6 balls. Place butter ball in centre of each piece of chicken. Fold over 2 short ends, then the long ends, making sure no butter is showing. Fasten each piece with toothpicks or skewers. (This is important; it keeps the herb butter inside during frying.) Roll each chicken piece in flour. Dip each in beaten egg, then roll in crumbs, coating pieces evenly. Refrigerate, covered, for approximately 1 hour.

In Dutch oven or large heavy saucepan, heat oil or shortening (3 inches deep) to 360°F on deep-frying thermometer. Add chicken pieces, 3 at a time. Fry, turning with tongs, until browned, approximately 5 minutes. Do not pierce chicken. Keep warm in pre-heated 200°F oven (no more) in pan lined with paper towels. Remove skewers or toothpicks carefully. Garnish with lemon wedges and parsley sprigs, if desired. *Serves 4 to 6.*

BROILED CHICKEN

4 Tbsp. butter
1 Tbsp. chopped fresh parsley
2 Tbsp. grated Parmesan cheese
1 Tbsp. lemon juice
1 tsp. paprika
salt and pepper to taste
4 chicken breasts

Melt butter in small pan and add parsley, cheese, lemon juice, paprika, salt and pepper.

Place chicken, meat side down, on cookie sheet that has been covered with foil and lightly brushed with oil. Brush bone side with marinade and place 6 to 7 inches from broiler. Cook for approximately 10 minutes. Turn breasts and brush remaining marinade liberally on the meaty side. Broil for approximately 10 to 15 minutes more. *Serves 4.*

TARRAGON CHICKEN TREAT

$1/4$ cup butter
$1/2$ lb. fresh mushrooms, sliced
salt and pepper to taste
6 chicken breasts
$1/2$ tsp. dried tarragon
1 cup dry white wine
1 cup sour cream
3 green onions, chopped
tomato wedges, for garnish

Heat 2 Tbsp. of the butter in large Dutch oven. Sauté mushrooms until tender but not browned. Season with salt and pepper. Remove mushrooms with slotted spoon, leaving juices in pan. Add remaining 2 Tbsp. butter to pan and sauté chicken gently until golden on all sides. Return mushrooms to Dutch oven; sprinkle with tarragon. Pour wine over chicken. Cover and simmer for 45 minutes or until tender.

Spoon sour cream into pan juices. Heat gently. Do not allow to boil. Sprinkle with green onions and garnish with tomato wedges. Serve immediately. Delicious over hot noodles. *Serves 6.*

CHICKEN KABOBS

$2^1/2$ to 3 lbs. boneless, skinless chicken breasts
1 lb. chicken livers
1 bunch green onions
1 cup soy sauce
$1/4$ cup sugar
1 Tbsp. salad oil
2 cloves garlic, crushed
$1/2$ tsp. ground ginger

Cut chicken into 1-inch pieces. Cut livers into 1-inch pieces and onions into 1-inch lengths. Thread on skewers, alternating pieces of chicken, green onion (spear through side) and chicken liver.

Blend soy sauce, sugar, oil, garlic and ginger.

Place kabobs in large shallow baking pan; pour sauce over. Brush each kabob thoroughly with sauce. Marinate kabobs for about 1 hour.

Preheat broiler. Remove kabobs from the pan, reserving marinade. Cook kabobs 5 inches below broiler for 3 minutes on each side, brushing with marinade after turning. Serve immediately. *Serves 6.*

Note: If using for appetizers, use smaller skewers.

JEAN'S FAVOURITE CHICKEN

5 whole chicken breasts, halved
butter
salt and pepper to taste
pinch paprika
1 package dehydrated onion soup mix
1 can (10 oz.) mushroom soup
1 cup sour cream
1 1/2 tsp. dill seed
2 tsp. lemon juice

Preheat oven to 350°F. Place chicken breasts in buttered baking dish, skin side up. Rub with butter, sprinkle with salt, pepper and paprika. Combine onion soup mix, mushroom soup, sour cream, dill seed and lemon juice; pour over chicken. Bake for approximately 1 1/4 hours or until done. *Serves 8 to 10.*

CURRY CHICKEN BREASTS

3 large whole skinless chicken breasts, halved
3/4 tsp. seasoning salt, or to taste
pinch paprika
1 cup chicken broth (or 1 chicken bouillon cube
    dissolved in 1 cup boiling water)
1/4 cup dry white wine
1/2 cup finely chopped onion
1/2 tsp. curry powder, or to taste
pinch pepper
1 cup sliced fresh mushrooms
1 Tbsp. butter or margarine
2 Tbsp. all-purpose flour
1/4 cup cold water
2 to 3 Tbsp. toasted slivered almonds
watercress, for garnish

Preheat oven to 350°F. Sprinkle chicken with salt and paprika. Place in single layer in shallow baking dish. Combine broth, wine, onion, curry powder and pepper and pour mixture over chicken. Cover with foil and bake for 30 minutes. Uncover and continue baking for 45 minutes longer or until tender.

Sauté mushrooms in butter or margarine until just tender. Set aside.

When chicken is done, remove to warm serving platter and keep warm. Strain juices and reserve. To make sauce, blend flour with water in saucepan. Slowly stir in pan juices. Cook and stir until sauce thickens; boil and stir for several minutes. Add the sautéed mushrooms (with juices); heat through. Spoon over chicken breasts (reserving some sauce to pass). Sprinkle almonds over top. Garnish with watercress. *Serves 6.*

MANDARIN CHICKEN

4 large whole skinless, boneless chicken breasts,
    halved
6 green onions
1 stalk celery
1 large green pepper
2 Tbsp. cooking oil
1 3/4 cups well-seasoned chicken broth
1 can (10 oz.) mandarin oranges
1/4 cup soy sauce
1/4 cup packed brown sugar
3 Tbsp. vinegar
1/3 cup cornstarch
pinch ground ginger

Cut chicken breasts in 1/2-inch-wide strips. Cut green onions in 1/2-inch lengths on the bias. Cut celery into 1/2-inch pieces on the bias. Cut green pepper into julienne strips.

Heat oil in wok or skillet over medium-high heat; stir-fry chicken until golden brown. Add green onions, celery, green pepper and broth. Bring mixture to a boil. Cover, reduce heat and simmer for 2 minutes.

Drain oranges, reserving syrup; set oranges aside. Combine orange syrup, soy sauce, brown sugar and vinegar in bowl; blend cornstarch into mixture slowly until smooth. Add ginger. Stir mixture into chicken; cook, stirring constantly, until thickened. Add reserved orange segments. Cover and heat through. Serve over hot cooked rice with extra soy sauce, if desired. *Serves 8.*

CHINESE PINEAPPLE CHICKEN

1 large whole skinless, boneless chicken breast

1 egg, beaten

1 Tbsp. all-purpose flour

1/2 tsp. salt

1/3 cup salad oil (approximately)

1 cup tomato juice

1 clove garlic, crushed

2/3 cup fresh or canned pineapple chunks
    (drained thoroughly, if using canned)

1/3 cup celery, cut on the bias

1/4 cup green pepper strips

1 Tbsp. cornstarch

1/4 cup honey

1/2 tsp. ground ginger, or to taste

1 Tbsp. soy sauce

1 Tbsp. sherry

Cut the chicken into long slivers. Combine egg, flour and salt in bowl. Roll chicken pieces in mixture to coat evenly. Heat oil in large skillet. Add prepared chicken. Cook, stirring constantly, over medium heat until chicken is lightly golden. Add tomato juice, garlic, pineapple chunks, celery and green pepper. Mix well. Cover and simmer for 15 minutes. Thoroughly mix cornstarch, honey, ginger, soy sauce and sherry. Pour over chicken mixture. Stir until sauce is thickened, approximately 2 minutes. Serve immediately over hot cooked rice. *Serves 4.*

CHICKEN-ASPARAGUS STIR-FRY

3 whole skinless, boneless chicken breasts, halved

6 Tbsp. salad oil

1/2 lb. asparagus

2/3 cup thinly sliced green onions

1 cup sliced fresh mushrooms

1 1/3 cups well-seasoned chicken broth (or 2 chicken
    bouillon cubes dissolved in 1 1/3 cups boiling water)

1/2 tsp. ground ginger

salt to taste

1 tsp. sugar

1/4 tsp. garlic powder

2 Tbsp. cornstarch

1/3 cup dry sherry

3 Tbsp. soy sauce

Slice chicken into thin strips approximately 1 1/2 inches long. In large skillet or wok heat 4 Tbsp. of the oil. Add chicken and stir-fry until lightly golden. Remove from skillet and keep warm, reserving pan drippings.

Break tough, woody ends from asparagus. Split each stalk lengthwise, then cut into 1 1/2-inch lengths on the bias. Heat remaining 2 Tbsp. oil in skillet or wok along with chicken drippings. Stir in asparagus, green onions and mushrooms. Stir-fry on high heat for 2 minutes. Add broth to asparagus mixture along with cooked chicken, ginger, salt, sugar and garlic powder. Cover and simmer for 3 minutes.

In small bowl, blend cornstarch, sherry and soy sauce until smooth. Stir into mixture in skillet. Cook, stirring constantly, until mixture thickens and bubbles. Cook for 1 minute longer. Serve immediately over hot cooked rice. *Serves 6.*

A recipe sheet headline from the time of Canada's conversion to metric.

SNOW PEAS WITH CHICKEN

3 whole skinless, boneless chicken breasts, sliced
    horizontally in $1/8$-inch-thick slices, then cut into
    1-inch squares
$1/2$ lb. snow peas, tips and strings removed
$1/2$ cup green onions, cut into 1-inch lengths
1 cup sliced mushrooms
1 cup bamboo shoots, drained
$1/2$ cup water chestnuts, sliced
3 Tbsp. soy sauce
1 Tbsp. water
2 Tbsp. cornstarch
$1/2$ tsp. sugar
$1/2$ tsp. salt
$1/4$ cup salad or peanut oil
$1/4$ cup cashews
1 cup well-seasoned chicken broth

Arrange prepared chicken, snow peas, green onions, mushrooms, bamboo shoots and water chestnuts on tray. In small bowl, mix soy sauce, water, cornstarch, sugar and salt. Heat 1 Tbsp. of the oil in wok or skillet over medium heat. Sauté cashews, stirring constantly, until lightly toasted, approximately 1 minute; remove from pan. Heat remaining 3 Tbsp. oil, add chicken and cook quickly. Add snow peas, green onions and mushrooms. Stir in broth. Cover and simmer for 2 minutes. Add bamboo shoots and water chestnuts. Stir soy-cornstarch mixture into pan juices. Cook, stirring constantly, until sauce is thickened; simmer for 1 minute. Sprinkle with cashews. Serve immediately. *Serves 6.*

KIKKO BROILED CHICKEN

$1/4$ cup soy sauce
$1/4$ cup lemon juice
$1/2$ tsp. onion powder
$1/4$ tsp. dried tarragon, crushed
2 broiler-fryers (about 2 lbs. each), halved or quartered

Combine soy sauce, lemon juice, onion powder and tarragon. Place chickens, skin side down, in broiler pan. Broil 5 to 7 inches from heat for about 20 minutes. Brush with sauce, turn over and broil for 20 minutes longer or until chicken is tender, brushing frequently with sauce. *Serves 4 to 6.*

CRUNCHY CHICKEN-NUT SAUTÉ

This is another of my favourites!

2 whole skinless, boneless chicken breasts
1 tsp. sake or dry white wine
1 tsp. grated fresh ginger
1 Tbsp. cornstarch
1 cup cashews or peanuts
3 Tbsp. salad oil
2 Tbsp. soy sauce
1 Tbsp. sake
1 tsp. sugar
$1/2$ tsp. cornstarch
1 Tbsp. water

Cut chicken into $1/2$-inch cubes. Sprinkle the 1 tsp. sake or wine and ginger over chicken. Coat with the 1 Tbsp. cornstarch.

Sauté nuts in 1 Tbsp. of the oil over low heat until golden brown. Remove from pan and set aside. Heat remaining 2 Tbsp. oil, add chicken and stir-fry for about 5 minutes or until chicken is cooked. Season with soy sauce, the 1 Tbsp. sake and sugar. Dissolve the $1/2$ tsp. cornstarch in water; stir into chicken mixture and cook until sauce thickens. Remove from heat and stir in nuts. *Serves 3 to 4.*

CHICKEN VERONIQUE

1 broiler-fryer ($2^{1}/_{2}$ to 3 lbs.), cut into serving-
    size portions
1 small lemon, halved
salt to taste
$1/3$ cup butter (approximately)
$1/3$ cup dry white wine
1 cup seedless grapes, washed and halved
chopped fresh parsley, for garnish (optional)

Rub chicken pieces well with cut lemon; set lemon halves aside. Sprinkle salt over chicken. Allow to stand and dry on rack for 15 minutes. Melt butter in skillet. Squeeze remaining juice from lemon halves into butter. Add chicken and brown well on all sides. Add wine and spoon sauce over chicken. Cover and simmer for 35 to 40 minutes or until chicken is tender (spoon sauce over chicken occasionally). Several minutes before serving, add grapes; heat thoroughly. Garnish with parsley, if desired. Serve immediately. *Serves 4.*

NAPOLEON'S CHICKEN

3 Tbsp. olive oil
1 frying chicken (3 to 3½ lbs.), cut into serving-size portions
¼ cup butter
¾ lb. mushrooms (slice if large)
½ cup white wine
2 tomatoes, chopped (peel and seed tomatoes, if desired)
1 cup chicken broth (or 1 chicken or vegetable bouillon cube dissolved in 1 cup boiling water)
2 cloves garlic, crushed
1 Tbsp. chopped fresh parsley
4 slices white bread, crusts removed
3 Tbsp. butter
4 eggs
salt and pepper to taste

Heat oil in large skillet, add chicken pieces and sauté over medium heat until completely cooked and golden brown on all sides. (Remove white portions before dark meat so they will not dry out.) Remove chicken from skillet; place on large warmed serving platter and keep warm.

Drain oil from skillet. Add the ¼ cup butter to pan; sauté mushrooms until tender. Remove mushrooms from pan with slotted spoon, leaving juices and butter in pan. Keep mushrooms warm. Add wine to pan juices. Simmer for 1 minute. Add tomatoes, chicken broth, garlic and parsley. Simmer quickly to reduce. Keep mixture warm.

In another skillet, sauté bread in 2 Tbsp. of the butter until golden on both sides. Keep warm.

Add the remaining 1 Tbsp. butter and fry eggs. Season with salt and pepper. Place eggs on fried bread. Spoon sauce over chicken. Arrange eggs on bread around chicken. Garnish with mushrooms. Serve immediately. *Serves 4.*

STAN'S JAMAICAN CHICKEN

This recipe is from BCTV's Jamaican cameraman. The crew loved it!

3- to 4-lb. chicken, cut into serving-size portions
1 Tbsp. Worcestershire sauce
½ tsp. garlic powder
2 Tbsp. soy sauce
½ tsp. ground thyme
1 Tbsp. ketchup
salt and pepper to taste
1½ tsp. ground ginger
1 egg
1 Tbsp. milk
1 tsp. soy sauce
1½ cups (approximately) fine dry bread crumbs
oil, for frying

Place chicken in large bowl. Combine Worcestershire sauce, garlic powder, the 2 Tbsp. soy sauce, thyme, ketchup, salt, pepper and ginger. Pour mixture over chicken. Cover and marinate in fridge 10 to 12 hours, turning occasionally.

Beat egg and milk together and add the 1 tsp. soy sauce. Dip marinated chicken in mixture, then roll in bread crumbs. Fry in pan over medium heat until done, or bake in preheated 375°F oven for about 1 hour. *Serves 6 to 8.*

COUNTRY GOOD CHICKEN

3/4 cup sour cream
1 Tbsp. lemon juice
1 tsp. salt
1 tsp. paprika
1/2 tsp. Worcestershire sauce
pinch garlic powder
1 broiler-fryer (2 1/2 to 3 lbs.), cut into serving-
    size portions
1 cup fine dry bread crumbs
1/4 cup butter

Preheat oven to 350°F. Combine sour cream, lemon juice, salt, paprika, Worcestershire sauce and garlic powder. Dip chicken pieces in mixture, roll in crumbs and place in broad, shallow baking dish. Dot with butter. Bake, covered, for 45 to 50 minutes. Remove cover and continue baking for another 40 to 50 minutes or until chicken is golden brown and tender. Baste occasionally with pan drippings. *Serves 4.*

CHICKEN STROGANOFF

1 broiler-fryer (2 1/2 to 3 lbs.), cut into serving-
    size portions
salt and pepper to taste
1/4 cup butter
1 medium onion, chopped
1 cup sliced fresh mushrooms
3 Tbsp. all-purpose flour
1/4 tsp. salt
1/4 tsp. ground thyme
3 chicken bouillon cubes
1 3/4 cups boiling water
1 cup sour cream
paprika, for garnish
chopped fresh parsley, for garnish

Sprinkle chicken pieces with salt and pepper. Melt butter in large skillet; brown chicken on all sides. Cover skillet; cook chicken over low heat for 30 to 40 minutes or until tender, turning occasionally. Remove chicken from skillet; keep warm.

Sauté onion and mushrooms in pan drippings until tender but not browned. Remove from heat; blend in flour, 1/4 tsp. salt and thyme.

Dissolve bouillon cubes in boiling water; gradually add to flour mixture. Cook over medium heat, stirring constantly, until smooth and thickened. Stir in sour cream; heat gently. Do not boil.

Pour half of sauce over chicken. Sprinkle lightly with paprika and parsley. Serve immediately with remaining sauce as gravy. Delicious with hot cooked rice or noodles. *Serves 4.*

CALCUTTA CHICKEN

1/3 cup all-purpose flour
1 tsp. salt
pinch pepper
1 tsp. paprika
1 broiler-fryer (2 1/2- to 3-lb.), cut into serving-
    size portions
1/4 cup butter or margarine
1 medium onion, thinly sliced
4 chicken bouillon cubes
3 1/2 cups boiling water
1 cup uncooked long-grain rice
1/2 cup light raisins
1/2 cup flaked coconut
1/4 cup coarsely chopped peanuts
1 tsp. curry powder

Preheat oven to 350°F. Mix flour, salt, pepper and paprika and coat chicken with mixture. Melt butter or margarine in skillet and brown chicken pieces. Remove chicken. Cook onion in remaining butter until tender but not brown. Dissolve bouillon cubes in boiling water; add to onions. Stir in remaining ingredients.

Turn mixture into 12 x 7 1/2 x 2-inch baking dish. Top with chicken. Bake, covered, for about 1 1/4 hours or until rice is cooked and chicken is tender. *Serves 4.*

PICK-UP CHICKEN STICKS

3 lbs. chicken wings (about 25)
1 cup margarine or butter
1 1/2 cups sifted all-purpose flour
1/3 cup finely crushed toasted almonds
1 Tbsp. salt
1/2 tsp. ground ginger

Preheat oven to 350°F. Divide each chicken wing in half by cutting through joint with sharp knife.

Melt margarine or butter in large shallow baking pan. Mix flour, almonds, salt and ginger in pie plate. Roll chicken pieces, one at a time, in margarine or butter, letting excess drip back, then roll in flour mixture to coat generously. Set aside on waxed paper until all are coated. Arrange without touching in a single layer in the baking pan.

Bake for 1 hour or until tender and golden on bottom. Brown under broiler for 3 to 5 minutes.

COMPANY CHICKEN WINGS

2 lbs. chicken wings
2 to 3 tsp. sugar
1/2 to 3/4 cup soy sauce
2 tsp. minced fresh ginger
1 clove garlic, minced
1/4 tsp. pepper
1/2 tsp. paprika
1/2 tsp. chili powder

Trim tips off wings. Sprinkle chicken wings with sugar and allow to sit at room temperature for 15 to 20 minutes. Place chicken wings on baking sheet. Combine soy sauce, ginger, garlic, pepper, paprika and chili powder in small bowl. Pour over chicken and allow to sit for 30 minutes, turning occasionally to completely coat chicken with the mixture.

Preheat oven to 350°F. Bake chicken for 45 minutes to 1 hour or until done. Delicious hot or cold. *Serves 4.*

Note: Chicken wings can be left in one piece after the tips have been cut off or can be cut in two.

ROAST DUCK WITH APRICOT GLAZE

1 small orange
salt
1 3- to 5-lb. duck
1 medium onion, cut into wedges
1 small apple, halved and cored
1 1/2 cups apricot nectar
2 crumbled chicken or vegetable bouillon cubes
1 Tbsp. cornstarch

Preheat oven to 375°F. Peel and quarter orange, reserving the peel.

Lightly salt cavity of duck. Stuff loosely with onion, apple and quartered orange. Tie legs of duck to tail. Prick legs and wings with fork to allow fat to escape. Place duck on rack in shallow roasting pan. Roast for 1 1/2 to 2 hours, spooning off excess fat.

Scrape white membrane from orange peel; cut remaining peel portion into thin strips.

To make apricot glaze, combine orange peel with remaining ingredients in saucepan. Cook and stir until thick and bubbly.

Brush duck with apricot glaze. Roast for 15 minutes more or until done. Serve remaining glaze as an accompaniment with duck. *Serves 3 to 4.*

A Canada Day salute from the mascot bear.

APPLESAUCE TURKEY BAKE

1 turkey (approximately 6 lbs., or equivalent in turkey
  pieces), cut up
1 cup apple sauce
$1/3$ cup soy sauce
1 Tbsp. brown sugar
$1/4$ tsp. garlic powder

Preheat oven to 350°F. Place turkey in baking pan.
Combine apple sauce, soy sauce, brown sugar and garlic powder; spoon mixture over turkey. Cover and bake
for $1^1/2$ hours or until turkey is tender. Thicken juices
and serve with turkey as a sauce or gravy. *Serves 6 to 8.*

TASTY TURKEY MARYLAND

1 small turkey, approximately 5 to 6 lbs.
1 egg
$1/3$ cup milk
$1/3$ cup all-purpose flour
$1^1/2$ cups fine dry bread crumbs
$1/4$ cup salad oil (more, if needed)
$1^1/2$ tsp salt, or to taste
$1/4$ tsp. pepper
pinch poultry seasoning
3 Tbsp. water
$2/3$ cup cream
2 Tbsp. all-purpose flour
$1/2$ cup water

Preheat oven to 350°F.

Cut turkey into serving-size portions. Beat egg with
milk in bowl. Place the $1/3$ cup flour and bread crumbs
on two separate sheets of waxed paper. Dip turkey
pieces first into flour, then egg mixture, then crumbs.

Heat oil in large skillet over medium heat. Cook
turkey pieces, several at a time, until golden brown
on all sides. Arrange turkey in shallow roasting pan.
Season with salt, pepper and poultry seasoning.
Add the 3 Tbsp. water and cover pan with foil. Bake
for approximately $1^1/2$ to $1^3/4$ hours or until fork-
tender. Remove foil cover during last 30 minutes of
cooking time.

When turkey is cooked, remove from pan and
place on warm serving platter. Keep warm. Stir
cream into pan drippings (loosen any crusty brown
bits in pan). Blend the 2 Tbsp. flour and $1/2$ cup
water until smooth. Gradually stir into hot liquid in
pan. Cook over medium heat, stirring constantly,
until mixture is thickened. *Serves 6 to 8.*

TURKEY CACCIATORE

1 skinless, boneless turkey breast, halved
  (about 3 lbs.)
all-purpose flour, for coating
3 Tbsp. butter (more, if necessary)
3 Tbsp. salad oil
2 cloves garlic, crushed
2 medium onions, cut into $1/4$-inch-thick slices and
  separated into rings
1 can (19 oz.) tomatoes, crushed
1 can ($7^1/2$ oz.) tomato sauce
2 tsp. chopped fresh parsley
1 tsp. salt, or to taste
$1/4$ tsp. pepper
$1/2$ tsp. dried oregano, or to taste
$1/2$ tsp. celery seed
1 bay leaf
$1/4$ cup dry white wine

Slice turkey into serving-size portions. Coat with
flour. Heat butter and oil in skillet, add turkey and
cook until golden on both sides. Remove from skillet. Add more butter, if necessary, and cook garlic
and onions until tender but not browned. Add tomatoes with their liquid, tomato sauce, parsley, salt,
pepper, oregano, celery seed and bay leaf. Stir to
blend seasonings. Cover and simmer for 15 minutes.
Add turkey and baste with sauce. Cover and continue simmering for 20 minutes longer, basting
occasionally. Add wine and cook for 15 minutes
longer or until turkey is tender, turning occasionally.
Remove bay leaf and skim off any excess fat. Ladle
sauce over turkey on serving platter. Serve with hot
cooked spaghetti, topped with grated Parmesan
cheese. *Serves 4 to 6.*

PARMESAN TURKEY AND BROCCOLI BAKE
A great recipe to use up leftover turkey!

2 packages (10 oz. each) frozen broccoli spears, or
    fresh cooked broccoli
4 Tbsp. butter or margarine
4 Tbsp. all-purpose flour
1 cup chicken broth (or 1 chicken bouillon cube
    dissolved in 1 cup boiling water)
1 cup light cream
3/4 cup grated Parmesan cheese
1/4 tsp. dry mustard
2 tsp. chopped fresh parsley
12 thin wide turkey slices
paprika

Cook broccoli in boiling salted water until tender-crisp. Drain well and place in bottom of greased 1 1/2-quart casserole dish; keep warm.

In medium-size saucepan over low heat, melt butter or margarine; stir in flour until mixture is smooth. Add chicken broth and cream. Cook over medium heat, stirring constantly, until mixture is thickened and bubbly. Remove from heat. Stir in half the cheese. Add mustard and parsley and combine well. Arrange turkey slices over broccoli to cover completely. Pour sauce over all, covering turkey completely. Sprinkle with remaining cheese and dust with paprika. Broil moderately slowly until heated through and top is browned, approximately 10 minutes. Serve with a green salad and hot rolls. *Serves 6.*

The mascot bear in party-preparation mode.

DOROTHY'S GOUGÈRE
This great recipe comes from Dorothy of the Oakridge Food Floor. It is a super Boxing Day meal!

3 Tbsp. turkey drippings, butter or margarine
4 Tbsp. all-purpose flour
2 cups turkey giblet broth, consommé or milk
2 Tbsp. capers (optional)
1/4 tsp. ground sage
salt and pepper to taste
1 to 2 cups diced cooked turkey
1/2 cup water
1/4 cup butter or margarine
1/2 cup all-purpose flour
pinch salt
2 eggs

Preheat oven to 375°F.

To make sauce, melt the drippings, butter or margarine and blend in the 4 Tbsp. flour. Slowly stir in broth, consommé or milk and cook, stirring constantly, until sauce is bubbly and creamy. Remove from heat and add capers, if desired, and sage. Season with salt and pepper. Fold in turkey. Set aside.

To make choux pastry, place water and butter or margarine in saucepan and bring to a boil. Add the 1/2 cup flour and salt. Cook, stirring hard, until dough pulls away from side of pan.

Remove from heat and beat in eggs one at a time, stirring vigorously after each addition. Use a knife to shape pastry into a circle around a shallow baking dish. Fill centre with creamed turkey mixture. With a fork, gently pull pastry slightly over turkey mixture. Bake for 30 to 40 minutes or until pastry is light, fluffy and golden, and creamed turkey is bubbly. *Serves 4.*

GOURMET RICE STUFFING

½ cup butter

2¼ cups finely chopped onion

2 cups finely chopped celery

1 green pepper, finely chopped

turkey liver, gizzard and heart, finely chopped or ground

1 Tbsp. salt

¼ tsp. pepper

1 tsp. dried marjoram

½ tsp. dried savory

1 tsp. dried sage

½ tsp. dried thyme

8 cups cooked, chilled rice (2⅔ cups raw or 4 cups quick-cooking)

1 cup chopped pecans

½ cup finely chopped celery leaves

2 eggs, well beaten

Melt butter in large frying pan; sauté onion, celery, green pepper, liver, gizzard and heart until thoroughly cooked. Blend in salt, pepper, marjoram, savory, sage and thyme. Add rice, nuts and celery leaves. Stir in beaten eggs; mix thoroughly. Loosely stuff turkey. Any extra stuffing can be baked in covered casserole or in aluminum foil during the last 45 minutes of roasting. *Makes approximately 12 cups.*

Note: When storing leftover turkey in freezer or refrigerator, remove dressing from bird and store separately.

SAUSAGE APPLE STUFFING

1 lb. pork sausage meat

1 large onion, chopped

1 cup chopped celery

1 large tart apple, peeled, cored and chopped

6 cups day-old bread cubes (approximately 11 to 12 slices bread)

2 eggs, slightly beaten

1 tsp. poultry seasoning

1½ tsp. salt, or to taste

pepper to taste

1 Tbsp. chopped fresh parsley

Brown sausage in large skillet over medium heat until cooked, breaking it apart until crumbly. Remove from skillet; drain meat well.

Remove all but ¼ cup drippings from skillet. Gently sauté onion and celery until almost tender but not browned. Add apple during last few minutes; sauté gently, stirring frequently. Remove pan from heat and stir in bread cubes. Add eggs, poultry seasoning, salt, pepper and parsley. Mix well. Add reserved sausage. Stir until ingredients are well distributed. Stuff turkey just before roasting. *Makes enough stuffing for a 13- to 15-lb. turkey.*

BRANDIED CRANBERRIES

4 cups fresh cranberries

1½ cups sugar

¼ cup brandy

Preheat oven to 300°F. Place cranberries in a shallow baking dish. Sprinkle sugar over top. Cover and bake for 1 hour. Remove from oven. Gently stir in brandy. Store in covered container in refrigerator. *Makes approximately 3 cups.*

CRANBERRY-ORANGE-LEMON RELISH
This is a delicately spiced, refreshing accompaniment to a holiday meal.

4 cups fresh or frozen cranberries (thawed and well drained, if using frozen)

1 large orange, quartered

1 medium lemon, quartered

1½ cups sugar

1 tsp. ground cinnamon

½ tsp. ground cloves

Wash cranberries; drain thoroughly. Remove any stems. Put cranberries, orange and lemon quarters in food processor and chop coarsely. Place prepared fruits in large bowl. Add sugar, cinnamon and cloves; mix thoroughly. Cover. Refrigerate for several hours or overnight to allow flavours to blend. *Makes about 4 cups.*

mona says . . .

- When using egg whites in a recipe, remove eggs from refrigerator several hours before needed. Egg whites beat up lighter and more readily when at room temperature (this gives angel-food cakes a finer grain and more delicate texture).
- Top a one-crust pie, baked pudding or fruit crisp with a 2 or 3 egg-white meringue. Bake dessert until almost cooked, top with meringue, and continue baking until meringue is lightly browned.
- Make a dessert that calls for yolks only—custard pies, some Bavarian creams, French ice creams, soufflés, mousses and lemon meringue pies. Instead of topping them with meringue, top them with ice cream or whipping cream.
- Poach egg whites in hot water until firm. Drain and shred. Add to casseroles, soups, sauces and salads.
- Beat egg whites slightly and brush over bread dough and pastries to put a shine on the crusts.
- For creamier icings, especially chocolate icing, replace part of the liquid with 1 or 2 egg yolks.
- Add 1 or 2 egg yolks to oil and vinegar salad dressings. Place in a screw-top jar and shake well.
- Drop egg yolks into boiling water and turn heat to low. Cook until yolk is firm. Drain. Mash or chop yolk for use in sandwiches, fish sauces and casseroles.

- For a golden crust on breads and pies, beat each egg yolk with 1 Tbsp. milk, cream or water and brush on before baking.
- Add leftover egg whites or yolks to whole eggs when scrambling or making omelets.

COOKING EGGS IN THE SHELL

Place the eggs in a single layer in a saucepan. Add enough cold water to come at least 1 inch above the eggs. Cover and quickly bring to a boil. Immediately remove from the heat.

- For Soft-Cooked Eggs: Let the eggs stand in hot water, covered, for 2 to 5 minutes, depending upon their size and how soft you like them. Lift out and rinse under cold water. Cut off the larger, rounded end with a knife and place in an egg cup, or scoop egg out into a dish.
- For Hard-Cooked Eggs: Bring the eggs to a boil, remove from heat and let stand in hot water, covered, for 20 to 25 minutes. Drain and immediately run cold water over the eggs until they are cooled. (This helps eggs to peel more easily.) This method stops the dark colouring around yolks.

EGGS LYONNAISE

This recipe was given to me by the late Muriel Downes of the Cordon Bleu of London.

3 Tbsp. butter or margarine
2 to 4 large onions, peeled and cut into ¼-inch slices
¾ tsp. salt, or to taste
6 eggs
⅓ cup light cream
freshly ground black pepper to taste
chopped fresh parsley, for garnish

Heat butter or margarine in large skillet. Place onion slices in single layer over bottom of skillet. (The number of onions used will depend upon their size.) Season with ½ tsp. of the salt. Cover and cook over low heat until onion slices are transparent, approximately 12 to 15 minutes. Carefully turn slices over with pancake turner, taking care to keep each slice intact. Break eggs into small container, one at a time, and slide carefully onto onion slices. Drizzle cream around edges. Season with remaining ¼ tsp. salt. Sprinkle with pepper. Cover and continue cooking over medium heat until eggs are set to desired preference. Sprinkle with parsley. Serve immediately. *Serves 6.*

GOURMET SPANISH EGGS

3 Tbsp. butter
2 Tbsp. salad oil
3 medium onions, chopped
2 large green peppers, chopped
3 large tomatoes, chopped (peeled, if desired)
½ cup chili sauce
⅛ tsp. chili powder
salt and pepper to taste
1 garlic sausage ring, sliced
8 to 10 cooked shrimp
5 to 6 eggs
1 Tbsp. finely chopped green onion

Preheat oven to 350°F. Heat butter and oil in skillet, add onion and green pepper and sauté until almost tender. Add tomatoes and continue cooking just until tomatoes are heated through and softened. Stir in chili sauce and chili powder. Season with salt and pepper.

Spread mixture in bottom of wide, shallow 1-quart casserole. Arrange sausage slices and shrimp around edge of dish. Carefully break eggs into casserole over vegetable layer. Sprinkle with green onion. Bake for approximately 10 to 15 minutes or until eggs are done according to personal preference. Serve with hot buttered rolls. *Serves 5 to 6.*

"SCOTCH" EGGS

Granny from Scotland gave us this family favourite.

1 lb. pork sausage meat
½ cup finely chopped onion
2 Tbsp. bottled steak sauce
½ tsp. salt, or to taste
¼ tsp. pepper
1 Tbsp. chopped fresh parsley
2 Tbsp. milk
6 hard-cooked eggs, peeled
1 egg, slightly beaten
1 cup fine dry bread crumbs
vegetable shortening or oil, for deep-frying

Lightly mix sausage meat, onion, steak sauce, salt, pepper, parsley and milk in bowl until well blended. Divide mixture into 6 and shape each piece around one hard-cooked egg, covering egg completely. Roll each meat-covered egg in slightly beaten egg, then coat in bread crumbs.

Heat shortening or oil to a 2-inch depth in deep saucepan. Heat to 365°F.

Process Scotch eggs two or three at a time, turning once or twice, until crumb coating is golden brown, approximately 5 minutes. Lift eggs out with slotted spoon and drain thoroughly. Serve hot with french fries and crisp green salad. *Serves 3 to 6.*

Note: To cook Scotch eggs in oven, omit shortening or oil; place prepared breaded eggs in shallow baking dish. Bake in preheated 400°F oven for 30 to 40 minutes or until meat is cooked and crumbs are golden.

Variation: Substitute ground beef for sausage meat; or a combination of half ground beef and half sausage; or add chopped bacon to sausage meat or ground beef.

EGGS MORNAY

6 thin slices cooked ham
1 Tbsp. butter or margarine
3 English muffins
1/2 cup whole cranberry sauce
6 eggs
salt and pepper to taste
1 recipe Mornay Sauce

Lightly brown ham in butter or margarine. Split muffins; toast and lightly butter. Place ham slice on each muffin half; top with cranberry sauce. Poach eggs; place on top of cranberry sauce. Season with salt and pepper. Pour Mornay Sauce over top. *Serves 6.*

Mornay Sauce
3 Tbsp. butter or margarine
3 Tbsp. all-purpose flour
3/4 tsp. salt
pinch pepper
1 cup light cream
1/4 cup dry white wine
1/3 cup shredded Swiss cheese

Melt butter or margarine in saucepan. Blend in flour, salt and pepper. Add cream all at once. Cook and stir until mixture is thickened and bubbles. Stir in wine; add cheese and stir until melted. *Makes 1 1/2 cups.*

PERFECT SCRAMBLE

6 eggs
1/3 cup milk or light cream
1/2 tsp. salt, or to taste
pinch pepper
1 1/2 Tbsp. butter, margarine or bacon drippings

Combine eggs, milk or cream, salt and pepper (mix lightly for streaked gold and white effect or mix thoroughly for all-over yellow). Heat butter, margarine or drippings in skillet just until hot enough to make a drop of water sizzle. Pour in egg mixture and reduce heat—this is important for tender eggs. Do not disturb mixture until it starts to set on bottom and sides, then lift and fold over with wide spatula so uncooked part goes to bottom. Avoid breaking up eggs more than necessary. Cook until eggs are just set, about 5 to 8 minutes. Remove skillet from heat just before all the moist part is cooked. Do not allow eggs to stand in skillet—the hot pan continues to cook them. Serve at once on warm platter. *Serves 3 to 4.*

Note: To scramble eggs in top of double boiler, omit butter, margarine or bacon drippings; use a spoon to stir. The water in bottom of double boiler should only simmer and not touch top pan. This method takes approximately twice as long as in a skillet.

The mascot bear in cowboy guise.

YUMMY CHEESE OMELET

1 Tbsp. butter or margarine
1 cup cottage cheese
3/4 cup shredded Swiss cheese
1 medium tomato, diced
1 Tbsp. all-purpose flour
1 tsp. dried dill weed
1 tsp. chopped fresh parsley
pinch salt
pepper to taste
4 eggs
fresh parsley, for garnish
tomato wedges, for garnish

Preheat oven to 350°F. Melt butter or margarine in 9-inch pie plate. Slightly beat cottage cheese; stir in Swiss cheese, tomato, flour, dill, parsley, salt and pepper. Beat eggs slightly and add to cheese mixture. Pour into prepared pie plate. Bake for 25 to 30 minutes. Cut into wedges and serve immediately. Garnish with parsley and tomato wedges, if desired. *Serves 4 to 6.*

MASHED BROWN OMELET

4 slices bacon
2 cups shredded cooked potatoes
1/3 cup chopped onion
1/3 cup chopped green pepper
4 eggs
1/4 cup milk
1/2 tsp. salt
pepper to taste
1 cup shredded sharp Cheddar cheese

Cook bacon until crisp in large skillet. Remove bacon, drain and crumble. Set aside. Mix potatoes, onion and green pepper with bacon drippings. Pat into skillet. Cook over low heat until underside is crisp and brown.

Blend eggs, milk, salt and pepper in bowl. Pour mixture over potatoes. Top with cheese and crumbled bacon. Cover and cook over low heat. When egg is cooked, loosen omelet and fold. *Serves 4.*

From brunch to cocktails, Woodward's recipe sheets offered advice for every holiday need.

SPANISH OMELET

FOR THE SAUCE:

3 Tbsp. chopped onion

3 Tbsp. chopped celery

3 Tbsp. chopped green pepper

2 Tbsp. salad oil

1 Tbsp. all-purpose flour

1 cup canned tomatoes

1/4 tsp. chili powder

1/4 tsp. salt

Sauté onion, celery and green pepper in oil until tender. Blend in flour and tomatoes gradually; cook and stir until thickened. Add chili powder and salt; simmer slowly for 5 minutes, stirring occasionally. Keep hot while preparing omelet.

FOR THE OMELET:

4 eggs

1/4 cup milk

1/2 tsp. salt

few grains pepper

Mix eggs, milk, salt and pepper together. Pour mixture into moderately hot, buttered skillet. As egg cooks at edge, lift with spatula to let uncooked portion flow to sides. Do not stir. When mixture has set but is still moist (about 3 minutes), increase heat to brown bottom quickly. Add sauce on one half of omelet and fold over. Serve at once. *Serves 3.*

QUICK QUICHE LORRAINE

1 9-inch unbaked pastry shell

8 slices bacon, diced

1/2 lb. Swiss cheese, shredded

1 Tbsp. all-purpose flour

1/2 tsp. salt

pinch ground nutmeg

3 eggs, beaten

1 1/3 cups milk

Preheat oven to 450°F. Bake pastry shell for 7 minutes or until lightly browned. Remove from oven and reduce heat to 325°F.

Fry bacon until crisp. Drain and crumble. Reserve 2 Tbsp. for garnish. Place remaining bacon in pie shell; add cheese.

Combine flour, salt, nutmeg, eggs and milk; pour over cheese and bacon. Sprinkle reserved bacon on top in circle. Bake for 35 to 40 minutes, or until almost set in centre. Cool for 15 to 30 minutes before serving. *Serves 6.*

DEVILLED EGGS IN ZESTY SAUCE

This recipe is one of our family favourites—especially for Christmas morning.

3 Tbsp. butter or margarine

1 small onion, chopped

3 Tbsp. all-purpose flour

2 tsp. sugar

3/4 tsp. salt, or to taste

freshly ground black pepper

1 can (28 oz.) diced tomatoes

1 bay leaf

6 eggs, hard-cooked

1/4 cup mayonnaise

1 tsp. Dijon-style mustard

salt and pepper to taste

3/4 cup fine dry bread crumbs

2 Tbsp. melted butter or margarine

Melt the 3 Tbsp. butter or margarine in skillet. Add onion and cook until tender. Stir in flour, sugar, salt, pepper, tomatoes and bay leaf. Cook, stirring, until thick and bubbly. Remove bay leaf. Pour sauce into 10 x 6 x 1 1/2-inch (or similar size) baking dish.

Cut eggs in half; remove yolks and mash. Blend in mayonnaise, mustard, salt and pepper. Fill egg whites. Nestle stuffed eggs in sauce.

Preheat oven to 425°F. Combine bread crumbs and the 2 Tbsp. melted butter or margarine. Sprinkle over eggs. Bake for 10 minutes or until piping hot. *Serves 6.*

This 1929 children's wagon race in Vancouver was sponsored by Woodward's.

rice and pasta

mona says . . .

Rice and pasta are particularly well-suited to casserole dinners, which are a favourite at our house for a number of reasons.

- They are delicious and simple family budget stretchers. Remember to suit the style of food to the purpose and avoid buying fancy quality when it really isn't necessary. Don't use fancy whole tomatoes if they will be broken up and cooked into a sauce or casserole; expensive white tuna meat isn't necessary if it will be flaked and baked in a casserole.
- Rice and pasta can be transformed from simple homey meals to elegant company fare when enhanced by a variety of garnishes.
- Casseroles are time savers when prepared in advance and frozen.

To Freeze Casserole Dishes
- Do not overcook foods. More cooking time is to come after you take the dish from the freezer. Cook vegetables, rice or noodles until just barely tender.
- Add toppings such as grated cheese when you are ready to bake the casserole.
- Thaw casseroles in the refrigerator for 12 to 24 hours before serving.

- Keep casserole dishes in home freezers for no longer than 2 months or in the freezer compartment of your refrigerator for no longer than 2 weeks.
- Freeze and store casseroles in the baking dish or in metal or glass containers, waxed cartons or plastic containers. Ensure that the package is airtight.
- If freezing food in casserole dish, cover and wrap completely with aluminum foil or plastic wrap.

A portrait of Mona from a Woodward's recipe sheet.

CORN NOODLE BAKE

2 cups noodles
½ to 1 lb. ground beef
2 stalks celery, chopped
1 medium onion, chopped
1 can (10 oz.) creamed corn
1 can (10 oz.) cream of mushroom soup
1 can (10 oz.) sliced mushrooms, drained
salt and pepper to taste
dash Worcestershire sauce
pinch garlic powder (optional)
1 cup grated Cheddar cheese

Preheat oven to 350°F. Cook noodles in boiling salted water according to package instructions. Drain. Brown ground beef with celery and onion. Place noodles, meat mixture, corn, mushroom soup, mushrooms, salt, pepper, Worcestershire sauce and garlic powder, if using, in large casserole dish. Mix thoroughly. Top with cheese. Bake for approximately 30 minutes or until cheese has melted and casserole is bubbly. Delicious with a crisp green salad or coleslaw. *Serves 4 to 6.*

SPAGHETTI MILANO

2 Tbsp. salad oil
1 lb. boneless pork loin, cut into 1-inch strips
½ cup chopped onion
½ cup chopped celery
1 medium green pepper, cut into thin strips
1 can (10 oz.) sliced mushrooms, undrained
1 tsp. Worcestershire sauce
1 tsp. salt
⅛ tsp. pepper
½ tsp. dried basil
1 can (10 oz.) condensed cream of mushroom soup, undiluted
½ cup milk
1 package (1 lb.) spaghetti
2 tomatoes, peeled, thinly sliced and cut in half
1½ cups bread cubes
2 Tbsp. melted butter
1 cup grated sharp Cheddar cheese

Heat oil in large skillet and brown pork. Add onion, celery and green pepper. Cook until tender. Mix in mushrooms, Worcestershire sauce, salt, pepper and basil. Simmer, covered, for 25 minutes. Blend in mushroom soup and milk; simmer, covered, for 5 minutes. Preheat oven to 350°F.

Cook spaghetti according to package directions. Drain and combine in an ungreased 2-quart baking dish with pork mixture. Overlap tomatoes around edge of casserole. Toss bread cubes with melted butter and sprinkle over casserole. Bake, covered, for 20 minutes. Remove from oven and top croutons with cheese. Bake, uncovered, for 10 minutes longer or until cheese melts and casserole is piping hot. *Serves 6 to 8.*

SEPARATING NOODLES

To prevent gummy noodles, rice, macaroni and spaghetti, add 2 tsp. of cooking oil to the water before cooking and your problems will be solved. You will find it makes the noodles glisten and stand apart.

SAUCY SPAGHETTI AND MEATBALLS

FOR THE SAUCE:
3 Tbsp. salad oil
1 medium onion, chopped
1 large clove garlic, crushed
1 can (28 oz.) tomatoes, undrained, crushed and broken up
2 cans (5½ oz. each) tomato paste
2 cups water
1½ tsp. dried oregano, crushed
1½ tsp. salt, or to taste
1 tsp. sugar
½ tsp. pepper, or to taste
1 bay leaf

Heat oil in skillet, add onion and garlic and cook until tender but not browned. Stir in remaining ingredients. Simmer, uncovered, for 30 minutes, stirring occasionally. Remove bay leaf before adding meatballs.

FOR THE MEATBALLS:

4 slices bread

$^1/_2$ cup water

2 eggs

1 lb. ground beef

$^1/_4$ cup grated Parmesan cheese

2 Tbsp. chopped fresh parsley

1 tsp. salt, or to taste

$^1/_4$ tsp. dried oregano, crushed

2 Tbsp. salad oil

Soak bread in water for several minutes. Add eggs, mixing well. Combine with ground beef, Parmesan cheese, parsley, salt and oregano. Form mixture into small balls (approximately 24). Brown slowly in hot oil.

Add meatballs to prepared sauce. Simmer, loosely covered, for 30 minutes. Serve over hot cooked spaghetti and sprinkle with extra grated Parmesan cheese. *Serves 6.*

SPAGHETTI SAUCE FROM LEFTOVERS

3 Tbsp. salad oil

1 large onion, chopped

2 cloves garlic, minced

2 stalks celery, thinly sliced

$^1/_2$ green pepper, coarsely chopped

1 cup fresh mushrooms, sliced

2 cups cooked beef, ground medium fine

1 can (28 oz.) tomatoes

1 can (7$^1/_2$ oz.) tomato sauce

salt and pepper to taste

$^1/_2$ tsp. ground oregano

2 Tbsp. dried parsley

$^1/_4$ cup Parmesan cheese

1 package (1 lb.) spaghetti

extra Parmesan cheese

Heat oil in large skillet. Sauté onion, garlic and celery until tender but not browned. Add green pepper, mushrooms and cooked beef; sauté quickly, stirring constantly. Add tomatoes, tomato sauce, salt, pepper, oregano, parsley and Parmesan cheese. Allow to sim-

mer gently, covered, for 45 minutes, stirring occasionally. Add a little water if necessary.

Cook spaghetti according to package directions; drain. Serve sauce over hot noodles. Pass **extra** Parmesan cheese at the table. *Serves 6.*

DEVILLED SPAGHETTI

1 package ($^1/_2$ lb.) spaghetti

1 onion, cut fine

1 small clove garlic, crushed

2 Tbsp. oil

2$^1/_2$ cups cooked tomatoes

salt and pepper

1 Tbsp. sugar

pinch cayenne pepper

$^1/_2$ cup diced cooked chicken

1 cup fresh mushrooms, sautéed

grated cheese, for topping

Preheat oven to 350°F. Cook spaghetti in boiling salted water until tender. Drain and place in greased casserole. Sauté onion and garlic in oil until tender but not brown. Add tomatoes, salt, pepper, sugar and cayenne pepper. Heat to boiling, then add chicken and mushrooms. Pour mixture over spaghetti and toss with a fork. Sprinkle with grated cheese and bake until mixture is heated through and cheese is melted, about 20 minutes. *Serves 6.*

An early recipe sheet headline.

HAM AND NOODLE BAKE

1 cup egg noodles

2 Tbsp. butter

1/4 cup chopped green pepper

1/2 cup chopped celery

1 small onion, chopped

2 Tbsp. all-purpose flour

1/2 tsp. salt

1/4 tsp. pepper

2 cups milk

1 cup diced cooked ham

1 1/2 cups cottage cheese

Preheat oven to 350°F. Cook noodles in boiling salted water until tender. Rinse and drain.

Melt butter in saucepan. Sauté green pepper, celery and onion in butter. Blend in flour, salt and pepper. Gradually add milk and mix until well blended. Cook, stirring constantly, until smooth and thickened. Remove from heat; add ham, cottage cheese and noodles. Pour into buttered 2-quart casserole and bake for 30 minutes or until top is bubbly and brown. *Serves 6.*

BEEF-A-RONI

1 lb. ground beef

1 large onion, chopped

3 stalks celery, sliced on the bias

1/2 green pepper, slivered

1 large clove garlic, crushed

1 can (28 oz.) tomatoes

2 tsp. chopped fresh parsley

salt and pepper to taste

2 tsp. Worcestershire sauce, or to taste

3 cups hot cooked elbow macaroni, well drained

1 cup shredded sharp Cheddar cheese

1/4 cup grated Parmesan cheese

In large skillet, sauté ground beef, onion, celery and green pepper until meat is no longer pink and vegetables are tender but not browned (if meat is very lean, add a small amount of oil to prevent sticking).

Add garlic and undrained tomatoes. Crush tomatoes with a fork. Add parsley, salt, pepper and Worcestershire sauce. Stir to distribute seasonings. Cover and simmer for 5 minutes. Add macaroni and both cheeses. Stir to combine well. Cover and simmer for 10 to 12 minutes longer or until piping hot and cheese has melted. Serve immediately. This dish reheats very well. *Serves 6.*

LASAGNA

1 1/2 lbs. ground beef

1 clove garlic, minced

1 medium onion, chopped

1 can (19 oz.) tomatoes

1 can (5 1/2 oz.) tomato paste

salt and pepper to taste

1/2 tsp. ground oregano

1 egg, slightly beaten

1 lb. cottage cheese

1/2 lb. lasagna noodles, cooked

1 lb. Swiss cheese, thinly sliced

1/2 cup grated Parmesan cheese

Preheat oven to 350°F. Sauté ground beef (if using a very lean ground beef, add a little cooking oil), garlic and onion in skillet until beef is crumbly and onion soft but not brown. Add tomatoes, tomato paste, salt, pepper and oregano. Cover and simmer gently for 20 minutes.

Combine egg and cottage cheese. Place several tablespoons of meat sauce in 10 x 17 x 2-inch (or similar size) baking dish, then half the noodles, half the cottage cheese mixture, half the remaining meat sauce and half the Swiss cheese. Repeat layers with remaining ingredients, ending with Swiss cheese and topping with Parmesan cheese. Bake for approximately 35 minutes; allow to set for 10 minutes before serving. *Serves 10.*

PACIFIC PASTA CASSEROLE

3 Tbsp. butter or margarine
1/4 cup chopped onion
2 Tbsp. all-purpose flour
1/4 tsp. pepper
1 package (1/2 lb.) shell macaroni, cooked and
    drained
2 cans (7 1/2 oz. each) pink salmon (or seafood of
    your choice)
1 1/2 cups buttermilk
1 cup cottage cheese
1 Tbsp. melted butter or margarine
3 Tbsp. fine dry bread crumbs

Preheat oven to 350°F. Melt the 3 Tbsp. butter or margarine in small frying pan; add onion and cook until tender and golden brown. Blend in flour and pepper. Stir mixture into cooked macaroni. Add salmon, buttermilk and cottage cheese and toss lightly. Turn into buttered 1-quart baking dish. Combine 1 Tbsp. melted butter or margarine and bread crumbs; sprinkle over macaroni mixture. Bake for about 30 minutes, until golden brown on top. *Serves 6.*

CHINESE FRIED RICE

3 slices bacon, diced
2 Tbsp. finely chopped onion
2 Tbsp. finely chopped green pepper
2 cups cold, cooked long-grain rice
2 eggs, slightly beaten
soy sauce

Cook bacon until crisp. Using slotted spoon, remove bacon from skillet and set aside to drain on paper towels. Pour off all but 2 Tbsp. hot bacon drippings from skillet. In remaining drippings, stir-fry onion, green pepper and rice for approximately 5 minutes. Add eggs and bacon bits. Cook, stirring constantly, until eggs are firm. Sprinkle with soy sauce. Serve piping hot. *Serves 3 to 4.*

SAVOURY RICE

1 cup long-grain rice
2 Tbsp. butter or margarine
1 medium onion, chopped
1 stalk celery, chopped
1 cup sliced fresh mushrooms
1/4 tsp. poultry seasoning
salt and pepper to taste

Cook rice according to package directions and set aside. Melt butter or margarine in medium saucepan. Sauté onion and celery until onion is transparent and celery is tender-crisp. Add mushrooms and sauté until tender. Stir in rice, poultry seasoning, salt and pepper. Heat through. A delicious accompaniment to poultry dishes. *Serves 4 to 6.*

RICE EXTRA-ORDINARY

To 4 servings of hot fluffy rice (prepared according to package directions), add any of the following, tossing until well mixed.

- 1 small stalk celery, chopped.
- 1/4 to 1/2 cup mushroom slices (canned or cooked, drained).
- 1 shredded raw carrot and 2 Tbsp. chopped fresh parsley.
- 1/2 cup shredded mild or sharp Cheddar cheese.
- 1/4 cup sliced ripe or pimiento-stuffed olives.
- 1/4 cup drained, diced chutney and 1/4 cup seedless raisins.

GARDEN-FLAVOURED RICE

1 1/2 lbs. zucchini, thinly sliced

3/4 cup chopped onion

3 Tbsp. butter or margarine

1 can (12 oz.) whole kernel corn, drained

1 can (14 oz.) tomatoes

3 cups cooked rice

1 1/2 tsp. salt

1/4 tsp. pepper

1/4 tsp. ground coriander

1/4 tsp. dried oregano

Sauté zucchini and onion in butter or margarine until tender. Add corn, tomatoes, rice, salt, pepper, coriander and oregano. Simmer, covered, for 15 minutes. (This dish freezes well.) *Serves 8.*

SWEET ONION BAKE

4 tsp. butter

7 1/2 cups sliced large sweet onions

1/2 cup uncooked rice

2 cups boiling salted water

1 cup grated Swiss cheese

2/3 cup cream

Preheat oven to 300°F. Melt butter in large skillet and sauté onions until almost tender. Cook rice in water for 5 minutes. Drain rice and mix with onions in casserole dish. Stir cheese and cream into mixture. Bake, covered, for 1 hour or until done. *Serves 8.*

LAZY CABBAGE ROLLS

1 can (approximately 28 oz.) sauerkraut, drained and rinsed in cold water

3/4 cup quick-cooking rice

1 large onion, finely chopped

1/2 lb. bacon, cut up

salt and pepper to taste

1/2 cup water (more, if necessary)

Mix all ingredients together in Dutch oven. Bring mixture to a boil. Simmer on stovetop or bake in preheated 325°F oven for approximately 1 hour or until rice is soft but not mushy. Add more water during cooking process if casserole becomes too dry. *Serves 4.*

An original copy of an early recipe sheet.

mona says . . .

ABOUT BEETS

- There are two basic ways to prepare beets.
  - Cut off all of the greens to within 1 inch of root. Scrub thoroughly. Cook, covered, in boiling salted water for 35 to 60 minutes or until tender. Peel beets when cooked.
  - Peel beets and slice, cube or shred them. Cook, covered, in small amount of boiling salted water, for 10 minutes if shredded or 15 to 20 minutes if sliced or cubed.
- Try seasoning beets with one or more of the following: a little lemon juice, a pinch of cloves or allspice, a little horseradish, a few sautéed onions.
- For an attractive garnish, marinate separated onion rings in beet juice for 30 minutes. Alternate with white onion rings in a chain. Garnish a salad, open-face sandwiches or casserole.

ABOUT BEANS

- To prepare beans, use either of these methods.
  - Wash beans well. Cut off ends and string. Cut into 1-inch pieces or cook whole in small amount of boiling salted water for 20 to 30 minutes or until tender-crisp.
  - Wash beans well. Cut off ends and string. Slit lengthwise. Cook in small amount of boiling salted water for 10 to 12 minutes or until tender-crisp.
- To avoid making beans tough, add salt halfway through cooking process.
- Beans lend themselves to a great variety of spices and combinations. Try one or more of the following: toasted almonds, chili sauce, a pinch of curry powder, snipped fresh parsley, lemon juice, Parmesan cheese, soy sauce, prepared mustard, sautéed mushrooms, slivered cooked carrots or chopped canned pimientos.

ABOUT MUSHROOMS

- Purchase mushrooms that are firm and dry to the touch. Small brown spots or opened caps merely indicate that the mushrooms are mature—their flavour is still delicate and delicious.
- Store fresh mushrooms on a rack or shallow tray in the refrigerator. Place a dampened paper towel over them—redampen the towel each day.
- Store cooked mushrooms in a covered dish in the refrigerator. Use as soon as possible.
- To prepare mushrooms, wash them gently; do not soak. Dry thoroughly; otherwise they will steam when sautéed, rather than browning nicely.
- Sprinkling mushrooms lightly with lemon juice prevents darkening.

BAKED POTATO VARIATIONS

6 potatoes
2 Tbsp. butter
1/4 to 1/3 cup milk
salt and pepper to taste

Bake potatoes. Cut a slice from top of each potato. Scoop out centre (leave shell intact). Mash potato with butter and milk; season with salt and pepper. Refill shells. Place stuffed potatoes in shallow baking dish and bake in preheated 400°F oven for 15 minutes or until browned. *Serves 6.*

Variations

- Add 2 to 4 Tbsp. raw or sautéed onion to potato filling.
- Mix mashed potatoes with sour cream instead of milk; add chopped green onions or chives.
- Add crumbled Roquefort cheese to potato mixture when mashing.
- Add 2/3 cup grated sharp Cheddar cheese to potato filling.
- Add 3/4 to 1 cup finely diced cooked ham to potato filling.
- Add 6 to 8 slices crisp-cooked, crumbled bacon to potato filling.
- Add 1 cup sliced, sautéed mushrooms to potato filling.
- Refill potato shells, forming a 1/2-inch-high ring around opening and leaving a depression in centre. Into this, place 1 tsp. butter (for each potato); sprinkle with salt and pepper to taste. Break an egg into centre of each hollow. Bake in preheated 350°F oven for about 15 minutes, or until egg is done as you like it. Garnish with chopped fresh parsley or green onions.

POTATO TIP

If you peel more potatoes than you need, cover them with cold water to which a few drops of vinegar have been added. Keep in refrigerator and they will last for several days.

MASHED POTATO CASSEROLE

6 medium potatoes
1 medium onion
2 eggs, well beaten
1 Tbsp. chopped fresh parsley
1 Tbsp. chopped fresh chives
salt and pepper to taste
1 tsp. Worcestershire sauce
1/4 cup butter
1 1/4 cups grated Cheddar cheese
freshly cracked black pepper
chopped fresh parsley and cherry tomato halves, for garnish (optional)

Peel and quarter potatoes and onion. Cook in boiling salted water until tender. Meanwhile, in medium bowl, beat eggs; add parsley, chives, salt, pepper and Worcestershire sauce. Beat to combine well. Drain potatoes and onion thoroughly. Add butter and 1 cup of the grated cheese. Mash to a smooth consistency. Add egg mixture and combine well. Pour into buttered 1 1/2-quart casserole dish. Sprinkle with remaining 1/4 cup cheese and cracked black pepper; cover.

Approximately 1 hour before serving time preheat oven to 350°F. Bake casserole, covered, for 30 minutes; remove cover and bake for 15 minutes longer. Garnish with parsley and cherry tomato halves, if desired. *Serves 6.*

OVERNIGHT POTATO CASSEROLE

Overnight potato casserole was the one the crew devoured. This was one show that went on air without a finished product. Never mind—it gave us all a big laugh.

6 large potatoes, peeled
2 cups sour cream
1 bunch green onions, chopped
2 Tbsp. chopped fresh parsley
1 1/2 tsp. salt, or to taste
1/4 tsp. pepper, or to taste
1 cup shredded sharp Cheddar cheese

Cook potatoes in boiling salted water until tender; drain well. Mash potatoes thoroughly. Stir in sour cream, green onions, parsley, salt and pepper. Blend well. Turn into a buttered casserole dish. Top with cheese. Cover with plastic wrap and refrigerate overnight.

Allow to stand at room temperature for approximately 1 hour before baking.

Preheat oven to 350°F. Bake, uncovered, until piping hot, about 30 to 40 minutes. *Makes 6 generous servings.*

BASQUE POTATOES

2 Tbsp. olive oil
1 medium onion, chopped ($\frac{1}{2}$ cup)
1 small clove garlic, crushed
$\frac{3}{4}$ cup chopped fresh parsley
$\frac{1}{4}$ cup chopped pimiento
1 tsp. salt
$\frac{1}{8}$ tsp. pepper
1 cup chicken broth (or 1 chicken or vegetable
    bouillon cube dissolved in 1 cup boiling water)
1 cup water
6 medium potatoes

Heat oil in medium skillet and sauté onion and garlic until soft. Stir in parsley, pimiento, salt, pepper, chicken broth and water. Remove from heat; set aside. Peel potatoes and slice thinly (you should have about 6 cups). Layer potato slices in the broth; heat to boiling. Reduce heat and simmer, covered, for about 20 minutes, or until tender. Using a slotted spoon, remove potatoes to a heated serving dish. Spoon remaining cooking liquid over potatoes. *Serves 6 to 8.*

POTATOES WITH ONION CAPS

This recipe goes perfectly with a cooked roast, steak or turkey.

12 medium potatoes, peeled and cut up
$\frac{1}{2}$ cup butter or margarine
1 cup milk, scalded
3 Tbsp. parsley flakes
salt and pepper to taste
2 Bermuda onions or other sweet onions, peeled and
    cut into 6 thick slices each
3 Tbsp. melted butter or margarine
sliced olives and pimiento, for garnish (optional)

Cook potatoes in boiling salted water until tender. Drain well. Mash and stir in the $\frac{1}{2}$ cup butter or margarine. Beat in scalded milk slowly, as needed, until creamy smooth. Add parsley flakes, salt and pepper. Cover pan and keep hot. Brush onion slices with the 3 Tbsp. melted butter or margarine and broil, without turning, for approximately 8 to 10 minutes or until tender and lightly browned. Spoon hot potatoes in 12 even mounds on platter around the cooked meat. Top each mound with onion slice. (Rings will separate to make cap.) Garnish with olives and pimiento, if desired. *Serves 12.*

BROCCOLI ITALIANO

2 lbs. fresh broccoli
$\frac{1}{2}$ tsp. dried oregano, crushed
$\frac{1}{2}$ cup mayonnaise or salad dressing
$\frac{1}{4}$ cup shredded sharp Cheddar cheese
1 Tbsp. milk

Cook broccoli with oregano in boiling salted water until tender. In top of double boiler, mix mayonnaise or salad dressing, cheese and milk; heat over hot—not boiling—water, stirring until cheese melts and mixture is hot. Serve with broccoli. *Serves 6.*

VEGETABLE PLATTER WITH FLUFFY HOLLANDAISE SAUCE

2 lbs. broccoli
2 lbs. carrots
1/2 cup butter or margarine
1/4 cup hot water
4 egg yolks
2 Tbsp. lemon juice
1/4 tsp. salt, or to taste
pinch cayenne pepper

Trim and discard outer leaves and tough ends of broccoli. If stalks are large, split lengthwise. Cook in boiling salted water until tender. Drain well and keep warm. Peel carrots and cut into julienne strips. Cook in boiling salted water until tender. Drain and keep warm.

Melt butter or margarine in top of double boiler over simmering water. When melted, stir in hot water. Remove top of double boiler from heat (keep water in bottom of double boiler simmering). Add egg yolks all at once; beat with electric mixer until mixture is almost double in bulk (this will take several minutes). Stir in lemon juice, salt and cayenne pepper. Return to stove and place over simmering water. Cook, stirring constantly, until thickened, approximately 5 minutes. Remove from heat.

Arrange vegetables attractively on warmed serving platter and spoon hollandaise sauce over top. *Serves 4 generously.*

TIPS ON MAKING HOLLANDAISE SAUCE

- Ensure water in bottom part of double boiler never boils during cooking time.
- Do not allow water to touch bottom of upper pan of double boiler.
- If cooking sauce in advance, let it stand, uncovered, after cooking. To reheat, place pan over simmering water again and stir gently for several minutes. Sauce may lose some of its fluffiness in reheating but will still be creamy and delicious.
- If your hollandaise sauce curdles when you are preparing it, remove sauce from heat and beat in

1 tsp. hot water, a few drops at a time. Do not return sauce to heat. Serve warm or at room temperature.

GLAZED CARROTS AND ONIONS

2 lbs. small carrots
2 Tbsp. water
1/2 tsp. salt, or to taste
1/4 tsp. pepper
1/4 cup butter
1/4 cup brown sugar
1 Tbsp. lemon juice
1 tsp. grated lemon rind
1 large onion, sliced and separated into rings
chopped fresh parsley, for garnish

Wash and scrape small carrots (if carrots are large, peel and cut into julienne strips). Combine water, salt, pepper, butter, sugar, lemon juice and rind in saucepan. Heat until butter melts. Stir to combine. Add carrots and onion. Cook over low heat until vegetables are tender and nicely glazed. Sprinkle with parsley. *Serves 4 to 6.*

ONIONS ITALIANO

1 lb. small white onions
1 can (7 1/2 oz.) tomato sauce
1/2 tsp. Worcestershire sauce
1/2 tsp. ground oregano
1 bay leaf
salt and pepper to taste
coarsely chopped green pepper, for garnish (optional)

Peel onions; cook in lightly salted boiling water until almost tender. Drain well. Meanwhile, thoroughly combine tomato sauce, Worcestershire sauce, oregano and bay leaf in saucepan. Season with salt and pepper. Simmer for 10 minutes to blend flavours, stirring occasionally. Remove bay leaf. Add hot cooked unions. Cover and simmer gently until onions are tender. To serve, place in a heated dish and garnish with green pepper, if desired. *Serves 4.*

GOURMET SHERRY ONION RINGS

1/4 cup butter or margarine

6 medium onions, sliced and separated into rings

1/2 tsp. salt

1/2 tsp. freshly ground black pepper

1/2 cup cooking sherry

1 Tbsp. chopped fresh parsley

1/4 cup grated Parmesan cheese

Melt butter or margarine in medium saucepan. Add onions, salt and pepper. Cook onions, stirring frequently, until tender but not browned, approximately 7 to 9 minutes. Add sherry and parsley. Cook for several minutes longer. Sprinkle with cheese and serve immediately. *Serves 8.*

CHEDDAR SCALLOPED ONIONS

4 large onions, cut into 1/2-inch-thick slices

1 clove garlic, crushed

1/4 cup butter

1/4 cup all-purpose flour

salt and pepper to taste

1/2 tsp. dry mustard

2 1/4 cups milk

2 cups shredded sharp Cheddar cheese

2 tsp. Worcestershire sauce

paprika, for garnish

2 Tbsp. butter, melted

1 tsp. lemon juice

1 Tbsp. chopped fresh parsley

1/3 cup bread crumbs

Cook onion slices with garlic in boiling salted water until onions are tender but still firm. Drain well. Arrange slices in well-buttered casserole dish. Melt the 1/4 cup butter in medium saucepan. Blend in flour, salt, pepper and mustard. Cook, stirring constantly, until bubbly. Stir in milk and cook, stirring constantly, until thickened. Allow to bubble for 2 minutes. Add cheese and Worcestershire sauce and stir until cheese melts. Pour sauce over prepared onions. Gently stir to combine. Sprinkle top lightly with paprika.

Preheat oven to 350°F.

Melt the 2 Tbsp. butter in saucepan. Add lemon juice and parsley and toss with bread crumbs until well coated. Sprinkle crumbs over top of casserole and bake for 30 minutes or until casserole is piping hot and crumbs are golden. Serve immediately. *Serves 4.*

Variations: Add 1 1/2 cups cooked cubed ham, chicken or turkey to cheese sauce; or toss bread crumbs with cooked, crumbled bacon; or add 1 cup coarsely chopped oysters to sauce. Serve piping hot over toast points or toasted English muffins.

CHEESE ONION BROIL

2 Tbsp. butter

1/4 tsp. salt

pinch pepper

2 medium onions, thinly sliced

6 slices white bread, toasted and buttered

6 Tbsp. chili sauce

6 thick slices Swiss cheese

3 slices bacon, cooked, drained and crumbled

6 thinly sliced green pepper rings

Melt butter; add salt and pepper. Sauté onions until tender but not browned. Spread each slice of hot buttered toast with 1 Tbsp. chili sauce. Top with onions and slice of cheese. Broil until cheese melts. Garnish with crumbled bacon and green pepper rings. A great lunch dish or late night snack. *Makes 6.*

BAKED STUFFED ONIONS

8 large sweet Spanish onions
1/2 lb. pork sausage meat
1 cup soft bread crumbs
2 Tbsp. chopped fresh parsley
2/3 cup canned whole kernel corn, well-drained
pinch pepper
2 Tbsp. butter or margarine
1/2 tsp. paprika

Preheat oven to 400°F.

Peel onions. Cut slice from top of each onion and remove enough onion to leave a cavity approximately 1 to 1 1/2 inches deep. Reserve scooped-out onion. Place onions in large saucepan with just enough salted water to cover; bring to a boil. Reduce heat; simmer, covered, for 18 to 20 minutes or until just tender. Do not overcook. Drain well.

Chop enough reserved onion to make 1/2 cup; set aside. In small skillet, brown sausage meat, crumbling it with a fork; drain off excess fat. Add chopped onion and continue cooking until onion is tender. Remove skillet from heat. Stir in bread crumbs, parsley, corn and pepper; set aside.

Melt butter or margarine and add paprika. Brush onions with mixture, coating well. Fill onion cavities with sausage mixture. Arrange stuffed onions in lightly greased, shallow baking dish. Cover loosely with foil. Bake for 15 minutes; remove foil and continue baking for 5 minutes longer or until onions and stuffing are hot and topping is lightly golden. *Serves 8.*

HARRY'S BARBECUED ONIONS

2 1/2 to 3 lbs. onions (the smallest you can find)
1/2 cup of your favourite barbecue sauce
1/2 cup Cabernet Sauvignon
2 Tbsp. oil
1 Tbsp. seasoning salt
1/4 tsp. dried oregano
dried parsley flakes to taste

Peel onions and place in casserole dish with lid. Blend remaining ingredients in bowl and pour over onions. Cover and place on barbecue at very low heat or in preheated 300° to 325°F oven for 45 minutes. *Serves 4 to 8.*

Harry was known as Harry the Clown at the PNE and was Santa's friend for the "Breakfast with Santa" shows at Woodward's. Great to work with, he is Harry Sumner to his friends.

SWEET POTATOES ON PINEAPPLE RINGS

2 cups mashed, cooked sweet potatoes
1/2 tsp. salt
1/2 cup brown sugar
4 Tbsp. butter
4 slices canned pineapple
4 marshmallows
4 maraschino cherries

Preheat oven to 400°F. Combine sweet potatoes, salt, sugar and 3 Tbsp. of the butter in a mixing bowl and beat until light and fluffy. Place slices of pineapple on a baking sheet. Dot with remaining 1 Tbsp. butter. Force sweet potato mixture through a pastry bag, using the rose tip, onto the slices of pineapple. Top each serving with a marshmallow and a cherry. Bake until heated through, about 10 minutes. *Serves 4.*

YAM-STUFFED APPLES

5 to 6 large apples
3 cooked yams, peeled and mashed
1 Tbsp. lemon juice
1/4 cup brown sugar
2 Tbsp. melted butter
1/2 tsp. ground cinnamon
1/8 tsp. ground nutmeg

Preheat oven to 350°F. Hollow out apples, leaving shell about 3/4 inch thick. Thoroughly combine yams, lemon juice, sugar, butter, cinnamon and nutmeg. Stuff prepared apples with filling. Bake for approximately 25 minutes. *Serves 5 to 6.*

SUSAN MAYO'S MAIN DISH SWEET POTATO PIE

This recipe comes to us from Susan Mayo, Norfolk, Virginia.

4 medium sweet potatoes
1/2 cup butter or margarine, softened
3 eggs, separated
3 Tbsp. sugar
1/4 cup chopped onion
1/4 cup chopped fresh parsley
1 tsp. salt
1/4 tsp. dried tarragon
1 Tbsp. lemon juice
1/2 cup milk
1 unbaked 9-inch pastry shell

Preheat oven to 400°F. Wash sweet potatoes thoroughly. Prick with fork and place in baking pan. Bake for 40 to 50 minutes or until soft. Lower oven temperature to 350°F.

Scoop out pulp and place in large bowl. Add butter or margarine and beat until smooth. Beat in egg yolks, sugar, onion, parsley, salt, tarragon, lemon juice and milk.

In separate bowl, beat egg whites until stiff but not dry. Fold into sweet potato mixture. Turn into unbaked pastry shell. Bake for about 50 minutes or until knife inserted in centre comes out clean.

Woodward's sent me to Norfolk, Virginia, to the Farm Fresh food chain to learn how to set up a consumer council. A wonderful way to get feedback from the consumer—I was extremely fortunate Susan Mayo was my instructor.

SCANDINAVIAN CABBAGE

6 cups shredded cabbage
1 cup sour cream
1/2 tsp. caraway seeds
1 tsp. salt, or to taste
1/4 tsp. pepper

Cook cabbage in boiling salted water to cover, until just tender, approximately 5 to 8 minutes. Drain very well. In top of double boiler, toss cabbage with sour cream. Season with caraway seeds, salt and pepper. Cook, covered, over boiling water until heated through, approximately 10 minutes. *Serves 4.*

SOUR CREAM TIP

To prevent sour cream from curdling when you're making sauces, bring it to room temperature before adding to hot mixture. Never allow mixture to boil after adding sour cream.

PHOEBE'S YAM CASSEROLE

Phoebe Hunt gave me this recipe and very kindly agreed to let me use it here. She has been a strong supporter for agriculture and we have worked together for years doing cooking shows. This is a great family favourite.

1 cup granulated sugar
2 eggs
$\frac{1}{2}$ cup butter
1 Tbsp. vanilla extract
3 cups cooked and mashed yams
1 cup firmly packed brown sugar
$\frac{1}{3}$ cup all-purpose flour
1 cup chopped pecans
$\frac{1}{3}$ cup butter

Combine sugar, eggs, the $\frac{1}{2}$ cup butter, vanilla and mashed yams. Mix well. Pour into 8- or 9-inch baking dish. Preheat oven to 350°F.

For the topping, combine brown sugar, flour, pecans and the $\frac{1}{3}$ cup butter. Mix well. Sprinkle over top of casserole. Bake for 45 to 60 minutes or until done.

Phoebe doing a cooking show with me.

SWEET 'N' SOUR RED CABBAGE

6 slices bacon
1 medium onion, chopped
1 medium red cabbage, finely shredded
1 tsp. salt
$\frac{1}{8}$ tsp. pepper
$\frac{1}{2}$ cup water
2 cups thinly sliced peeled and cored apples
$\frac{1}{2}$ cup vinegar
$\frac{1}{4}$ cup brown sugar

Preheat oven to 325°F. Cook bacon until crisp; drain and crumble. Set aside. Sauté onion in bacon drippings for 2 minutes. Stir in cabbage, salt, pepper, water, apples, vinegar and brown sugar. Add crumbled bacon. Place mixture in buttered casserole with lid. Cover and bake for approximately 1 hour or until vegetables are tender. *Serves 6.*

CABBAGE, PARSNIPS AND POTATOES

3 qts. water
1 Tbsp. salt
6 medium potatoes
$2\frac{1}{2}$ to 3 lbs. parsnips
1 head cabbage (approximately $2\frac{1}{2}$ lbs.)
$\frac{1}{2}$ cup butter or margarine
2 tsp. lemon juice
salt and pepper to taste
1 Tbsp. chopped fresh parsley

Place water and salt in large kettle; bring to a boil. Meanwhile, peel and halve potatoes; peel parsnips and halve parsnips lengthwise; cut cabbage into 6 wedges. Add vegetables to boiling water. Return to a boil, lower heat and simmer, covered, for 25 minutes or until vegetables are tender.

Drain vegetables and place in serving dish. Keep warm. Meanwhile, in small saucepan, melt butter or margarine. Add lemon juice, salt, pepper and parsley. Drizzle butter mixture over cooked vegetables. Serve immediately. *Serves 6.*

CABBAGE IN CREAM

3/4 cup milk

3 cups finely shredded cabbage

1/4 cup light cream

1/2 tsp. salt, or to taste

1/8 tsp. pepper

1 Tbsp. butter, softened

1 Tbsp. all-purpose flour

1/4 tsp. paprika

Bring milk just to boiling in saucepan. Add cabbage and boil for 2 minutes. Stir in cream, salt and pepper. Blend butter with flour and paprika. Add to cabbage mixture and stir to combine. Cook over medium heat until cabbage is tender and sauce thickened, about 3 to 5 minutes. *Serves 6.*

GLAZED SQUASH WITH ONIONS AND WALNUTS

3 acorn squash, cut in half lengthwise and seeds removed

salt to taste

2 cups small whole onions, cooked and drained

1/2 cup walnut pieces

1/3 cup butter or margarine

1/3 cup light molasses

1/4 tsp. ground cinnamon

1/4 tsp. salt, or to taste

Preheat oven to 350°F. Place squash in shallow baking pan, cut side down, and bake for 35 to 40 minutes or until almost tender.

Turn cut side up. Season cavities lightly with salt. Fill with onions and walnuts. In small saucepan, melt butter or margarine; add molasses, cinnamon and salt. Spoon part of mixture over squash and filling. Continue baking in oven for 15 to 20 minutes longer or until squash is tender, brushing several times with remaining sauce to glaze. *Serves 6.*

SQUASH—AN INTERESTING SELECTION

Winter squash comes in many sizes, colours and shapes, but all have a yellow-orange flesh. Good winter squash is heavy for its size, free from blemishes and has a hard shell. A pound of fresh squash makes approximately 1 cup when cooked. Here are some of the most popular kinds.

- Acorn squash is small, has a hard dark green or orange rind with distinct ridges and is shaped like an acorn. The flavour is faintly sweet and nutty. This squash bakes well; when peeled or cubed, it can be boiled and mashed or added to stews.
- Butternut squash is gourd shaped and may be as small as an acorn squash or as long as 10 to 12 inches. Its rind is smooth and thin, and ranges in colour from light tan to dark yellow. The flesh varies from creamy yellow to orange. The flavour is slightly nutty. This squash is best when baked or steamed.
- Hubbard squash is large, with a thick, warty rind. Its colour varies from dark green to slate blue to orange-red. The flesh is thick, deep yellow and sweet. It's delicious baked, steamed, or peeled, cubed and boiled until tender, then mashed with butter. Great in stews.

JIGG'S CORNED BEEF AND CABBAGE

2 cups chopped canned corned beef

1 medium onion, chopped

2 Tbsp. oil

salt and pepper to taste

2 Tbsp. chopped fresh parsley

1 cup diced cooked potatoes

1 cup canned tomatoes

1/2 cup chili sauce

2 cups shredded cabbage

Preheat oven to 350°F. In Dutch oven, brown corned beef and onion in oil. Season with salt and pepper. Sprinkle with parsley. Add potatoes, tomatoes, chili sauce and cabbage. Stir to combine well. Bake, covered, for approximately 45 minutes or until cabbage is tender. *Serves 4.*

MARINATED ASPARAGUS PLATTER

2 lbs. fresh asparagus spears, trimmed (or frozen or
    canned equivalent)
1 cup well-seasoned oil and vinegar salad dressing
1/4 cup finely chopped green pepper
1/4 cup finely chopped dill pickle
2 Tbsp. finely chopped fresh parsley
1 Tbsp. finely chopped green onion
1 Tbsp. chopped capers (optional)
1 hard-cooked egg, chopped
lettuce leaves
1 hard-cooked egg, sliced, for garnish
pimiento strips, for garnish

Cook asparagus until tender (if using canned, drain
thoroughly). Combine dressing, green pepper, dill
pickle, parsley, green onion and capers (if using) in
jar with lid. Shake vigorously. Stir chopped egg into
dressing.

Place asparagus in shallow dish. Pour prepared
dressing over top. Cover and refrigerate until well
chilled. To serve, place drained asparagus attractively over bed of lettuce. Garnish with hard-cooked
egg slices and pimiento strips. *Serves 6 to 8.*

BAKED SPINACH-TOPPED TOMATOES

1/4 cup butter or margarine
1 medium onion, finely chopped
1 large clove garlic, minced
2 1/2 cups frozen chopped spinach, thawed
2 tsp. lemon juice
1 cup fine dry bread crumbs
2 eggs, beaten
2 tsp. salt, or to taste
pepper to taste
4 large tomatoes, halved
grated Parmesan cheese

Melt butter or margarine in skillet over medium
heat. Sauté onion and garlic until tender but not
browned. Add spinach and lemon juice and cook for
7 to 8 minutes longer or until spinach is tender,
breaking spinach up with spoon and stirring frequently. Remove skillet from heat. Stir in bread
crumbs, eggs, salt and pepper and set aside.

Place tomato halves, cut side up, in greased baking
dish 13 x 9 x 2 inches (or similar size). If necessary,
cut a thin slice from bottom of tomato half so it
stands upright. Divide spinach mixture into 8 portions and mound onto each tomato half. Cover and
refrigerate.

To serve, preheat oven to 350°F. Lightly sprinkle
Parmesan cheese over spinach. Bake, uncovered, for
35 minutes or until piping hot. *Serves 8.*

VEGETABLE CASSEROLE

5 medium carrots, sliced (1 1/2 cups)
1 medium onion, sliced
1 package (12 oz.) frozen whole spinach
3 Tbsp. butter or margarine
3 Tbsp. all-purpose flour
1 1/2 cups milk
1 cup shredded Cheddar cheese
1/4 tsp. salt
pinch pepper
1/2 cup bread crumbs
2 Tbsp. melted butter

Preheat oven to 350°F. Cook carrots and onion in
small amount of boiling salted water, covered, until
almost tender, about 8 minutes. Drain. Cook
spinach according to package directions; drain.

For sauce, melt butter or margarine and mix in
flour. Gradually blend in milk. Cook and stir until
thick. Remove from heat and add cheese, salt and
pepper, stirring until cheese melts.

Place half the spinach in ungreased 1-quart casserole; cover with half the carrots and onion. Top with
half the cheese sauce. Repeat layers. Combine bread
crumbs and melted butter; sprinkle over top. Bake
for 15 to 20 minutes. *Serves 6.*

RATATOUILLE (VEGETABLE STEW)

1/4 cup oil

1 clove garlic, thinly sliced

1 medium onion, thinly sliced

1 green pepper, thinly sliced

1 medium eggplant, peeled and cut into
   1/4-inch-thick slices

1 medium (or 2 small) zucchini, cut into
   1/4-inch-thick slices

2 medium tomatoes, thinly sliced

salt and pepper to taste

Heat oil in large frying pan with lid over medium heat and sauté garlic. Remove and reserve 1 Tbsp. garlic-flavoured oil. Layer vegetables in pan in order given, seasoning each layer with salt and pepper. Sprinkle reserved Tbsp. of oil over layered vegetables; cover and simmer over medium-low heat for 30 minutes. Uncover and cook for an additional 10 minutes to reduce liquid to desired thickness. *Serves 6 to 8.*

TURNIP CASSEROLE

1 large turnip, cut into chunks

1 Tbsp. butter

2 large apples

1/4 cup lightly packed brown sugar

pinch ground cinnamon

1/3 cup all-purpose flour

1/3 cup brown sugar

2 Tbsp. butter

Preheat oven to 350°F. Cook turnip in salted water until tender; drain. Mash turnips with the 1 Tbsp. butter. Peel, core and slice apples; toss with the 1/4 cup brown sugar and cinnamon. Arrange alternate layers of turnip and apples, beginning and ending with turnips. Mix together flour, 1/3 cup brown sugar and 2 Tbsp. butter until crumbly. Sprinkle mixture over top of casserole. Bake for approximately 1 hour. Serve hot. *Serves 6 to 8.*

LEMON TURNIPS

2 cups julienned turnip

1 1/2 Tbsp. butter or margarine

1 tsp. lemon juice

2 tsp. chopped fresh parsley

1 tsp. very finely chopped onion

salt and pepper to taste

Cook turnip in boiling salted water just until tender, approximately 20 minutes; drain well. Keep hot. Meanwhile, in small saucepan, melt butter or margarine; add lemon juice, parsley and onion. Season with salt and pepper. Stir to combine. Toss with hot drained turnip. *Serves 4.*

LUAU BEANS

Joy Gonzales tells me that she tops the Luau Beans with a sprinkling of Crumb Coating (page 107).

1/2 lb. sliced bacon

2 sliced onions

8 cups beans with pork

1 cup crushed pineapple

1/4 cup chili sauce

2 Tbsp. molasses

1 1/2 tsp. dry mustard

1/2 tsp. salt

Fry bacon until crisp. Remove bacon from skillet and drain. Cook onions in drippings.

Crumble bacon and combine in Dutch oven with onions and remaining ingredients. Cover and bake on grill over medium-hot coals for 1 1/2 hours. Remove cover and cook for about 25 minutes longer. Stir occasionally. To cook in an oven, preheat oven to 350°F. Cover and bake for 45 minutes to 1 hour, or until done. Remove cover for last 15 minutes. *Serves 10 to 12.*

SWEET 'N' SOUR SOYBEANS

1 cup soybeans
3 cups water
2 Tbsp. salad oil
1 large onion, cut into 1-inch dice
2 large carrots, cut into 1/4-inch slices
1 clove garlic, minced or crushed
1 green pepper, cut into 1-inch dice
3/4 cup canned pineapple chunks, drained
2 small tomatoes, cut into 1-inch dice
1 recipe Sweet-Sour Sauce

Rinse soybeans; place in a large bowl. Add water. Cover and soak for 6 to 8 hours or overnight. Place beans and liquid in a 3-quart saucepan, adding additional water, if necessary, to cover beans. Simmer, covered, for 3 hours, or until beans are tender. Stir several times; add a little additional water if needed to prevent sticking. Drain, reserving liquid for sauce. Set beans aside.

In a large frying pan or wok, heat oil over high heat. Add onion, carrots and garlic. Cook, stirring, for about 3 minutes or until slightly tender but still crisp. Add green pepper; cook for 1 minute, then add pineapple, tomatoes, soy beans and Sweet-Sour Sauce. Continue to cook, stirring, until mixture boils and all ingredients are covered with sauce, about 2 minutes. *Serves 4 to 6.*

Sweet-Sour Sauce
1 Tbsp. cornstarch
1/3 cup firmly packed brown sugar
1/4 tsp. ground ginger
1 Tbsp. soy sauce
1 Tbsp. sherry
5 Tbsp. wine vinegar
1/4 cup reserved cooking liquid or beef broth

Stir all ingredients together. *Makes 3/4 cup.*

BEANS AMANDINE

3 cups green beans (French cut)
1/2 cup almonds, slivered
2 Tbsp. butter
1/4 tsp. salt
1/8 tsp. pepper
1/8 tsp. ground nutmeg

Cook beans until tender. Sauté almonds in butter until golden. Drain beans. Pour almonds and butter over beans; add salt, pepper and nutmeg. Toss to mix. *Serves 4 to 5.*

ORANGE BEETS

1 can (14 oz.) sliced beets, well drained
2 Tbsp. orange marmalade
1 Tbsp. cider vinegar
2 Tbsp. butter or margarine
1/2 tsp. salt

Combine all ingredients in medium saucepan. Cook over low heat, stirring occasionally, until beets are heated through. Serve immediately. *Serves 4.*

TOMATO-MUSHROOM BAKE

2 large tomatoes, quartered
Italian salad dressing, for brushing
salt and pepper to taste
chopped fresh parsley to taste
pinch dried basil
12 medium mushrooms
1 Tbsp. melted butter
salt and pepper to taste
1 Tbsp. grated Parmesan cheese

Place tomato quarters cut side up on foil pie plate. Brush with salad dressing. Season with salt and pepper. Sprinkle parsley and basil on top. Dip mushrooms in melted butter and place on foil plate with tomatoes. Season with salt and pepper and sprinkle with cheese. Place, uncovered, on grill and cook for 10 minutes. Do not turn. *Serves 4.*

MUSHROOMS ROMANOFF

1/2 lb. mushrooms
2 Tbsp. butter or margarine
1 cup sour cream
1 tsp. dill seed
1/4 tsp. salt, or to taste
pinch freshly ground pepper
pinch ground nutmeg
paprika
hot toast points

Wash mushrooms and dry well. Slice larger mushrooms through cap and stem. In skillet, melt butter or margarine, add mushrooms and cover. Cook over medium heat, stirring occasionally, for approximately 6 to 8 minutes or until lightly browned. Stir in sour cream, dill seed, salt, pepper and nutmeg. Reduce heat; cook and stir over low heat just until heated through. Do not boil. Sprinkle with paprika. Serve over hot toast points. *Serves 3 to 4.*

SOUR CREAM MUSTARD SAUCE
A great topping for your favourite vegetables. This sauce also brightens up heated leftover vegetables.

1 cup sour cream
1 Tbsp. minced onion
1 Tbsp. prepared mustard
1/4 tsp. salt
pinch pepper
1 Tbsp. chopped fresh parsley

Heat sour cream, onion, mustard, salt and pepper in small saucepan over very low heat, just until hot. Sprinkle with parsley. *Makes approximately 1 cup.*

CRUMB COATING
Joan Smith from the Bea Wright kitchen at Main Store gave us this useful recipe. It is an excellent recipe for coating fish, chicken and veal.

1 cup very fine bread crumbs
1/4 cup all-purpose flour
1/2 tsp. sugar
1 tsp. paprika
1/2 tsp. white pepper or cayenne pepper
1/2 tsp. salt or seasoning salt

Combine all ingredients in small bowl, mixing well. Buzz in a blender or use finest blade of food chopper as crumbs must be very fine. If you wish, a package of dry spaghetti sauce mix may be blended into the crumbs. *Makes approximately 1 1/4 cups.*

Variation: Omit salt and use celery salt, garlic salt, thyme or rosemary. A hint of curry is a pleasant seasoning with chicken.

SPICY CHEESE SPREAD
This is a versatile spread to have on hand. Serve as a stuffing or topper for baked tomatoes, a spread for crackers, a condiment with hamburgers, a stuffing for celery stalks or a sandwich spread.

2 cups sharp Cheddar cheese, grated medium-fine
1/3 cup pimiento-stuffed green olives, chopped medium-fine
1/2 cup chopped walnuts
2 Tbsp. finely chopped green onion
1 Tbsp. chopped fresh parsley
1/2 cup mayonnaise
2 Tbsp. prepared mustard
1 Tbsp. prepared horseradish
pinch pepper

Combine all ingredients in medium bowl. Mix well. *Makes approximately 2 cups.*

CHOW CHOW

16 cups sliced green tomatoes

4 cups chopped onions

3 or 4 sweet red peppers, finely chopped

1 to 2 Tbsp. salt

ice water to cover

4 cups chopped apples

3 cups vinegar

3 cups white sugar

1 Tbsp. turmeric

1 cup whole mixed pickling spices, tied in a cheesecloth bag

Cover tomatoes, onions and peppers with 1 to 2 Tbsp. salt and ice water; refrigerate overnight. Drain thoroughly. Add apples, vinegar, sugar, turmeric and spice bag. Bring to a boil; simmer for 45 minutes. Remove spice bag. Pour mixture into hot sterilized jars. Seal according to manufacturer's directions. *Makes approximately 8 pints.*

CHILI SAUCE

24 large red-ripe tomatoes

8 large onions, chopped

6 green peppers, chopped

2 cups vinegar

1 Tbsp. salt

1 tsp. ground cinnamon

1 tsp. ground cloves

1 tsp. ground ginger

1 Tbsp. celery seed

1 tsp. crushed chili flakes

1 tsp. dry mustard

3 cups sugar

Peel, core and chop tomatoes; combine with remaining ingredients. Gently boil, uncovered, for 4 hours or until sauce is thickened, stirring frequently to prevent sticking. Pour into hot sterilized jars, leaving $1/4$ inch head space. Seal according to manufacturer's directions. *Makes about 13 cups.*

These lampshade-wearing, cocktail-drinking revellers were part of an entertaining feature in the Bea Wright sheets.

FREEZER TOMATO SAUCE

Keep this in the freezer to quickly whip up a recipe when unexpected guests arrive—it's a lifesaver.

3 Tbsp. salad oil

4 medium onions, chopped

2 large cloves garlic, crushed

4 cans (28 oz. each) tomatoes

4 cans (5½ oz. each) tomato paste

¾ cup chopped fresh parsley

1 lb. fresh mushrooms, sliced

3 Tbsp. sugar

1 Tbsp. ground oregano

3 Tbsp. salt

pepper to taste

2 bay leaves

Heat oil in large saucepan over medium heat. Cook onions and garlic until tender but not browned. Add remaining ingredients and bring to a boil. Reduce heat to low; cover and simmer for 2 hours. Remove and discard bay leaves. Place sauce in 2-cup freezer containers, leaving at least 1 inch head space. Cover and refrigerate until well chilled. Label and freeze. *Makes approximately 16 cups sauce.*

QUICK MELTED BUTTER SAUCES

Try one of these melted butter sauces to perk up your menu.

- **Clarified or Drawn Butter:** Great for sautéeing chicken or fish. Serve with broiled shrimp or lobster. Melt ½ cup butter over medium heat. Skim off foam. Pour off clear yellow butter, leaving milky residue in bottom of pan.
- **Lemon Butter:** Delicious on vegetables. Add 3 Tbsp. lemon juice to above recipe for clarified butter.
- **Brown Butter:** Heat ½ cup clarified butter until it turns a delicate brown colour.
- **Crunchy Crumb Butter:** Delicious over broccoli or cauliflower and topped with chopped hard-cooked egg. Sauté ⅓ cup toasted bread crumbs in ½ cup brown butter; add 1½ Tbsp. lemon juice and 1 Tbsp. chopped fresh parsley.

A sample of Woodward's brand vegetables.

- **White Butter:** Wonderful on salmon. Simmer 2 Tbsp. finely chopped green onion, 2 Tbsp. white wine vinegar and ¼ cup chicken bouillon until reduced to 2 Tbsp. Remove from heat. Gradually add ½ cup chilled butter (cut into pieces), beating until light and creamy. Season to taste with salt and pepper.
- **Mushroom Butter:** Great on vegetables. Sauté 2 cups sliced fresh mushrooms and 2 Tbsp. finely chopped green onion in ½ cup butter until lightly browned.
- **Nut Butter:** Try this on green beans, squash or sweet potatoes. Sauté ⅔ cup sliced nuts (almonds, Brazil nuts, peanuts, walnuts) in ½ cup butter until golden brown. Season to taste with salt and pepper.

The original Woodward's store in Vancouver.

seafood

mona says . . .

- Before broiling fish, dot with butter to bring out the flavour.
- Season cod fillets, clams, oysters and prawns before dipping in batter.
- Garnish these luscious morsels with lemon wedges, strips of pimiento, radish roses, parsley sprigs or tomato wedges.

- Fish can be baked, broiled, poached, fried, smoked, barbecued, pickled and made into chowders. Fish is a good source of mineral salts and iodine.
- Whole baked, stuffed salmon has an aroma not soon forgotten. Oysters, clams, prawns and shrimp whet our appetites and lend elegance to holiday dining. Seafood is well worth that extra bit of work and attention.

BROILED SALMON STEAKS WITH LEMON-PARSLEY BUTTER

4 salmon steaks, cut $1/2$ inch thick
$1/4$ cup butter
1 tsp. seasoning salt, or to taste
pinch pepper
1 recipe Lemon-Parsley Butter

Wipe salmon steaks with damp cloth; pat dry with paper towels. Place salmon steaks on rack of broiler pan. Melt butter; add seasoning salt and pepper. Brush top side of salmon with 2 Tbsp. seasoned butter. Broil 4 inches from heat for 10 minutes. Turn steaks; brush with remaining seasoned butter. Broil for approximately 8 minutes longer or until fish flakes easily when tested with a fork.

Remove cooked salmon to a warm serving platter. Drizzle Lemon-Parsley Butter over top. *Serves 4.*

Lemon-Parsley Butter

$1/4$ cup butter
2 Tbsp. lemon juice
2 Tbsp. chopped fresh parsley
$1/2$ tsp. grated lemon rind (optional)

In small saucepan, melt butter; add lemon juice, parsley and lemon rind, if using. Stir to combine. Keep warm. *Makes $1/2$ cup.*

Variation: For a taste change, omit the parsley and substitute 2 Tbsp. chopped chives.

CREAMED SALMON ON MUFFIN

1 can ($7^1/2$ oz.) salmon
3 Tbsp. butter or margarine
3 Tbsp. all-purpose flour
$1/2$ tsp. salt
$1/4$ tsp. dry mustard
1 cup liquid (salmon juice plus milk)
2 green onions, chopped
2 English muffins
2 hard-cooked eggs, sliced
$1/4$ tsp. paprika

Drain salmon, reserving juice, and flake. Melt butter or margarine in saucepan. Combine flour, salt and mustard and add to pan. Add salmon juice/milk slowly, stirring constantly, until thickened. Fold in flaked salmon and green onions. Split muffins and toast. Top muffin halves with creamed salmon. Garnish with egg slices and sprinkle with paprika. Serve immediately. *Serves 2.*

SALMON BRUNCH

1 can ($7^1/2$ oz.) salmon
$3/4$ cup grated Swiss cheese
2 Tbsp. chopped green onion
3 Tbsp. chopped stuffed olives
$1/4$ tsp. dried dill weed
$1/8$ tsp. pepper
2 tsp. lemon juice
$1/4$ cup mayonnaise
1 package (8 oz.) refrigerated crescent rolls
1 recipe Parsley Sauce

Preheat oven to 375°F. Drain salmon, reserving juice for parsley sauce. Flake salmon with fork and combine with remaining ingredients, except crescent roll dough and sauce.

Pinch edges of refrigerated rolls together to make one rectangle. Spread with salmon filling. Roll up from long side. Cut into 12 pinwheels. Place pinwheels cut-side down in buttered baking dish. Bake for 20 to 25 minutes or until golden. Serve with Parsley Sauce. *Serves 4 to 6.*

Variation

• To make salmon pinwheel hors d'oeuvre, prepare salmon mixture as above. Divide dough into 4 rectangles, pinching seams together. Spread $1/4$ of the salmon filling over each rectangle. Roll up from long side. Cut each roll into 10 pinwheels. Bake as above, but only for 12 to 15 minutes.

Parsley Sauce

    2 Tbsp. butter
    2 Tbsp. all-purpose flour
    $\frac{1}{2}$ tsp. salt
    $\frac{1}{8}$ tsp. pepper
    $\frac{1}{4}$ tsp. dry mustard
    reserved salmon juice
    1 $\frac{1}{2}$ cups milk
    2 egg yolks, beaten
    2 Tbsp. snipped fresh parsley

Melt butter. Blend in flour, salt, pepper and mustard. Add salmon juice and milk. Cook, stirring constantly, until thickened and smooth. Add small amount of sauce to beaten egg yolks, then add egg yolks to remaining sauce. Cook, stirring constantly, until thickened. Add parsley and serve. *Makes about 2 cups.*

SALMON CRUNCH

    2 cans (7$\frac{1}{2}$ oz. each) salmon
    3 eggs, beaten
    1 cup sour cream
    $\frac{1}{2}$ cup shredded sharp Cheddar cheese
    $\frac{1}{4}$ cup mayonnaise
    1 Tbsp. grated onion
    3 drops hot pepper sauce
    $\frac{1}{4}$ tsp. dried dill weed
    1 $\frac{1}{2}$ cups whole wheat flour
    1 cup shredded sharp Cheddar cheese
    $\frac{1}{2}$ tsp. salt
    $\frac{1}{2}$ tsp. paprika
    $\frac{1}{2}$ cup butter
    $\frac{1}{3}$ cup finely chopped almonds

Preheat oven to 400°F. Flake salmon, including juice and mashed bones. Add eggs, sour cream, the $\frac{1}{2}$ cup cheese, mayonnaise, onion, hot pepper sauce and dill to salmon, mixing thoroughly.

Combine flour, the 1 cup cheese, salt and paprika. Cut in butter until mixture is crumbly. Add almonds and distribute evenly throughout mixture. Reserve 1 cup crumb mixture for topping. Press remaining crumb mixture into 9-inch pie plate.

Turn salmon mixture into whole wheat crust. Sprinkle with reserved crumbs. Bake for 45 minutes or until filling is set. Serves 6.

SALMON-ZUCCHINI WEDGES
A delicious appetizer or luncheon dish.

    1$\frac{2}{3}$ cups shredded zucchini (about $\frac{1}{2}$ lb.)
    $\frac{1}{3}$ cup finely chopped onion
    3 eggs, well-beaten
    $\frac{1}{2}$ cup grated Parmesan cheese
    4 tsp. lemon juice
    3 Tbsp. chopped fresh parsley
    $\frac{1}{4}$ tsp. dried dill weed
    salt and pepper to taste
    1 can (7$\frac{1}{2}$ oz.) salmon, drained and flaked

Preheat oven to 350°F. In small saucepan, combine zucchini and onion; add water to cover and bring to a boil. Reduce heat and simmer, covered, just until vegetables are tender, approximately 3 minutes. Drain well, squeezing out any excess liquid.

Combine eggs, cheese and lemon juice in bowl. Stir in prepared vegetables, parsley and dill. Season with salt and pepper. Fold in salmon. Turn mixture into ungreased 11-inch pie plate. Bake until set, about 25 to 30 minutes. To serve as an appetizer, cut into 8 to 10 wedges. If serving as a luncheon dish, cut into 4 wedges and serve with a crisp salad and hot crusty rolls.

Note: To make in advance, cool and refrigerate cooked dish. Reheat in a preheated 300°F oven for 10 to 12 minutes before serving.

SALMON STEAKS WITH ALMOND SAUCE

2 lbs. salmon steaks, approximately 1 inch thick
2 tsp. minced green onions
1 Tbsp. chopped fresh parsley
1 Tbsp. lemon juice
$\frac{1}{2}$ cup mayonnaise
$\frac{1}{3}$ cup unblanched almonds, finely minced
whole almonds, for garnish (optional)

Wipe fish with damp cloth. If fish is frozen, do not thaw. Place salmon steaks on lightly greased steamer rack. Bring 2 inches of water to a rapid boil in steamer pot. Place salmon on rack in steamer and cover tightly. Steam fresh salmon for 10 minutes per inch of thickness, frozen salmon for 20 minutes per inch of thickness, or until fish flakes when fork tested. Remove from steamer to heated serving platter.

Combine green onions, parsley, lemon juice, mayonnaise and almonds in bowl. Spread mixture over hot steaks. Garnish with whole almonds, if desired. Serve immediately. *Serves 6.*

MÈRE'S SALMON POTATO LOAF

2 cans ($7\frac{1}{2}$ oz. each) pink salmon
1 cup grated cooked potato, packed
1 cup grated carrot
2 Tbsp. finely chopped onion
2 eggs, well beaten
2 Tbsp. melted margarine
3 Tbsp. lemon juice
2 to 3 Tbsp. fine dry bread crumbs
$\frac{3}{4}$ tsp. salt
pinch pepper

Preheat oven to 350°F. Mash salmon and juice together in large bowl. Discard dark skin, if desired. Add remaining ingredients and toss lightly together. Spread in greased loaf pan and set in pan of hot water. Bake for approximately 50 to 60 minutes, or until loaf is set.

Cool slightly and unmould. Serve in slices with tomato sauce or your favourite cream sauce to which you have added one chopped egg. *Serves 5 to 6.*

HALIBUT STEAKS WITH CHINESE SAUCE

$1\frac{1}{2}$ lbs. halibut steaks, approximately 1 inch thick
2 Tbsp. dry sherry
2 Tbsp. lemon juice
2 Tbsp. soy sauce
2 Tbsp. salad oil
1 tsp. salt
$\frac{1}{2}$ tsp. pepper
$\frac{1}{2}$ tsp. ground ginger
2 scallions or green onions, cut into pieces

Fill steamer with water to $1\frac{1}{2}$ inches below steamer rack. Bring to a rapid boil. Wipe fresh halibut with damp cloth. If frozen, do not thaw. Place halibut on large piece of double thickness heavy-duty foil. Turn edges of foil up all around fish (to contain liquids). Place fish on steamer rack over rapidly boiling water. Combine remaining ingredients and pour over fish. Cover tightly. Steam fresh fish for 15 minutes, frozen for 25 minutes, or until fish flakes easily. Baste fish occasionally with sauce during cooking. *Serves 4.*

BAKED HALIBUT

2 lbs. halibut fillets, $\frac{3}{4}$ inch thick
$1\frac{1}{2}$ tsp. salt
1 tsp. paprika
1 medium to large lemon, peeled and finely chopped
$\frac{1}{2}$ cup sliced ripe olives
$\frac{1}{2}$ cup snipped fresh parsley
1 large tomato, sliced
sour cream, for garnish
lemon wedges

Thaw fillets if frozen. Preheat oven to 400°F. Cut fillets into serving-size pieces, season with salt and paprika, and place in covered baking dish. Combine chopped lemon and its juice with olives and parsley. Spread half of mixture over fillets; top each serving with tomato slice and then remaining lemon mixture. Cover and bake for 25 minutes; uncover and bake for another 10 minutes. Garnish each serving with sour cream; serve with lemon wedges. *Serves 4 to 6.*

BAKED HALIBUT ROYALE

2 lbs. halibut steak, about 1 inch thick
1 tsp. salt
1/2 tsp. paprika
few grains cayenne pepper
juice of 1 lemon
1/2 cup chopped onion
1 Tbsp. butter or margarine
green pepper strips, for garnish

Place fresh or frozen halibut steaks in shallow baking dish. Combine salt, paprika and cayenne pepper with lemon juice and pour over steaks. Marinate in refrigerator for 1 hour, turning the steaks halfway through so seasonings penetrate both sides.

Preheat oven to 450°F. Sauté onion in butter or margarine until tender. Spread onion over steaks. Top with green pepper strips and baste with marinade. Bake for 10 minutes for fresh fish, 20 minutes for frozen, or until fish flakes easily when tested with a fork. *Serves 8.*

CHEDDAR COD BAKE

2 Tbsp. butter
1/4 cup all-purpose flour
1/2 tsp. salt
1/8 tsp. pepper
1 tsp. dry mustard
1 1/2 cups milk
2 cups shredded Cheddar cheese
1 1/2 lbs. cod fillets
3 Tbsp. snipped fresh parsley

Preheat oven to 400°F. Butter a 9-inch-square baking dish. Melt butter in saucepan; blend in flour, salt, pepper and mustard. Gradually stir in milk. Cook over medium heat, stirring constantly, until smooth and thickened. Add cheese and stir until melted. Wipe fillets with damp cloth and cut in serving pieces. Arrange fish in prepared baking dish, cover with cheese sauce and sprinkle with parsley. Bake for 20 minutes. *Serves 6.*

SOLE THERMIDOR

5 Tbsp. butter or margarine
2 tsp. salt
1/2 tsp. seasoning salt
pepper to taste
4 medium sole fillets (approximately 1 1/2 lbs.)
lemon juice
1/4 cup chopped green onions
1 1/4 cups milk
3 Tbsp. all-purpose flour
1/2 tsp. dry mustard
1 cup grated sharp Cheddar cheese
3 Tbsp. dry sherry
paprika
chopped fresh parsley, for garnish

In small saucepan over low heat, melt 2 Tbsp. of the butter or margarine. Add salt, seasoning salt and pepper.

Preheat oven to 350°F. Sprinkle sole fillets with lemon juice. Brush fillets with butter mixture on both sides. Sprinkle each fillet with 1 Tbsp. green onions. Roll up fillets from narrow end and place seam side down in baking dish. Pour 1/2 cup of the milk over fillets and bake for 25 minutes or until fish flakes easily when tested with a fork.

Meanwhile, melt remaining 3 Tbsp. butter in saucepan; stir in flour and mustard until well blended. Gradually stir in remaining 3/4 cup milk and cook, stirring constantly, until mixture thickens. Reduce heat and stir in cheese until it melts. Stir in sherry.

When fish is done, remove from oven. Pour off pan liquid, reserving 1/4 cup. Stir it into cheese sauce.

Preheat broiler. Place sole fillets on ovenproof serving dish. Pour sauce over fish; sprinkle with paprika. Broil for approximately 1 minute or until sauce is slightly golden. Sprinkle with parsley and serve immediately. *Serves 4.*

FILLET OF SOLE BONNE FEMME

1/4 cup butter or margarine

3 green onions, chopped

6 fillets of sole, haddock or flounder (about 2 1/2 lbs.)

1/2 lb. mushrooms, sliced

1/2 tsp. salt, or to taste

1/8 tsp. pepper, or to taste

1 cup white wine

1 Tbsp. chopped fresh parsley

1 1/2 Tbsp. all-purpose flour

lemon wedges and parsley sprigs, for garnish
    (optional)

In large skillet, melt 2 Tbsp. of the butter. Add green onions and sauté gently for 1 minute. Arrange fish over green onions. Place sliced mushrooms over fish. Season with salt and pepper. Add wine and bring to a boil; reduce heat and simmer, covered, for 10 minutes. Add parsley and continue cooking until fish flakes easily with a fork, about 5 minutes. Drain fish well, reserving 1 cup liquid.

Arrange fish, mushrooms and green onions in large shallow baking dish. In skillet, melt remaining 2 Tbsp. butter; remove from heat. Stir in flour until mixture is smooth. Gradually stir in reserved liquid. Cook over medium heat, stirring constantly, until mixture is thickened. Pour sauce over fish and vegetables. Place under broiler for several minutes, just until top is golden brown. Serve immediately. Garnish with lemon and parsley, if desired. *Serves 6.*

FRIED FISH IN BATTER

2 lbs. fish fillets

1 tsp. salt

1 egg

1 cup water

1 1/4 cups all-purpose flour

oil, for frying

Season fish with 1/2 tsp. of the salt and cut into serving-size portions. If the pieces are more than 1/2 inch thick but not thick enough to slice conveniently,

make 3 or 4 slits in the side. The fish will cook more evenly and quickly.

To make batter, beat egg and add water. Stir in 1 cup of the flour and the remaining 1/2 tsp. salt, until just dampened; batter will be lumpy. Dip fish in the remaining 1/4 cup flour, then into batter. Fry fish in deep oil at 375°F until golden brown, turning once. This will take about 7 minutes. Drain. *Serves 4 to 6.*

Note: As a general rule, a batter made with water will be crisp while a batter made with milk will be tender.

ENGLISH-STYLE FISH AND CHIPS
Reminds me of the many incredible pub lunches one can have in Britain.

1 cup all-purpose flour

1 egg yolk

2 Tbsp. beer

1/4 tsp. salt

3 Tbsp. milk

3 Tbsp. water

1 egg white

vegetable oil or shortening, for deep-frying

8 medium potatoes, sliced lengthwise into strips
    1/2 inch thick and 1/2 inch wide

1 1/2 lbs. white fish fillets (haddock, sole, flounder or
    cod), skinned and cut into 3 x 5-inch serving pieces

Pour flour into large mixing bowl, make a well in centre and add egg yolk, beer and salt. Stir ingredients together until well mixed. Combine milk and water and gradually add to batter. Continue to stir until batter is smooth. Beat egg white until stiff peaks form and gently but thoroughly fold it into batter. For a light texture, let batter rest at room temperature for at least 30 minutes, although it may be used at once if necessary.

Heat 4 to 5 inches of oil or shortening in deep-fryer to 375°F. Preheat oven to 250°F, and line large shallow roasting pan with paper towels. Dry potatoes thoroughly and deep-fry in 3 or 4 batches until crisp and light brown. Transfer to lined pan to drain and place in oven to keep warm.

Wash fish under cold running water and pat completely dry with paper towels. Drop 2 or 3 pieces at a time into batter. When well coated, plunge into hot oil. Fry for 4 or 5 minutes or until golden brown, turning pieces occasionally with spoon to prevent sticking together or to pan.

To serve, heap fish in centre of large heated platter and arrange chips around outside. Traditionally, fish and chips are served sprinkled with malt vinegar and salt. *Serves 4.*

CRAB CASSEROLE

1 cup finely chopped onion
1 cup finely chopped green pepper
1 cup finely chopped celery
1/2 cup finely chopped fresh parsley
6 Tbsp. butter or cooking oil
1 can (10 oz.) condensed cream of mushroom soup
1 cup milk
1 1/2 tsp. salt
1 tsp. dry mustard
1 1/2 tsp. curry powder
2 tsp. Worcestershire sauce
4 cups day-old bread crumbs
2 lbs. crabmeat
pinch paprika
1/2 cup bread crumbs, browned in 1 Tbsp. butter
chopped fresh parsley, for garnish

Preheat oven to 350°F. Sauté the onion, green pepper, celery and parsley in butter or oil. Blend soup and milk in saucepan over medium heat. At simmering stage, add salt, mustard, curry powder and Worcestershire sauce. Blend well. Add sautéed vegetables and stir in the 4 cups bread crumbs and crabmeat. Pour mixture into casserole dish. Sprinkle lightly with paprika and the 1/2 cup buttered bread crumbs. Bake until lightly browned, about 40 minutes. Garnish with parsley before serving. *Serves 12 to 16.*

CURRY OF SHRIMP

1/3 cup butter
1/2 cup chopped onions
1/2 cup chopped green pepper
2 cloves garlic, minced
2 cups sour cream
2 tsp. lemon juice
2 tsp. curry powder
1/2 tsp. ground ginger
pinch pepper
3/4 tsp. salt
pinch chili powder
3 cups cleaned cooked or canned shrimp

Melt butter; add onions, green pepper and garlic. Cook until tender but not brown, about 5 minutes. Stir in sour cream, lemon juice and seasonings; add shrimp. Cook over low heat, stirring constantly, just until heated through. (Sauce is traditionally thin.) Serve over hot rice. *Serves 6.*

SAUCY OYSTER COCKTAIL

3/4 cup chili sauce
2 Tbsp. lemon juice
2 Tbsp. prepared horseradish
2 tsp. Worcestershire sauce
1 tsp. grated onion
salt to taste
dash hot pepper sauce
2 cups shucked oysters, chilled well
lettuce
lemon twists and fresh parsley sprigs, for garnish

Combine chili sauce, lemon juice, horseradish, Worcestershire sauce, onion, salt and hot pepper sauce. Mix well and chill thoroughly.

Halve or quarter oysters if large. Line cocktail glasses with lettuce. Arrange oysters attractively on lettuce. Spoon prepared sauce over oysters. Garnish with lemon and parsley. *Serves 6.*

OYSTER SCALLOP

2 cups fresh oysters

1 tsp. lemon juice

2 cups medium-coarse cracker crumbs

$\frac{1}{2}$ cup butter or margarine, melted

2 cups sliced fresh mushrooms

$\frac{3}{4}$ cup light cream

1 tsp. chopped fresh parsley

$\frac{1}{4}$ tsp. Worcestershire sauce

freshly cracked black pepper to taste

pimiento strips and green pepper rings, for garnish
   (optional)

Preheat oven to 350°F. Drain oysters; reserve $\frac{1}{4}$ cup oyster liquid. Sprinkle oysters with lemon juice. Combine crumbs with melted butter or margarine. Reserve $\frac{1}{2}$ cup of crumbs for topping. In large bowl, combine drained oysters, remaining crumbs, mushrooms, cream, parsley, Worcestershire sauce and pepper. Stir gently to combine. Place mixture into 8-inch round baking dish. Top with reserved crumbs. Bake for 30 to 40 minutes or until oysters are cooked and sauce is bubbly. Serve hot. Garnish with pimiento and green pepper, if desired. *Serves 8.*

PACIFIC OYSTER STEW

$1\frac{1}{2}$ Tbsp. all-purpose flour

$1\frac{1}{2}$ tsp. salt

dash hot pepper sauce

2 Tbsp. cold water

2 cups oysters and oyster liquor

$\frac{1}{4}$ cup butter or margarine

3 cups milk

1 cup light cream

extra pats of butter, for garnish (optional)

paprika and chopped fresh parsley, for garnish
   (optional)

Combine flour, salt, hot pepper sauce and cold water in small bowl; blend to a smooth paste. Place oysters and oyster liquor in saucepan. Stir in flour paste; add butter or margarine and simmer over low heat,

stirring gently, for approximately 5 minutes or until edges of oysters begin to curl. Meanwhile, in large saucepan, scald milk and light cream. Pour in oyster mixture. Remove from heat. Cover and allow to stand for 20 minutes to blend flavours.

Reheat stew to serving temperature and pour into heated tureen. If desired, garnish with butter pats, paprika and parsley. *Serves 4.*

Note: If oysters are small, prepare whole. If they are large, cut them accordingly.

SEAFOOD COCKTAIL

$1\frac{1}{2}$ lbs. seafood (crab, shrimp, lobster, oyster
   or salmon)

$\frac{1}{4}$ cup thinly sliced celery

$\frac{1}{4}$ cup chopped green pepper

2 green onions, chopped

1 Tbsp. lemon juice

$\frac{3}{4}$ cup chili sauce

2 Tbsp. prepared horseradish

2 Tbsp. lemon juice

2 Tbsp. Worcestershire sauce

$\frac{1}{4}$ tsp. salt

1 tsp. grated onion

dash hot pepper sauce

shredded lettuce

6 lemon slices, for garnish

Select any one seafood or a combination. Combine with celery, green pepper, green onions and the 1 Tbsp. lemon juice. Cover and chill.

In a small bowl, combine chili sauce, horseradish, the 2 Tbsp. lemon juice, Worcestershire sauce, salt, grated onion and hot pepper sauce. Mix well. Refrigerate, covered, for at least 3 hours.

To serve, arrange shredded lettuce in 6 sherbet glasses. Place seafood mixture over lettuce. Spoon some sauce over each. Garnish with lemon slices. *Serves 6.*

GARDEN VEGETABLE STUFFING

1 cup finely chopped onion

$\frac{1}{4}$ cup butter or margarine

2 cups dry bread cubes

1 cup shredded carrot

1 cup fresh mushrooms, cleaned, trimmed and
    chopped

$\frac{1}{2}$ cup snipped fresh parsley

$1\frac{1}{2}$ Tbsp. lemon juice

1 egg

1 clove garlic, crushed

2 tsp. salt, or to taste

$\frac{1}{4}$ tsp. dried marjoram

$\frac{1}{4}$ tsp. pepper

Sauté onion in butter or margarine until onion is tender. Place in bowl and lightly mix with remaining ingredients. If you have extra stuffing, wrap in aluminum foil and heat on grill for 20 minutes before serving. Great for fish, especially salmon. *Makes 5 cups.*

TARTAR SAUCE

1 cup mayonnaise

1 Tbsp. chopped capers (optional)

1 Tbsp. chopped olives

1 Tbsp. chopped pickles

1 Tbsp. minced fresh parsley

Mix together and serve with fish. *Makes $1\frac{1}{4}$ cups.*

SEAFOOD SAUCE

1 cup tomato ketchup

$\frac{1}{3}$ cup lemon juice

1 Tbsp. minced onion

1 Tbsp. soy sauce

1 Tbsp. prepared horseradish

$\frac{1}{2}$ tsp. anise seed, crushed

Combine all ingredients and blend thoroughly. Cover and refrigerate for several hours. *Makes about $1\frac{1}{2}$ cups.*

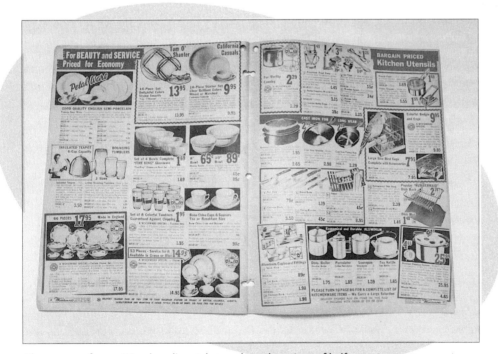

These pages from a Woodward's catalogue show the prices of half a century ago.

BÉARNAISE SAUCE

1/4 cup dry white wine

1/4 cup tarragon vinegar

2 tsp. dried tarragon

1 Tbsp. chopped shallot or green onion

1 Tbsp. chopped fresh parsley

1/8 tsp. coarsely ground black pepper

3 egg yolks

1/2 cup butter or margarine (do not use "soft" style margarine)

1 Tbsp. chopped fresh parsley or tarragon

In saucepan, combine wine, vinegar, dried tarragon, shallot or green onion, 1 Tbsp. parsley and pepper. Bring mixture to a boil, stirring constantly. Reduce heat; simmer, uncovered, until mixture has reduced to 1/4 cup, about 8 to 9 minutes. Strain mixture, squeezing herbs with back of spoon to extract juices; discard herbs. Allow mixture to cool completely.

In top of double boiler, beat egg yolks with 2 Tbsp. of prepared liquid with wire whisk, just until blended. Cook over hot—not boiling—water until mixture begins to thicken, approximately 1 minute. Add butter 1 Tbsp. at a time (for convenience, divide butter into 8 pieces in advance), beating constantly after each addition until butter is melted and mixture is a smooth consistency before adding next Tbsp. butter. This process should take approximately 5 minutes. The sauce can curdle quickly over high heat, so do not allow water in bottom pan to boil. If it starts to boil, immediately add small amount of cold water to cool it down. Water should not touch bottom of top pan.

After all butter has been added, remove top of double boiler. Using wire whisk, slowly beat in remaining 2 Tbsp. prepared liquid, then the 1 Tbsp. fresh parsley or tarragon. Beat until sauce is as thick as mayonnaise. Serve warm or cold. *Makes approximately 1 cup.*

This embroidered tag was once part of a Woodward's employee's uniform.

PIQUANT SAUCE FOR FISH STICKS

1 cup mayonnaise or salad dressing

1 Tbsp. chopped fresh parsley

2 tsp. prepared mustard

2 tsp. minced onion

1/4 cup crumbled blue cheese

chopped fresh chives or green onions, for garnish

Combine mayonnaise or salad dressing, parsley, mustard, onion and blue cheese in bowl. Refrigerate. Before serving, sprinkle with chives or green onions. Delicious over hot fish sticks. *Serves 4 to 5.*

LEMON DILL BUTTER

A super topping for your salmon steaks or sole fillets.

1/4 cup soft butter

1/2 Tbsp. lemon juice

1/4 tsp. finely grated lemon rind

1 Tbsp. chopped fresh parsley

1/4 tsp. dried dill weed

pinch white pepper

Cream butter in small bowl; gradually beat in lemon juice and rind until all juice is absorbed. Stir in parsley, dill and pepper. Place in covered container and refrigerate. Remove from refrigerator 30 minutes before serving. *Serves 4.*

yeast doughs, quick breads and pancakes

mona says . . .

Nothing so commands respect for the cook as freshly baked bread. Nothing so captures the imagination as its aroma and no culinary achievement gives greater satisfaction.

Using a pair of flat stones, the early settlers ground their own wheat into flour. Sourdough served in place of yeast and pans of dough were wrapped in woollen coats and blankets to protect them from the cold. Today, skillfully milled and blended flour, fast-rising yeast and thermostatically controlled temperatures in the home have taken the guesswork out of breadmaking. The challenge becomes not so much how the thing is done as how to create family favourites by putting to use good basic recipes.

Yeast doughs lend themselves to experimentation: with a knowledge of some rules you'll be in command of the magic.

- Flour: Use an all-purpose flour. Pastry flour does not contain enough gluten to produce an elastic dough. Use only enough flour to keep dough from sticking to your hands. For best nutrition, use enriched flours.
- Yeast: A living thing, yeast responds to gentle treatment. Too much yeast hastens the rising of the dough but detracts from the flavour of the bread; too little shortens the time required for the yeast to be fully active. To ensure the best yeast activity and to reduce the time lapse between the mixing and the finished product, begin with utensils and ingredients at room temperature. Any closed space with a bowl of hot water inside it makes an ideal place to set dough to rise.
- Salt: Not only necessary for flavour, but also to control fermentation.
- Sugar: Not only sweetens, but also encourages yeast activity.
- Liquids and fats: Potato water, shortening, milk and butter all improve the flavour and quality of the loaf.
- Rising: Grease dough to prevent crust forming on surface. Let rise in warm place (85°F) free from any drafts.
- Texture: Thorough kneading ensures a fine and even texture. Knead on a floured board and use three motions repeatedly: fold, press and turn; fold, press and turn.
- Baking: If tops brown too quickly, cover loaves with foil during the last 20 minutes of cooking time. When done, brush with butter. For a crisp crust, leave the loaf uncovered. Cool on a rack.

NEVER FAIL WHITE BREAD

When I lived in the Yukon I had to make my own bread. Baked and cooled, I would wrap and hang it out on the clothesline to freeze in winter. I called the clothesline my Whitehorse deep freeze!

2 Tbsp. sugar
1/4 cup warm water (about 110°F)
1 package active dry yeast
2 cups milk, scalded
2 tsp. salt
1 Tbsp. shortening
6 to 6 1/4 cups sifted all-purpose flour
butter or margarine

Dissolve sugar in warm water. Sprinkle yeast over top. Set aside until frothy. In large bowl, combine scalded milk, salt and shortening. Cool to lukewarm. Add softened yeast. Gradually beat in flour, adding enough to make a moderately stiff dough.

Turn dough out on a lightly floured surface. Knead until smooth and satiny, about 8 to 10 minutes. Shape into a ball.

Place dough in lightly greased bowl and turn to grease top surface. Cover and set in warm place. Let rise until doubled in bulk, about 1 1/2 hours.

Punch down and allow to double in size again, about 45 minutes. Cut into two equal portions and form into balls. Let rest 10 minutes.

Shape loaves by rolling balls into 7 x 15-inch rectangle on lightly floured surface. Roll up jelly-roll fashion, starting at narrow end. Tuck ends under as you roll. Place seam side down in greased 8 1/2 x 4 1/2 x 2 1/2-inch loaf pan. Grease tops of loaves, cover with greased waxed paper and let rise until dough reaches 1 1/2 inches above top of pan in centre, and corners are filled (1 to 1 1/2 hours).

Preheat oven to 400°F and bake 35 to 40 minutes. Remove from pans at once and cool on wire rack. Brush tops with butter or margarine. *Makes 2 loaves.*

WHOLE-WHEAT BREAD

1 package active dry yeast
1/4 cup warm water (about 110°F)
2 1/2 cups hot water
1/2 cup brown sugar
3 tsp. salt
1/4 cup shortening
3 cups whole-wheat flour
5 cups sifted all-purpose white flour

Soften yeast in the 1/4 cup warm water. Combine the 2 1/2 cups hot water, sugar, salt and shortening; cool to lukewarm.

Stir in whole-wheat flour and 1 cup of the white flour; beat well. Stir in softened yeast. Add enough of the remaining flour to make a moderately stiff dough. Turn out on a lightly floured surface; knead until smooth and satiny, 10 to 12 minutes. Shape into a ball. Place dough in lightly greased bowl and turn to grease top surface. Cover and set in warm place until doubled in bulk, approximately 1 1/2 hours.

Punch down and cut in two equal portions. Shape each into a smooth ball. Cover and let rest 10 minutes.

Shape loaves by rolling balls into 7 x 15-inch rectangle on lightly floured surface. Roll up jelly-roll fashion, starting at narrow end. Tuck ends under as you roll. Place seam side down in greased 8 1/2 x 4 1/2 x 2 1/2-inch loaf pan. Let rise until double in bulk, approximately 1 1/4 hours.

Preheat oven to 375°F. Bake for approximately 45 minutes. Cover with foil during last 20 minutes if necessary to prevent overbrowning. Remove from pans and cool on wire rack. *Makes 2 loaves.*

SWEET DOUGH

This is one of my favourite recipes. It's so rewarding to make and I love the applause from the family.

2 tsp. sugar
$\frac{1}{2}$ cup warm water (about 110°F)
2 packages active dry yeast
1 cup milk
$\frac{1}{2}$ cup sugar
2 tsp. salt
$\frac{3}{4}$ cup cold water
$\frac{1}{4}$ cup softened butter or margarine
2 eggs
7 to $7\frac{1}{2}$ cups all-purpose flour

Dissolve the 2 tsp. sugar in the warm water in large warm bowl. Sprinkle yeast into water mixture and let stand for 10 minutes, then stir well. Scald milk and mix in the $\frac{1}{2}$ cup sugar and salt. Add cold water and cool to lukewarm. Add milk mixture, butter or margarine, eggs and 2 cups of the flour to dissolved yeast mixture. Beat until smooth. Add 5 cups of remaining flour gradually, adding more if necessary to make a soft dough that pulls away from sides of bowl. Turn out on floured surface.

Form into ball and knead 5 to 10 minutes or until dough is smooth, elastic and no longer sticky, adding flour as necessary.

Place in lightly greased bowl, turn to grease top surface of dough and cover with greased waxed paper. Set in warm place until doubled in bulk, about $1\frac{1}{2}$ hours.

Punch down and cut into 4 equal portions. Form each portion into a ball, cover and let rest 10 minutes. Shape each portion into rolls. Brush with melted butter or shortening. Cover with greased waxed paper.

Let rise in warm place until doubled in bulk, 30 to 60 minutes. Preheat oven to 375°F. Bake for 12 to 15 minutes. Brush with butter, if desired. Rolls can also be brushed with a glaze of 1 Tbsp. sugar dissolved in 1 Tbsp. water 5 minutes before end of baking time. *Makes 5 to 6 dozen rolls or 4 coffee cakes.*

Variations

- **Pan Buns:** Roll $\frac{1}{4}$ recipe sweet dough with palms of hands into a cylinder about 12 inches long. Cut dough into 16 equal portions; roll each into a ball. Place evenly in well-greased 8-inch square pan. *Makes 16 buns.*

- **Parkerhouse Rolls:** Roll $\frac{1}{4}$ recipe sweet dough to $\frac{1}{4}$ inch thickness. Cut into circles using floured $2\frac{1}{2}$-inch round cookie cutter. Make off-centre crease and fold so top overlaps slightly; seal end edges of each roll. Place on well-greased baking sheet. *Makes 12 to 16 rolls.*

- **Fan Tans:** Roll $\frac{1}{4}$ recipe sweet dough into 9 x 14-inch rectangle; spread with softened butter. Cut into 6 strips lengthwise. Stack strips and cut into 9 pieces. Place cut-side down in well-greased muffin cups. *Makes 9 rolls.*

- **Cloverleaf Rolls:** Use $\frac{1}{4}$ recipe sweet dough and form dough into 1-inch balls. Place 3 balls in each well-greased muffin cup. Brush with melted butter. *Makes 12 to 16 rolls.*

- **Crescent Rolls:** Roll $\frac{1}{4}$ recipe sweet dough into 12-inch circle; cut into 12 wedges. Beginning at rounded edge, roll up each piece. Place point down on greased baking sheet. Curve into crescents. *Makes 12 rolls.*

In its heyday, Woodward's Food Floor carried products from around the world. There were even pastries flown in from the famous Paris restaurant, Maxim's.

OATMEAL LOAF

1 1/2 cups boiling water
1 Tbsp. butter or margarine
1 1/2 tsp. salt
1/3 cup brown sugar
1 1/2 cups rolled oats
1 package active dry yeast
1/4 cup warm water (about 110°F)
3 cups all-purpose flour

Pour boiling water into large bowl. Add butter or margarine, salt, sugar and oats; mix well; cool to lukewarm. Dissolve yeast in warm water. Add dissolved yeast mixture to oat mixture. Stir in flour and mix well. Knead dough about 20 times. Shape into a round loaf (1 large or 2 small) and place on greased cookie sheet. Let rise for 1 1/2 hours in warm place. Preheat oven to 375°F and bake for 30 to 50 minutes, depending on size of loaf, or until bread sounds hollow when tapped on bottom. *Makes 1 large or 2 small loaves.*

POTATO BREAD

2 packages active dry yeast
2 cups warm water (about 110°F)
1/4 cup sugar
1 Tbsp. salt
1 cup mashed potatoes (do not season or
   add butter)
1/2 cup butter, softened
6 1/2 to 6 3/4 cups all-purpose flour
2 Tbsp. melted butter

Sprinkle yeast over warm water in large bowl. Stir until dissolved. Stir in sugar and salt until dissolved. Add mashed potatoes, softened butter and 3 cups of the flour. With electric mixer at medium speed, beat until smooth, approximately 2 minutes. Clean dough from beaters with spatula if mixer does not have dough attachment. Mix dough by hand, gradually adding balance of flour, as needed, to make smooth dough stiff enough to leave sides of bowl.

Turn dough out onto lightly floured surface. Knead until smooth and elastic and small blisters appear on the surface, about 10 minutes. Place in lightly greased large bowl and turn to grease top surface. Cover with damp cloth to prevent crust from forming. Let rise in warm place until doubled in bulk, approximately 1 hour.

Turn dough out onto lightly floured surface and divide in half. Shape each piece into loaf by rolling into 16 x 8-inch rectangle. Roll up jelly-roll fashion, starting at narrow end. Press ends even and pinch to seal. Place seam side down in greased 9 x 5 x 3-inch loaf pans. Brush surface lightly with melted butter and let rise in warm place until sides come to top of pan and tops are rounded.

Preheat oven to 400°F. Set oven rack on lowest level (otherwise loaf may look done, but bottom may not be baked). Bake for 35 to 45 minutes or until crust is deep golden brown and loaves sound hollow when tapped. If crust becomes too brown, cover with foil. Turn out of pans onto wire racks. Brush tops with remaining melted butter. Let cool completely. *Makes 2 loaves.*

BACON AND CHEESE BREAD

1 can (10 oz.) condensed Cheddar cheese soup,
   undiluted
1/2 cup milk
1/4 cup butter or margarine
3 1/2 cups all-purpose flour
1 package active dry yeast
1 tsp. salt
1 large egg
6 slices bacon, cooked and crumbled

Place soup in medium saucepan and gradually stir in milk. Add butter or margarine and heat over low heat until warm (120 to 130°F). Combine 2 cups of the flour, undissolved yeast and salt in large bowl of mixer. Add soup mixture. Beat on low speed until dry ingredients are moistened. Add egg and 1/2 cup of the flour. Beat 2 minutes at medium speed, scraping bowl with rubber spatula. Remove from mixer. Stir in remaining 1 cup flour and crumbled bacon with spoon to make a firm but sticky dough. Cover bowl with plastic wrap; refrigerate for 1 hour or until dough is doubled in bulk.

Grease 2-quart casserole. Grease hands well and shape dough into ball. Place in prepared casserole. Cover and let rise in warm place for 1 hour or until doubled in bulk.

Preheat oven to 350°F. Bake for 50 minutes or until golden brown. Remove from casserole immediately and cool completely on wire rack. *Makes 1 loaf.*

OVERNIGHT BUNS

These buns are as light as balls of fluff. My husband, Claude, keeps searching the freezer in case there's more left!

1 package active dry yeast
$1/2$ tsp. granulated sugar
$1/2$ cup warm water (about 110°F)
11 to 12 cups all-purpose flour
4 cups cold water
$3/4$ cup salad oil
1 cup berry sugar
$1 1/2$ tsp. salt

Prepare this dough in late afternoon. Dissolve yeast and $1/2$ tsp. sugar in warm water; let stand for 5 to 10 minutes. Stir well.

In large bowl combine flour, cold water, oil, berry sugar and salt. Blend well. Add yeast mixture. Mix until completely moistened. Turn out on lightly floured surface and knead well, for approximately 10 minutes. Place in greased bowl and turn to grease top surface of dough. Allow to rise at room temperature. When dough is doubled in size, shape into buns and place on lightly greased cookie sheet. Cover and leave overnight in very cool place.

Preheat oven to 375° to 400°F. While breakfast is cooking, bake buns for 15 minutes. *Makes approximately 6 dozen.*

RAISIN BREAD

2 tsp. sugar
$1/2$ cup warm water (about 110°F)
2 packages active yeast
$3/4$ cup milk
$1/4$ cup sugar
2 tsp. salt
$1/4$ cup shortening
2 eggs
4 to $4 1/2$ cups all-purpose flour
2 cups raisins
melted margarine or butter

Dissolve the 2 tsp. sugar in warm water in large warm bowl. Sprinkle yeast over water and let stand for 10 minutes, then stir well. Scald milk; mix in the $1/4$ cup sugar and salt; cool to lukewarm. Add milk mixture, shortening, eggs and 1 cup of the flour to dissolved yeast mixture. Beat until smooth. Lightly coat raisins with a little of flour called for in recipe and stir into mixture. Add remaining flour gradually, adding more if necessary to make a soft dough that pulls away from sides of bowl. Turn out on floured surface and form into ball. Knead for 5 to 10 minutes or until dough is smooth, elastic and no longer sticky. Place in lightly greased bowl and turn to grease top surface. Cover with greased waxed paper and set in warm place until doubled in size, $1 1/2$ to 2 hours.

Punch down and turn out on work surface. Divide dough into 2 equal portions. Form each into ball, cover and let rest 10 minutes.

Shape each portion into loaf by rolling into 7 x 15-inch rectangle on lightly floured surface. Roll up jelly-roll fashion, starting at narrow end. Tuck ends under as you roll. Place seam side down in greased $8 1/2$ x $4 1/2$ x $2 1/2$-inch loaf pans. Grease loaves, cover with greased waxed paper and let rise in warm place until doubled, 1 to $1 1/2$ hours.

Preheat oven to 400°F. Bake for 35 to 40 minutes. Remove from pans and cool on wire racks. Brush top crust with margarine or butter for soft shiny crust. *Makes 2 loaves.*

STREUSEL COFFEE CAKE

1/4 recipe Sweet Dough (page 123)
1/3 cup all-purpose flour
1/3 cup brown sugar, packed
1/2 tsp. ground cinnamon
3 Tbsp. butter
1 egg yolk
2 tsp. milk

Depending on type of pan used (8- or 9-inch, square or round), roll dough into a square or circular shape, with dough just fitting pan. Place in greased pan; grease top of dough and cover with greased waxed paper. Set in warm place until doubled in size, 45 to 60 minutes.

Preheat oven to 375°F. In small bowl, combine flour, brown sugar and cinnamon; mix well. Cut in butter until mixture is crumbly; set aside. Prick top of risen dough with fork. Brush with mixture of egg yolk and milk. Sprinkle crumb mixture over top. Bake for 25 to 30 minutes. Loosen edges with spatula and lift out onto wire rack. Serve warm or cold. *Makes 1 coffee cake.*

EASTER BREAD WITH ALMOND FILLING

FOR THE DOUGH:
1 tsp. sugar
1/4 cup lukewarm water (about 110°F)
1 package active dry yeast
1/4 cup milk, at room temperature
1 tsp. vanilla extract
1/2 tsp. grated lemon rind
1/4 cup sugar
1/2 tsp. salt
3 egg yolks
2 cups all-purpose flour
4 Tbsp. butter, softened

Dissolve the 1 tsp. sugar in warm water. Sprinkle in yeast. Let stand for 2 to 3 minutes until yeast dissolves. Set in a warm draft-free place for about 5 minutes or until yeast has begun to bubble and has almost doubled in volume.

Combine yeast with milk, vanilla, lemon rind, the 1/4 cup sugar and salt. Stir in egg yolks one at a time. Beat in flour 1/2 cup at a time. Beat butter into dough 1 Tbsp. at a time. Turn dough out on floured surface and knead for about 10 minutes, until dough is smooth and elastic. Sprinkle more flour on dough or work surface if either becomes sticky. Form into ball, place in greased bowl and turn to grease top surface. Let rise in warm area for about 1 hour or until doubled in bulk.

FOR THE ALMOND FILLING:
4 Tbsp. butter, softened
1/4 cup sugar
1 egg yolk, lightly beaten
1/2 cup finely grated almonds
1 tsp. grated orange rind
1/2 cup raisins
1/2 tsp. vanilla extract

Cream butter and sugar. Beat in egg yolk and gradually stir in almonds, orange rind, raisins and vanilla. Blend thoroughly.

TO MAKE THE BREAD:
1 egg lightly beaten with 1 Tbsp. milk

Turn dough out on floured surface and knead for a minute. Roll dough into rectangle about 9 inches wide and 13 inches long; it should be about 1/4 inch thick. With metal spatula, spread almond filling over dough, leaving 3/4-inch border on each side. Starting with 13-inch side, roll dough up jelly-roll fashion. Place roll seam side down on lightly greased baking sheet. Brush top and sides with egg-milk mixture.

Let rise in warm place until doubled in bulk, about 45 minutes to 1 hour. Brush again with egg-milk mixture. Preheat oven to 350°F. Bake for 40 to 45 minutes or until light golden brown. *Makes 1 loaf.*

GREEK EASTER BREAD

$1/2$ cup milk

$1/4$ cup granulated sugar

$3/4$ tsp. salt

2 Tbsp. softened butter

$1/3$ cup warm water (about 110°F)

1 tsp. granulated sugar

1 package active dry yeast

1 egg, well beaten

$2^{1}/_2$ to 3 cups sifted all-purpose flour

$1/4$ cup currants

$1/2$ cup chopped almonds

melted butter

$3/4$ cup sifted icing sugar

1 Tbsp. milk

whole blanched almonds

candied cherries

Scald the $1/2$ cup milk; stir in the $1/4$ cup sugar, salt and softened butter. Cool to lukewarm. Meanwhile, measure warm water into a large warm bowl; stir in the 1 tsp. sugar. Sprinkle with yeast. Let stand for 10 minutes, then stir well. Stir in lukewarm milk mixture and egg. Add $1^{1}/_2$ cups of the flour and beat for 2 to 3 minutes with electric mixer at medium speed, until smooth. Mix in currants and chopped almonds. Gradually stir in 1 to 2 cups of remaining flour to make a soft dough. Turn dough onto lightly floured surface and knead until smooth and elastic, 5 to 10 minutes. Form into ball and place in buttered bowl, turning to grease top surface of dough. Cover and let rest in warm place for 30 minutes.

An early advertisement highlighting fashionable footwear.

Punch down dough and turn onto lightly floured surface. Divide into 3 equal portions and shape into 3 round loaves. Place loaves on buttered baking sheet in shape of 3-petalled flower. Brush top with melted butter. Cover loosely with plastic wrap and place in refrigerator set at moderately cold setting for 2 to 24 hours.

Preheat oven to 375°F. Remove dough, uncover and let rise in warm place for 20 minutes. Bake for 35 to 40 minutes.

Remove from baking sheet and cool on rack. Combine icing sugar and 1 Tbsp. milk and pour over each of the three loaves. Arrange almonds and cherries in flower shapes on frosting. Cut into thin slices and serve with butter. *Makes 1 flower-shaped loaf.*

APPLE OAT BREAD

1 egg, beaten

1 cup peeled, shredded apple, firmly packed

$3/4$ cup sour milk

2 Tbsp. molasses

$1/4$ cup margarine, melted

$1^{3}/_4$ cups sifted all-purpose flour

1 tsp. baking powder

1 tsp. salt

1 tsp. baking soda

$1/2$ cup brown sugar

$1/2$ cup quick-cooking oats

$1/3$ cup raisins

$1/3$ cup chopped walnuts

Preheat oven to 350°F. Grease a 9 x 5 x 3-inch loaf pan. Combine egg, apple, sour milk, molasses and melted margarine. In separate bowl, sift together flour, baking powder, salt and baking soda, then stir in sugar, oats, raisins and walnuts. Add liquid ingredients to dry ingredients all at once and stir just until mixture is blended. Turn batter into greased loaf pan and bake for 50 to 60 minutes, or until toothpick inserted in centre comes out clean. Cool pan on wire rack for 10 minutes, then turn bread out and cool completely on rack. Wrap and slice the next day. *Makes 1 loaf.*

PECAN BREAD

3 cups sifted all-purpose flour
1 cup sugar
4 tsp. baking powder
1 tsp. salt
1 cup very finely chopped pecans or walnuts
2 tsp. grated lemon rind
2 eggs
1 cup milk
¼ cup vegetable oil
pecan or walnut halves, for decoration

Preheat oven to 325°F. Grease an 9 x 5 x 3-inch loaf pan. Sift flour, sugar, baking powder and salt together in a large bowl. Stir in chopped nuts and lemon rind. In small bowl, beat eggs well with milk; mix in oil. Add to flour mixture, stirring until evenly moist. Turn into greased loaf pan; spread top even. To decorate, press pecan or walnut halves down centre of batter. Bake for 1 hour and 20 minutes, or until toothpick inserted in centre comes out clean.

Cool in pan on wire rack for 10 minutes, then loosen around edges with knife and turn out onto rack. Place right side up. Let cool completely. Wrap and store overnight to mellow flavours and for easier slicing. *Makes 1 loaf.*

MOLASSES NUT BREAD

3 cups sifted all-purpose flour
3 tsp. baking powder
1½ tsp. salt
½ tsp. baking soda
½ cup light brown sugar, firmly packed
½ cup molasses
1 egg, well beaten
1 cup milk
¼ cup shortening, melted
½ cup finely chopped nuts
1 cup raisins

Preheat oven to 350°F. Grease a 9 x 5 x 3-inch loaf pan. Sift together flour, baking powder, salt and baking soda. Add brown sugar. In separate bowl, combine molasses, egg and milk. Add milk mixture and melted shortening to flour mixture, mixing only enough to dampen flour. Fold in nuts and raisins. Turn into loaf pan and bake for 65 to 70 minutes, or until toothpick in centre comes out clean. Cool completely on wire rack. Wrap and store overnight to mellow flavours. *Makes 1 loaf.*

BANANA BREAD

1 cup sugar
½ cup shortening
2 eggs, well beaten
3 ripe, medium bananas, mashed
1¼ cups cake flour
½ tsp. salt
1 tsp. baking soda

Preheat oven to 350°F. Grease a 9 x 5 x 3-inch loaf pan. Cream sugar and shortening. Mix in eggs and bananas. Sift flour, salt and baking soda together. Blend wet and dry mixtures. Do not overmix. Pour evenly into pan and bake for approximately 45 minutes. Cool in loaf pan for 10 minutes. Remove from pan and cool on rack. *Makes 1 loaf.*

PUMPKIN LOAF

3 cups all-purpose flour
2 cups sugar
1½ cups oil
4 eggs
2 tsp. baking powder
2 tsp. baking soda
½ tsp. salt
2 tsp. ground cinnamon
1 can (14 oz.) pumpkin
1 cup raisins
½ cup chopped walnuts

Preheat oven to 350°F. Grease and flour two 9 x 5 x 3-inch loaf pans. Place all ingredients in large bowl. Mix until well combined. Turn batter into prepared pans. Bake for 50 to 60 minutes or until toothpick inserted in centre comes out clean. Remove from pans and cool on wire rack. *Makes 2 loaves.*

WALNUT LOAF

2 1/2 cups sifted all-purpose flour
3 tsp. baking powder
1/2 tsp. salt
1 egg, beaten
1 tsp. vanilla extract
3/4 cup sugar
1/4 cup butter or margarine, melted
1 1/4 cups milk
1 1/4 cups chopped walnuts
1 tsp. grated lemon rind

Preheat oven to 350°F. Grease and flour a 9 x 5 x 3-inch loaf pan. Sift flour with baking powder and salt. Combine egg, vanilla, sugar and melted butter or margarine in large bowl. Beat until well blended. Add milk and blend well. Add flour mixture and beat until smooth. Stir in walnuts and lemon rind. Pour batter into pan. Bake for 60 to 65 minutes. Allow to cool in loaf pan for 10 minutes. Remove from pan and cool completely on rack. *Makes one loaf.*

CARROT-DATE LOAF

2 cups sifted all-purpose flour
1 cup sugar
1 tsp. baking soda
3/4 tsp. salt
1/2 tsp. ground cinnamon
2 eggs, slightly beaten
1/2 cup oil
3/4 cup lemon-lime carbonated beverage
1 cup finely grated carrots
1 cup chopped dates

Preheat oven to 350°F. Grease and flour a 9 x 5 x 3-inch loaf pan. Mix flour, sugar, baking soda, salt and cinnamon. In separate large bowl, combine eggs, oil, carbonated beverage, carrots and dates. Mix in dry ingredients. Turn into pan and bake for 50 to 55 minutes or until cake tester inserted in centre comes out clean. Remove from pan immediately and cool on wire rack. *Makes 1 loaf.*

Note: This loaf freezes well. To serve, thaw wrapped loaf at room temperature.

GLAZED ORANGE LOAF

1 2/3 cups sifted all-purpose flour
1 1/2 tsp. baking powder
1/2 tsp. salt
2/3 cup chopped pecans
1/2 cup softened butter
1 cup sugar
2 eggs
2 tsp. grated orange rind
1/2 tsp. vanilla extract
2/3 cup milk
2 Tbsp. frozen orange juice concentrate, thawed
1/4 cup sugar

Preheat oven to 350°F. Butter a 9 x 5 x 3-inch loaf pan. Sift flour, baking powder and salt together; mix in pecans. Cream butter; gradually beat in the 1 cup sugar. Add eggs, one at a time, beating well after each addition. Mix in orange rind and vanilla. Add sifted dry ingredients to creamed mixture alternately with milk; combine lightly after each addition. Turn batter into prepared pan. Bake for 50 to 55 minutes. Combine orange juice concentrate and the 1/4 cup sugar. As soon as loaf is removed from oven, drizzle with orange juice mixture. Cool completely in pan on cake rack. Remove from pan. Wrap in foil and store for 24 hours. Slice and serve with butter. *Makes 1 loaf.*

SULTANA LOAF

Great for the lunch box!

2 lbs. sultana raisins
boiling water
1 cup softened butter
1 1/2 cups sugar
6 eggs
1 tsp. lemon extract
1 tsp. vanilla extract
1 tsp. almond extract
1/2 cup glacé cherries, coarsely chopped
3 cups all-purpose flour
1 tsp. baking powder

Preheat oven to 300°F. Grease two 9 x 5 x 3-inch pans. Place raisins in large bowl and cover with boiling water. Allow to stand for 5 minutes; drain and dry thoroughly. In large bowl, cream butter and sugar until light and fluffy. Add eggs, one at a time, beating well after each addition. Stir in lemon, vanilla and almond extracts. Place prepared raisins and cherries in bowl. Sift flour and baking powder over top. Stir until fruit is well coated with flour. Add fruit mixture to egg mixture one-third at a time, beating well after each addition. Pour batter into pans. Bake for 1 1/2 hours or until cake tester inserted in centre comes out clean. *Makes 2 loaves.*

Note: This recipe can be halved if desired.

SEED CAKE

3 cups all-purpose flour
1 Tbsp. baking powder
1/4 tsp. salt
3/4 cup butter
1 1/2 cups sugar
3 eggs, separated
1 cup milk
1 Tbsp. caraway seeds

Preheat oven to 325°F. Grease and flour a 9 x 5 x 3-inch loaf pan. Sift flour, baking powder and salt together. Cream butter and sugar until light. Add egg yolks, one at a time, beating after each addition. Alternately add sifted dry ingredients and milk. Mix in caraway seeds. Beat egg whites until stiff and fold into batter. Pour batter into pan and bake for 50 to 60 minutes. *Makes 1 loaf.*

POTATO SCONES

1 cup sifted all-purpose flour
4 tsp. baking powder
1/4 tsp. salt
1 cup well-mashed potatoes, unseasoned
2 Tbsp. butter or margarine
1/2 cup milk (approximately)

Preheat oven to 400°F. Sift flour, baking powder and salt twice, then add mashed potatoes. Work in butter or margarine lightly. Add milk gradually (amount may vary according to amount of moisture in potatoes). Dough should be soft. Turn out on lightly floured board. Roll out to 1/2-inch thickness. Cut with 2 1/2-inch cutter. Bake on greased baking sheet for about 15 minutes or until done. *Makes about 6 to 8 biscuits.*

TEA BISCUITS

1 3/4 cups all-purpose flour
3 tsp. baking powder
1 tsp. salt
1/4 cup shortening
3/4 cup milk

Preheat oven to 450°F. Combine flour, baking powder and salt, stirring well. Cut in shortening until mixture resembles coarse crumbs. Make a well in dry mixture. Add milk all at once. Stir with fork until all ingredients are moistened. Turn mixture out on lightly floured surface; gather up and knead gently about 20 times. Roll dough out with a floured rolling pin to 1/2-inch thickness. Cut with floured 2-inch biscuit cutter. Gather up leftover dough, pat together and cut with cutter. Do not re-roll.

Place on ungreased baking sheet ($^3/_4$ inch apart for crusty biscuits, or close together for soft sides). Bake for 8 to 10 minutes. *Makes 1 dozen.*

Variations

- **Drop Biscuits:** Increase flour to 2 cups and milk to 1 cup. Omit kneading; drop mixture by tablespoonfuls onto ungreased baking sheet. Bake for 12 to 15 minutes.
- **Buttermilk Biscuits:** Add $^1/_4$ tsp. baking soda to dry ingredients. Replace milk with buttermilk or sour milk.
- **Extra Rich Biscuits:** Add $^1/_4$ cup butter. Add 2 Tbsp. sugar to dry ingredients.
- **Cheese Biscuits:** Cut $^3/_4$ cup grated sharp cheese into dry ingredients after adding shortening.

MUFFINS

3 Tbsp. sugar
$2^1/_2$ cups Make-It-Yourself Mix (see next page)
$^3/_4$ cup raisins, cut-up dates or other fruit (optional)
$^3/_4$ cup milk
1 egg, beaten

Preheat oven to 400°F. Grease 12-cup muffin pan. Stir sugar into mix, and add fruit, if desired. Add milk and egg. Stir just until all ingredients are moistened. Batter will look lumpy. Fill muffin cups $^2/_3$ full. Bake for 20 to 25 minutes. Loosen edges and turn out on wire rack. Serve warm. *Makes 12.*

Another early recipe sheet headline.

BASIC MUFFIN MIX

2 cups sifted all-purpose flour
4 tsp. baking powder
$^1/_2$ tsp. salt
$^1/_4$ cup sugar
1 egg, beaten
$^1/_4$ cup melted shortening
1 cup milk

Sift dry ingredients together. Mix egg, shortening and milk together thoroughly. Combine mixtures, stirring just enough to dampen flour. Fill greased muffin pans $^2/_3$ full. Bake in preheated 400°F oven for 25 minutes. *Makes 12 to 15.*

Variations

- **Bacon or Ham Muffins:** Reduce sugar to 2 Tbsp. and add $^1/_2$ cup coarsely chopped, crisp bacon or fine-cut cooked ham to dry ingredients.
- **Blueberry Muffins:** Add 1 cup blueberries to dry ingredients. Drain frozen or canned berries.
- **Cheese Muffins:** Add $^1/_2$ cup grated cheese and $^1/_8$ tsp. paprika to dry ingredients.
- **Cherry Muffins:** Add $^2/_3$ cup drained, chopped cherries to dry ingredients.
- **Cornmeal Muffins:** Use 1 cup cornmeal and 1 cup flour instead of 2 cups flour.
- **Cranberry Muffins:** Add $^2/_3$ cup chopped cranberries mixed with 2 Tbsp. sugar to dry ingredients.
- **Fruited Muffins:** To dry ingredients add $^1/_2$ cup of dried fruits, chopped, sliced or whole. Use apricots, currants, dates, figs, peaches, prunes or a combination of two or more.
- **Nut Muffins:** Add $^1/_3$ cup chopped nuts of your choice to dry ingredients.
- **Pineapple Muffins:** Add 1 cup crushed pineapple, drained, to dry ingredients.
- **Raisin Muffins:** Add $^1/_3$ cup raisins to dry ingredients.
- **Whole-Wheat Muffins:** Use 1 cup whole-wheat flour and 1 cup all-purpose flour instead of 2 cups all-purpose flour.

MAKE-IT-YOURSELF MIX (QUANTITY RECIPE)

10 cups all-purpose flour
$1/3$ cup baking powder
1 Tbsp. salt
$2^1/3$ cups shortening

Combine flour with baking powder and salt; stir well to blend. Cut in shortening with pastry blender until mixture resembles coarse meal.

Store mix in closed container at room temperature for 4 to 6 weeks. (Note: When measuring mix, spoon into dry measuring cup. Do not pack.) *Makes about $16^1/2$ cups.*

CINNAMON RING

$1/4$ cup halved maraschino cherries
1 cup sugar
$1/3$ cup chopped nuts
4 tsp. ground cinnamon
$6^3/4$ cups Make-It-Yourself Mix
$1/2$ cup sugar
$1^3/4$ cups milk
$2/3$ cup melted butter
$1/4$ cup raisins

Preheat oven to 350°F. Grease a 9-inch tube pan well. Place cherries over bottom.

Combine the 1 cup sugar, nuts and cinnamon in small bowl. Combine mix and the $1/2$ cup sugar in large bowl. Add milk and stir with fork just until all ingredients are moistened.

Drop heaping tablespoons of dough in melted butter, then in cinnamon-sugar mixture. Place balls slightly apart in a single layer in bottom of pan; sprinkle with 2 Tbsp. raisins. Repeat for second layer. Press lightly in place to give an even surface. Bake for 50 to 60 minutes. Invert immediately onto serving plate. Serve warm or cold. *Makes 1 ring.*

QUICK PANCAKES

1 Tbsp. sugar
$1^1/2$ cups Make-It-Yourself Mix
1 cup milk
1 egg, beaten

Stir sugar into mix, then add milk and egg. Stir until blended. Pour batter by $1/4$-cupfuls onto lightly greased hot griddle. Cook until puffy and bubbly. Turn and cook other side. Serve hot with butter and syrup. *Makes about 12 fluffy 4-inch pancakes.*

ALEXANDER'S NUTRITIOUS PANCAKES
These are favourites of my three-and-a-half-year-old grandson Alexander Brun.

2 large eggs
1 cup milk
1 Tbsp. vegetable oil
$1^1/2$ cups multigrain flour
$1/2$ tsp. salt
3 tsp. baking powder
$1/2$ cup honey, at room temperature
$1/2$ cup softened butter

Beat or whisk together eggs, milk and oil. Mix flour, salt and baking powder. Add all at once to egg mixture, whisking or beating until blended. Using $1/4$-cup measure, drop pancakes onto hot, lightly greased frying pan. Flip to cook other side when batter bubbles pop. In small bowl, beat honey and softened butter with an electric mixer until light, about 2 minutes. Serve hot pancakes with dollops of honey butter. *Makes about 14 fluffy 4-inch pancakes.*

BLINTZ PANCAKES

1 cup sifted all-purpose flour
1 Tbsp. sugar
$\frac{1}{2}$ tsp. salt
1 cup sour cream
1 cup small-curd cottage cheese
4 eggs, well beaten
1 recipe Blueberry Sauce

Sift flour, sugar and salt together. Add sour cream, cottage cheese and eggs. Stir just until mixed. Drop by large spoonfuls on hot, greased griddle. Cook until bubbles appear, then flip and cook other side. Serve with Blueberry Sauce. *Makes about 24.*

Blueberry Sauce

1 can (14 oz.) blueberries (or frozen blueberries)
2 tsp. cornstarch
1 tsp. lemon juice

In saucepan, combine blueberries and cornstarch. Cook, stirring, until mixture thickens and bubbles. Blend in lemon juice. *Makes 1$\frac{1}{2}$ cups.*

PANCAKES WITH ORANGE SAUCE

1 $\frac{1}{4}$ cups all-purpose flour
2 Tbsp. sugar
$\frac{3}{4}$ tsp. salt
2 tsp. baking powder
3 Tbsp. oil
1 $\frac{1}{3}$ cups milk
1 egg
1 recipe Orange Sauce

In large bowl, mix flour, sugar, salt and baking powder. In small bowl, mix oil, milk and egg. Stir egg mixture into flour mixture just until combined. Lightly brush skillet or griddle with oil. Pour batter by scant $\frac{1}{4}$-cupfuls onto hot griddle, making a few pancakes at a time. Cook until bubbly and bubbles burst. Turn pancakes and cook until undersides are golden; place on heated platter and keep warm. Repeat until all the batter is used. Brush griddle with more oil if necessary. Serve pancakes with Orange Sauce. *Makes approximately 12 4-inch pancakes.*

Note: To make thicker pancakes, reduce milk to 1 cup.

Orange Sauce

$\frac{3}{4}$ cup sugar
4 tsp. cornstarch
1 $\frac{1}{2}$ cups orange juice (juice from about 4 medium oranges)
$\frac{1}{8}$ tsp. salt
2 Tbsp. butter or margarine
1 tsp. vanilla extract

Mix sugar and cornstarch in saucepan. Stir in orange juice and salt until well blended. Heat mixture to boiling over medium heat, stirring constantly. Remove from heat. Stir in butter or margarine and vanilla until blended. Keep warm. *Makes about 1$\frac{1}{2}$ cups.*

BUTTERMILK PANCAKES

2 cups sifted all-purpose flour
1 Tbsp. sugar
1 tsp. salt
1 tsp. baking soda
2 eggs, well beaten
2 cups buttermilk
2 Tbsp. oil

Sift together flour, sugar, salt and baking soda. In large bowl, combine eggs and buttermilk. Add sifted dry ingredients all at once to egg mixture. Beat until smooth. Stir in oil. Drop pancakes by $\frac{1}{4}$-cupfuls onto greased, medium-hot griddle. Cook until bubbles form and start to break. Turn and cook undersides until golden. Serve immediately. *Serves 4 to 6.*

SKILLET APPLE PANCAKE

2 Tbsp. butter

1 tsp. ground cinnamon

2 Tbsp. sugar

2 small apples, peeled, cored and sliced

3 Tbsp. all-purpose flour

$\frac{1}{4}$ tsp. baking powder

pinch salt

2 eggs, separated

3 Tbsp. milk

3 Tbsp. sugar

Preheat oven to 400°F. Melt butter in ovenproof skillet. Combine cinnamon with the 2 Tbsp. sugar; sprinkle over melted butter. Arrange apple slices in skillet and cook for 5 minutes.

Combine flour with baking powder and salt. Combine egg yolks and milk and add to dry ingredients. Beat egg whites until foamy, gradually adding the 3 Tbsp. sugar. Continue beating until soft peaks form. Fold into flour mixture. Pour over apple slices, being sure to spread batter to edge of pan all around. Bake for 10 minutes or until golden and puffy. Do not open the oven door for the first 8 minutes! Invert onto serving plate. *Serves 2 to 4.*

Note: It is important that the sides of the skillet are not greased, otherwise the pancake will not rise very high.

Variation: For breakfast or brunch, serve with bacon, sausage or ham. For dessert, top with sour cream, ice cream or whipped cream. Add fruit in season, if desired.

ORANGE DOUGHNUTS

When I made these on TV the crew had demolished them before we went into commercial break.

3 Tbsp. shortening, softened

1 cup sugar

2 eggs, well beaten

2 Tbsp. grated orange rind

3$\frac{1}{2}$ cups sifted all-purpose flour

4$\frac{1}{2}$ tsp. baking powder

1 tsp. ground cinnamon

$\frac{3}{4}$ tsp. salt

1 cup orange juice

1 recipe Orange Frosting

Blend shortening and sugar thoroughly. Add eggs and mix well, then orange rind. Sift flour, baking powder, cinnamon and salt together. Add to creamed mixture alternately with orange juice. The dough should be soft but still easily handled. Chill for at least an hour. Roll or pat dough on floured board to $\frac{1}{2}$-inch thickness. Cut with floured doughnut cutter.

Cook in deep salad or vegetable oil heated to 370°F (a cube of day-old bread will brown in it in 60 seconds). Cook only as many doughnuts at one time as will easily float on top of oil. As soon as doughnuts rise to surface, turn, then turn again, if necessary, to ensure even browning. Remove doughnuts from oil with long-handled fork and drain on paper towel. Ice with Orange Frosting. *Makes 2 dozen.*

Orange Frosting

4 oz. cream cheese

3$\frac{1}{2}$ cups icing sugar

3 Tbsp. orange juice

1 tsp. grated orange rind

Beat cheese until soft and smooth; add sugar and orange juice, mixing well; fold in orange rind. Red and yellow food colouring may be added for a deeper orange colour. *Makes 1$\frac{1}{2}$ cups.*

potpourri of cakes

mona says . . .

- To split a cake into layers, measure halfway up the side of the cake and mark perimeter with toothpicks. Using a serrated knife, cut across and through, using the toothpicks as guides.
- Basic rule for baking cakes and cookies: thick to bottom, thin to top. Place sponge and loaf cakes on the lowest shelf of the oven and cookies on the top shelf.
- Cake slices best when chilled, but tastes best at room temperature.
- To keep bowls steady when mixing or whipping, set them on a wet, folded cloth.

In 1981, Woodward's bakers competed in the Royal Wedding Cake Classic. Harry Smith and Bob Miller won with a 69-pound cake that took 56 hours to make. They flew with the cake to present it to Buckingham Palace.

BASIC CAKE BATTER

$^1\!/_2$ cup shortening

$^3\!/_4$ cup sugar

2 eggs, well beaten

1 tsp. vanilla extract

1 $^3\!/_4$ cups all-purpose flour, sifted

2 tsp. baking powder

$^1\!/_4$ tsp. cream of tartar

$^1\!/_2$ tsp. salt

$^2\!/_3$ cup milk

Preheat oven to 350°F. Grease 8- or 9-inch square cake pan or two 8-inch round layer pans and line the bottom with waxed paper (or dust lightly with flour). Cream shortening. Gradually blend in sugar; beat until light and fluffy. Add eggs and vanilla and beat until well combined. Sift flour, baking powder, cream of tartar and salt together. Add dry ingredients to the creamed mixture alternately with milk, mixing well. Pour into prepared pan or pans. Bake for 45 to 50 minutes for a square cake, or 30 to 35 minutes for layer cake. *Serves 9.*

Variations

- **Spice:** Add 1 tsp. ground cinnamon, $^1\!/_2$ tsp. ground ginger, $^1\!/_2$ tsp. ground nutmeg and $^1\!/_4$ tsp. allspice to the dry ingredients.
- **Marble:** Divide batter into two portions. Combine 1 square melted unsweetened chocolate, 2 tsp. sugar, $^1\!/_8$ tsp. baking soda and 2 tsp. hot water. Add to one portion of batter. Leave other portion plain. Alternately drop spoonfuls of the two batters into greased and floured pan. Swirl for a marbled effect.
- **Maple Nut:** Substitute 1 tsp. maple flavouring for vanilla extract. Add $^1\!/_2$ cup finely chopped walnuts to the batter.

Woodward's was the first major retailer to fly fresh strawberries in from California. Some of them were dipped in Pauline Johnson chocolate to make a favourite springtime treat.

CHOCOLATE ZUCCHINI CAKE

$2^1\!/_2$ cups all-purpose flour, unsifted

$^1\!/_2$ cup cocoa

$2^1\!/_2$ tsp. baking powder

$1^1\!/_2$ tsp. baking soda

1 tsp. salt

1 tsp. ground cinnamon

$^3\!/_4$ cup softened butter or margarine

2 cups sugar

3 eggs

2 tsp. vanilla extract

2 tsp. grated orange rind

2 cups coarsely shredded unpeeled zucchini

$^1\!/_2$ cup milk

1 cup chopped pecans or walnuts

1 recipe Glaze

Preheat oven to 350°F. Grease and flour 10-inch tube or Bundt pan. Combine flour, cocoa, baking powder, baking soda, salt and cinnamon; set aside.

Beat butter or margarine and sugar until smoothly blended. Add eggs one at a time, beating well after each addition. Stir in vanilla, orange rind and zucchini. Stir dry ingredients into zucchini mixture, alternating with milk. Include nuts with last addition.

Pour batter into pan. Bake for about 1 hour or until a toothpick inserted in centre comes out clean. Cool in pan for 15 minutes; turn cake onto wire rack to cool thoroughly. Drizzle glaze over cake. Cut into thin slices to serve. *Serves 10 to 12.*

Glaze

2 cups icing sugar

3 Tbsp. milk

1 tsp. vanilla extract

Mix icing sugar, milk and vanilla; beat until smooth. *Glazes one 10-inch cake.*

COCO-CHOCOLATE CAKE

2 egg whites
1/4 cup sugar
1 1/2 cups all-purpose flour
1 cup sugar
1/2 cup cocoa
1 1/4 tsp. baking soda
1 1/4 tsp. salt
2 egg yolks
2/3 cup oil
1 cup sour milk or buttermilk

Preheat oven to 350°F. Grease and flour two 8-inch round layer pans. Beat egg whites until foamy; gradually add the 1/4 cup sugar, 1 Tbsp. at a time, and beat to soft peaks. Set aside.

Combine flour, the 1 cup sugar, cocoa, baking soda and salt in large mixing bowl. Stir well to blend. Add egg yolks, oil and sour milk or buttermilk to dry ingredients. Blend with mixer until smooth. Fold egg white mixture into batter.

Pour batter evenly into pans. Bake for 25 to 30 minutes, or until tester inserted in centre comes out clean. Cool for 10 minutes in pans before turning out on wire rack. Frost with your favourite chocolate icing. *Serves 8 to 10.*

CHOCOLATE WACKY CAKE

Remember what fun we had making this cake? The children loved to help.

1 1/2 cups all-purpose flour
1 cup sugar
4 Tbsp. cocoa
1/2 tsp. salt
1 tsp. baking soda
1 Tbsp. vinegar
1 tsp. vanilla extract
6 Tbsp. vegetable oil
1 cup water
1 recipe Mocha Icing

Preheat oven to 350°F. Into an 8- or 9-inch square pan, stir flour, sugar, cocoa, salt and baking soda. Make 3 depressions in dry ingredients. Into one, pour vinegar, in second, vanilla and in third, oil. Pour water over all. Stir until dry ingredients are well blended. Bake for approximately 30 minutes, until tester inserted in centre comes out clean. Allow to cool before icing. *Serves 9.*

Note: This is a lovely moist cake that can be doubled.

Mocha Icing

3 to 4 Tbsp. butter
sifted icing sugar
1 tsp. instant coffee granules, dissolved in 1 Tbsp. hot water

Combine butter, icing sugar (use enough to obtain desired consistency) and coffee. Spread over cooled cake.

A commemorative shopping bag from the original Woodward's store in downtown Vancouver.

CHOCOLATE CREAM ROLL

³/₄ cup sifted cake flour

¹/₄ cup cocoa

1 tsp. baking powder

¹/₄ tsp. salt

3 eggs

1 cup sugar

5 Tbsp. water

1 tsp. vanilla extract

¹/₄ cup cocoa

2 cups whipping cream

¹/₃ cup sugar

Preheat oven to 375°F. Grease 10 x 15 x ³/₄-inch jelly roll pan and line with waxed paper. Sift flour, ¹/₄ cup cocoa, baking powder and salt together. Beat eggs until thick. Gradually beat in the 1 cup sugar. Stir in water and vanilla. Add flour mixture all at once. Beat just until smooth.

Spread batter in prepared pan and bake for 12 to 15 minutes. Remove from oven and immediately invert cake on tea towel sprinkled with icing sugar. Peel off paper. Roll up loosely in tea towel. Cool completely on wire rack.

To make frosting, combine ¹/₄ cup cocoa and cream. Refrigerate for at least 1 hour. Whip until soft peaks form. Beat in the ¹/₃ cup sugar.

Unroll cake and spread with half the chocolate whipped cream. Re-roll cake and frost top with remaining chocolate whipped cream. Chill until serving time. *Serves about 10.*

Use a towel when making a jelly-roll. When the cake is covered and ready for rolling, place it on a towel. Start the first tight turn with your hands, then lift the towel higher and the cake will roll off by itself.

HINTS FOR CHIFFON-TYPE CAKES

- Have all ingredients assembled and accurately measured before you start mixing your cake.
- Do not grease pans. Always use size of pan indicated in recipe.
- Sift dry ingredients into bowl—then add, in order, oil, yolks, liquid and flavouring—then beat until batter is very smooth.
- Egg whites should be very stiff—do not underbeat.
- Pour egg yolk batter over the entire surface of egg whites in a thin stream—then fold just until ingredients are blended.
- Cake is cooked when it springs back after being lightly touched with fingertips.
- After removing cake from oven invert tube pan over a bottle until cake cools to room temperature. Remove from pan by loosening cake around sides and tube with a knife or spatula. Turn cake upside down over wire rack or plate, then remove pan.

MOCHA CHIFFON CAKE

4 tsp. instant coffee granules

³/₄ cup boiling water

2¹/₄ cups sifted cake flour

1¹/₂ cups sugar

3 tsp. baking powder

1 tsp. salt

¹/₂ cup oil

5 egg yolks

1 tsp. vanilla extract

3 squares (1 oz. each) semi-sweet chocolate, thinly shaved

1 cup egg whites (approximately 8)

¹/₂ tsp. cream of tartar

Preheat oven to 325°F. Dissolve coffee in boiling water; allow to cool. Sift flour, sugar, baking powder and salt together. Make a well in centre. Add oil, egg yolks, vanilla and cooled coffee. Beat until smooth. Stir in shaved chocolate. In large clean mixing bowl, place egg whites and cream of tartar. Beat until stiff peaks form. Pour batter over whites in a thin stream, gently folding to blend. Pour into ungreased 10-inch tube pan and bake for 55 minutes. Increase oven temperature to 350°F and bake for 10 to 15 minutes longer. Invert pan and allow to cool before removing from pan. *Serves 8 to 10.*

ANGEL CAKE

1 cup sifted cake flour
$^3/_4$ cup sugar
12 egg whites (1 $^1/_2$ cups)
1 $^1/_2$ tsp. cream of tartar
$^1/_4$ tsp. salt
1 $^1/_2$ tsp. vanilla extract
$^3/_4$ cup sugar

Preheat oven to 375°F. Sift flour 4 times with $^3/_4$ cup sugar; set aside. Beat egg whites, cream of tartar, salt and vanilla until soft peaks form, but mixture is still moist and glossy. Add remaining $^3/_4$ cup sugar, 2 Tbsp. at a time, continuing to beat until egg whites hold stiff peaks. Sift about $^1/_4$ of flour mixture over whites; fold in. Repeat, folding in remaining flour, $^1/_4$ at a time. Bake in ungreased 10-inch tube pan for 35 to 40 minutes. Invert pan and allow cake to cool before removing from pan. *Serves 8 to 10.*

HEAVENLY BERRY CAKE

1 recipe Angel Cake
1 $^1/_4$ cups strawberries or raspberries
    (thawed if frozen)
2 cups whipping cream
$^1/_4$ cup sugar
1 tsp. vanilla extract
6 drops red food colouring
additional berries, for decoration

Cut openings 1 inch apart in a circle around the cake between centre and edge. Cut right through to bottom. With knife inserted, pull cake away slightly and spoon some berries and juice into each opening.

Whip cream with sugar, vanilla and food colouring until stiff. Frost cake; chill. Trim with additional berries. *Serves 10 to 12.*

JAMES BEARD'S STRAWBERRY ANGEL DELIGHT

This makes a beautiful "special" cake. It is our family's traditional birthday cake.

1 $^1/_4$ cups sugar
$^1/_2$ cup water
8 eggs, separated
1 cup sifted cake flour
$^1/_2$ tsp. salt
1 tsp. cream of tartar
1 tsp. almond flavouring
1 $^1/_4$ cups whipping cream
$^1/_4$ cup sugar
3 cups strawberries or raspberries, washed and hulled

Preheat oven to 300°F. Combine the 1 $^1/_4$ cups sugar and water. Boil over high heat until it spins a thread (230°F on candy thermometer). Beat egg yolks until light and lemon-coloured. While continuing to beat, pour hot syrup over yolks in a thin stream. The mixture should thicken noticeably. Sift flour and salt 7 or 8 times; measure. After egg mixture has cooled to room temperature, fold in flour. Beat egg whites until frothy. Add cream of tartar and continue beating until whites are stiff but not dry. Fold egg whites into flour mixture. Mix in almond flavouring. Pour into ungreased 10-inch tube pan. Bake for approximately 1 $^1/_2$ hours. Invert pan while cooling.

Whip the cream and sweeten with the $^1/_4$ cup sugar. Split cooled cake in half. On bottom layer, place half the berries and half the whipped cream. Place other layer on top; add remaining berries and decorate with remaining whipped cream. (If berries are out of season use your favourite frosting.) *Serves 6 to 8.*

HINTS FOR CONVENTIONAL CAKES

- When making cakes it is most important to follow recipe suggestions exactly. Never double a cake recipe, as you will not get proper beating and blending of ingredients.
- Use the size of pan recommended in the recipe. The batter should fill about $\frac{1}{2}$ the pan and should be evenly spread.
- For best results, add the dry ingredients $\frac{1}{3}$ at a time, the liquid $\frac{1}{2}$ at a time. Start and end with the dry ingredients and simply stir to combine the batter. Do not beat as this may result in a coarse, tough cake.
- Grease cake pans on bottoms only, using unsalted shortening or vegetable oil. Line with waxed paper cut to fit; or add about 1 tsp. flour and shake to coat the bottom. Discard excess flour. Sprinkle berry sugar lightly over flour.
- A cake is baked if the top springs back when pressed with the fingertips or when a cake tester inserted in the centre comes out clean.
- Let cake stand in the pan for about 10 minutes and then remove from the pan and cool on a rack.

APPLESAUCE CAKE

$\frac{1}{3}$ cup shortening
$\frac{1}{2}$ cup brown sugar
$\frac{1}{2}$ cup granulated sugar
1 egg
1 cup applesauce
1 $\frac{2}{3}$ cups sifted all-purpose flour
1 tsp. baking soda
1 tsp. salt
$\frac{1}{4}$ tsp. ground cloves
$\frac{1}{2}$ tsp. ground cinnamon
$\frac{1}{4}$ tsp. ground nutmeg
$\frac{1}{3}$ cup water
$\frac{1}{3}$ cup chopped nuts
$\frac{2}{3}$ cup raisins

Preheat oven to 350°F. Grease 9-inch square pan. Cream shortening. Add sugars and cream together until light and fluffy. Add egg, beating well. Stir in applesauce. In separate bowl, sift flour, baking soda, salt, cloves, cinnamon and nutmeg. Add dry ingredients to creamed mixture alternately with water. Stir in nuts and raisins when adding last portion of flour. Spread in pan. Bake for about 40 to 45 minutes, until tester inserted in centre comes out clean. *Serves 9.*

SUPERB APPLE CAKE

A winner at the PNE—and with our Scottish relatives!

4 cups apples, peeled and diced
2 cups sugar
$\frac{1}{2}$ cup oil
1 cup chopped nuts
2 eggs, well beaten
2 tsp. vanilla extract
2 cups all-purpose flour
2 tsp. ground cinnamon
2 tsp. baking soda
1 tsp. salt
1 recipe Cream Cheese Frosting

Preheat oven to 350°F. Grease 9 x 13-inch pan. Mix together apples, sugar, oil, nuts, eggs and vanilla. Sift flour, cinnamon, baking soda and salt into apple mixture. Stir until well combined. Pour batter into a pan. Bake for 45 to 60 minutes. Cool in pan on wire rack before frosting. *Serves 12.*

Cream Cheese Frosting

$\frac{1}{2}$ cup butter
1 package (9 oz.) cream cheese, softened
5 $\frac{1}{2}$ cups icing sugar (approximately)
1 tsp. vanilla extract

Beat butter and cream cheese together until light. Add icing sugar and beat until frosting reaches desired consistency. Add vanilla and continue blending until smooth. Spread on cooled cake. *Generously frosts a 9 x 13-inch cake.*

GLAZED GERMAN APPLE CAKE

2/3 cup margarine

2 cups sugar

2 eggs, well beaten

2 tsp. vanilla extract

2 cups all-purpose flour

2 tsp. baking soda

1 tsp. salt

2 tsp. ground cinnamon

6 medium apples

1/2 cup chopped walnuts

1 recipe Glaze Topping

Preheat oven to 375°F. Grease and flour 9 x 13-inch pan. In large bowl cream margarine and sugar. In small bowl, beat eggs; add vanilla. Combine egg and butter mixtures and mix thoroughly. In medium bowl, sift flour, baking soda, salt and cinnamon together. Peel, core and chop apples. Add dry ingredients to creamed mixture alternately with apples. Stir well after each addition. Add walnuts. Pour batter into pan and bake for 40 to 45 minutes. Allow to cool before spreading Glaze Topping over cake. *Serves 12.*

Glazed Topping

1/2 cup evaporated milk

1/2 cup sugar

1 egg yolk

1 1/2 tsp. butter

1 tsp. vanilla extract

1/2 cup coconut

1/2 cup chopped walnuts

In saucepan, combine evaporated milk, sugar, egg yolk, butter and vanilla. Cook until thickened, stirring constantly. Remove from heat. Beat until cool. Stir in coconut and walnuts. *Frosts one 9 x 13-inch cake.*

APPLE COFFEE CAKE

2 cups sifted all-purpose flour

2 tsp. baking powder

1 1/3 cups granulated sugar

2 eggs

2/3 cup milk

1/2 cup butter, melted

2 tsp. grated orange rind

2 1/4 cups coarsely chopped apples

1/2 cup chopped almonds

1/4 cup brown sugar, lightly packed

1/2 tsp. ground cinnamon

Preheat oven to 350°F. Butter 9-inch square cake pan. Sift flour, baking powder and granulated sugar together. Beat eggs well; stir in milk, melted butter and orange rind. Make a well in dry ingredients and add liquid all at once, mixing lightly until just combined; do not overmix. Turn into prepared pan; spread evenly. Bake for 20 minutes. Remove cake and top with apples. Sprinkle with almonds, brown sugar and cinnamon. Return to oven and continue baking for another 45 to 50 minutes. Cut into squares and serve warm. *Serves 9.*

To help promote local apples, Woodward's once created a giant apple pie using six boxes of fresh fruit. The completed pastry measured six feet in diameter.

PINEAPPLE UPSIDE-DOWN CAKE

3 Tbsp. butter or margarine

2½ cups pineapple (crushed or tidbits)

9 to 10 maraschino cherries

9 to 10 walnut halves

⅔ cup brown sugar

⅓ cup shortening

½ cup granulated sugar

1 egg

1 tsp. vanilla extract

1¼ cups sifted cake flour

1½ tsp. baking powder

½ tsp. salt

Melt butter or margarine in 9 x 1½-inch round pan. Drain pineapple, reserving ½ cup syrup. Arrange cherries and walnut halves in bottom of pan. Cover with brown sugar, then add pineapple.

Preheat oven to 350°F. Cream together shortening and granulated sugar. Add egg and vanilla; beat until fluffy. Sift flour, baking powder and salt together; add dry ingredients alternately with reserved syrup to mixture, beating well after each addition. Spread over pineapple. Bake for 45 to 50 minutes. Let stand for 5 minutes before inverting pan onto serving plate. Serve warm. *Serves 6 to 8.*

WATER CAKE

1 cup water

1 cup sugar

1 cup raisins

¾ cup margarine

2 cups all-purpose flour

1 tsp. baking powder

1 tsp. allspice

½ tsp. baking soda

Preheat oven to 350°F. Line 8-inch square baking pan with waxed paper. Combine water, sugar, raisins and margarine in saucepan and bring to a boil. Reduce heat. Simmer for 5 minutes. Allow mixture to cool slightly.

In mixing bowl, stir together flour, baking powder, allspice and baking soda. Add cooled water mixture and mix thoroughly. Pour batter into pan. Bake for 35 to 40 minutes. Ice cake when it is cooled, if desired. This cake is better when allowed to age for 12 hours before cutting. *Serves 6 to 8.*

LAZY DAISY CAKE

FOR THE CAKE:

2 eggs

1 tsp. vanilla extract

1 cup sugar

1 cup all-purpose flour

1 tsp. baking powder

1 tsp. salt

½ cup milk

2 Tbsp. butter or margarine

Preheat oven to 350°F. Beat eggs in bowl; beat in vanilla and sugar. Add flour, baking powder and salt. Heat milk with butter or margarine until butter or margarine melts. Add to egg-flour mixture and combine well. Pour into 8-inch square pan. Bake for 30 minutes or until cake tester inserted in centre comes out clean.

FOR THE ICING:

2 Tbsp. butter, softened

3 Tbsp. light cream

½ cup brown sugar

½ cup coconut

Combine butter, cream, brown sugar and coconut.

Spread over hot cake. Return cake to oven until topping is bubbly. *Serves 9.*

Before frosting a cake, always allow it to cool thoroughly and brush away all loose crumbs. To leave the cake plate clean, place strips of waxed paper under the bottom edge of the cake and remove paper when finished.

Woodward's famous Christmas catalogue.

RAY'S GINGERBREAD

$1/2$ cup sugar

$1/2$ cup molasses

$1/2$ cup butter or shortening

$1/2$ cup boiling water

1 egg

$1 1/2$ cups all-purpose flour

1 tsp. baking soda

1 tsp. ground ginger

$1/2$ tsp. ground cinnamon

$1/2$ tsp. ground nutmeg

$1/2$ tsp. ground cloves

pinch salt

Preheat oven to 375°F. Grease and flour 8- or 9-inch square pan. Place sugar in 1 cup measure; fill cup with molasses. Pour mixture into large bowl. Add butter or shortening and boiling water to molasses mixture. Add egg. Stir to combine ingredients.

In separate bowl, mix together flour, baking soda, ginger, cinnamon, nutmeg, cloves and salt. Add dry ingredients to molasses mixture. Mix well. Pour batter into pan. Bake for 25 minutes or until toothpick inserted in centre comes out clean. Delicious served with whipped cream. *Serves 9.*

BANANA SPICE CAKE WITH SEAFOAM FROSTING

$2 1/2$ cups sifted cake flour

$1 2/3$ cups sugar

$1 1/4$ tsp. baking powder

$1 1/4$ tsp. baking soda

1 tsp. salt

$1 1/2$ tsp. ground cinnamon

$3/4$ tsp. ground nutmeg

$1/2$ tsp. ground cloves

$2/3$ cup all-purpose cooking oil

$2/3$ cup buttermilk

$1 1/4$ cups mashed bananas

2 eggs

1 recipe Seafoam Frosting

1 large banana

Preheat oven to 350°F. Grease and flour three 8-inch round pans. Sift flour, sugar, baking powder, baking soda, salt, cinnamon, nutmeg and cloves into large mixing bowl. Add oil, buttermilk and mashed bananas and mix until all flour is dampened. Beat with mixer at high speed for 2 minutes. Add eggs and beat for 1 minute longer. Turn batter into pans. Bake for 30 to 35 minutes. Allow to cool completely before frosting.

Spread frosting on cooled layers of cake. Slice 1 large banana and place on bottom 2 layers. Stack layers and frost top and sides of cake. *Serves 12.*

Seafoam Frosting

2 egg whites

$1 1/2$ cups brown sugar

5 Tbsp. water

pinch salt

1 tsp. vanilla extract

Combine egg whites, sugar, water and salt in top of large double boiler. Place over boiling water and beat with mixer at high speed until frosting stands in peaks, about 7 minutes. Remove from heat and add vanilla. Beat for 1 to 2 minutes until frosting is thick enough to spread. *Frosts one 3-layer cake.*

BOSTON CREAM PIE

My mother-in-law, Mère, made this quite often and all the family loved it.

FOR THE CAKE:

2 egg whites
$\frac{1}{2}$ cup sugar
2$\frac{1}{4}$ cups sifted cake flour
1 cup sugar
3 tsp. baking powder
1 tsp. salt
$\frac{1}{3}$ cup oil
1 cup milk
1$\frac{1}{2}$ tsp. vanilla extract
2 egg yolks

Preheat oven to 350°F. Grease and lightly flour two 9-inch round pans. Beat egg whites until soft peaks form; gradually add the $\frac{1}{2}$ cup sugar, beating until very stiff peaks form. Sift flour, the 1 cup sugar, baking powder and salt in separate bowl. Add oil, $\frac{1}{2}$ cup of the milk and vanilla. Beat for 1 minute at medium mixer speed, scraping bowl often. Add remaining $\frac{1}{2}$ cup milk and egg yolks; beat for 1 minute, scraping bowl. Gently fold in egg white mixture. Pour batter into pans. Bake for about 25 minutes. Cool in pans for 20 minutes before removing. Cool completely on wire rack.

FOR THE FILLING:

1 package (4-serving size) regular vanilla pudding mix
1$\frac{3}{4}$ cups milk

Prepare pudding mix according to package directions, but use only 1$\frac{3}{4}$ cups milk. Place between cake layers.

FOR THE CHOCOLATE GLAZE:

1$\frac{1}{2}$ squares unsweetened chocolate
2 Tbsp. butter
1$\frac{1}{2}$ cups sifted icing sugar
1 tsp. vanilla extract
3 Tbsp. boiling water

Melt chocolate and butter over low heat, stirring constantly. Remove from heat and stir in icing sugar and vanilla, until mixture is crumbly. Mix in boiling water, adding enough water (about 2 tsp. at a time) to form medium glaze of pouring consistency. Quickly pour over cake and spread evenly over top and sides. *Serves 8.*

LEMON SUNSHINE CAKE

6 eggs, separated
1$\frac{1}{2}$ cups sifted cake flour
$\frac{1}{2}$ tsp. salt
$\frac{1}{2}$ tsp. cream of tartar
1$\frac{1}{2}$ cups sugar
3 Tbsp. freshly squeezed lemon juice
5 Tbsp. water
1 Tbsp. grated lemon rind
1 recipe Fresh Lemon Glaze

Place egg whites in large mixer bowl and egg yolks in small mixer bowl; let stand until they reach room temperature. Preheat oven to 325°F.

Measure sifted flour, then sift again with salt onto piece of waxed paper. Beat egg whites until frothy; add cream of tartar and beat at high speed until moist peaks form. Gradually add $\frac{1}{2}$ cup of the sugar, 2 Tbsp. at a time; continue beating until stiff, but not dry. Set aside.

Beat egg yolks a full 2 minutes until very thick and light. Add remaining 1 cup sugar very gradually; continue beating at high speed until thick. Beat in lemon juice and water, blending until smooth; stir in lemon rind. Add flour all at once; gently fold in, then partially stir until well blended. Add mixture to egg whites and fold in quickly but gently.

Pour into ungreased 10-inch tube pan; cut through batter with table knife to remove large air bubbles. Bake for about 1 hour, or until cake springs back when lightly touched. Immediately invert on wire rack; leave in pan until completely cool. Loosen cake around tube and sides with narrow spatula; turn onto cake plate. Glaze top with Fresh Lemon Glaze, allowing some to drizzle over edges. *Serves 8 to 10.*

Fresh Lemon Glaze

  1 1/2 cups sifted icing sugar

  1 1/2 to 2 Tbsp. freshly squeezed lemon juice

Blend sugar and lemon juice until smooth. *Glazes one 10-inch cake.*

CHERRY POUND CAKE

  3/4 lb. butter

  1 1/2 cups berry sugar

  6 egg yolks, well-beaten

  3 cups sifted all-purpose flour

  1/2 tsp. salt

  1 tsp. baking powder

  1 cup candied cherries, halved

  1 tsp. vanilla extract

  6 egg whites, beaten until stiff

Preheat oven to 325°F. Line 10-inch tube pan with 3 thicknesses of brown paper (or 2 thicknesses of foil wrap), greased on side next to cake. Cream butter with sugar until light and fluffy. Add well-beaten egg yolks; blend well. Sift flour, salt and baking powder together; add half to batter. Combine the other half with cherries to coat well, then add to batter. Stir in vanilla. Gently fold in egg whites. Bake for 1 hour and 45 minutes. *Serves 10 to 12.*

BUDGET POUND CAKE

  3 cups sifted cake flour

  1 1/2 tsp. baking powder

  1/4 tsp. mace

  1/8 tsp. salt

  1 cup butter

  1 1/2 cups sugar

  1 tsp. vanilla extract

  3 eggs, beaten

  1/2 cup milk

Preheat oven to 350°F. Grease 10-inch tube pan. Sift flour, baking powder, mace and salt together three times. Cream butter, sugar and vanilla until fluffy. Add eggs and beat thoroughly. Add sifted dry ingredients and milk alternately in small amounts, beating well after each addition. Pour into pan and bake for 60 minutes. Turn out and allow to cool on wire rack. *Serves 10 to 12.*

LAST-MINUTE FRUIT CAKE (EGGLESS)

  3 cups thick unsweetened applesauce

  1 cup shortening

  2 cups sugar

  3 2/3 cups chopped nuts

  2 1/2 cups dates, pitted and chopped

  3 cups light or dark raisins

  1/2 cup glacé cherries

  1/2 cup glacé pineapple

  1/2 cup citron, chopped

  4 1/2 cups sifted all-purpose flour

  4 tsp. baking soda

  1 tsp. ground nutmeg

  2 1/2 tsp. ground cinnamon

  1/2 tsp. ground cloves

  1 tsp. salt

Preheat oven to 250°F. Line 2 large loaf pans with 3 layers of brown paper greased on side next to batter. Combine applesauce, shortening and sugar in saucepan; bring to a boil. Boil for 5 minutes. Let stand until cool.

  Mix nuts and fruits in large mixing bowl. Sift flour, baking soda, nutmeg, cinnamon, cloves and salt over all; mix well with hands to coat fruits and nuts with flour. Stir in cooled applesauce mixture. Mix well. Spoon mixture into pans. Bake for 2 hours. When cooled wrap well and allow to mellow for 7 to 10 days before serving. *Makes 2 loaves.*

HINTS FOR FRUIT CAKES

- When making a light fruit cake, watch that your fruit and nut mix is all light-coloured.
- Chop or slice nuts for best results; electric blenders will grind the nuts too fine, releasing some of their natural oils.
- Set a pan of water on the bottom of the oven to keep the top of the cake moist and give it a shiny look.
- Lay a sheet of foil over cake during the last part of baking to prevent overbrowning.
- It is best to work with no more than a double recipe.
- Use an electric mixer only for creaming the butter or margarine with the sugar and beating in the eggs.

RICH FRUIT CAKE

$2^2/_3$ cups sifted all-purpose flour

1 tsp. salt

2 tsp. ground cinnamon

1 tsp. ground nutmeg

1 tsp. allspice

$^1/_4$ tsp. ground cloves

4 cups seedless raisins, washed and dried

2 cups currants, washed and dried

1 cup cut-up pitted dried prunes

1 cup cut-up dried apricots

$1^1/_2$ cups slivered mixed candied peel and citron

1 cup red and green candied or well-drained maraschino cherries, halved

$^1/_2$ cup slivered blanched almonds

$^1/_4$ cup coarsely chopped pecans

$1^1/_4$ cups softened butter

$1^1/_2$ cups brown sugar, lightly packed

8 eggs

$^1/_3$ cup grape juice

$^1/_3$ cup cold strong coffee

Line deep 9-inch round cake pan or 2 deep 6-inch round cake pans with 2 layers of foil. Preheat oven to 300°F. Sift flour, salt, cinnamon, nutmeg, allspice and cloves together in large bowl. Add prepared fruit and nuts and toss until all are coated with flour.

Cream butter; gradually beat in sugar. Add eggs, one at a time, beating well after each addition. Combine grape juice and coffee. Add to creamed mixture alternately with floured fruit, combining lightly after each addition. Turn batter into prepared pan or pans; spread evenly. Bake for about $2^1/_2$ hours for a large cake or $1^3/_4$ hours for smaller cakes. Allow cake to mellow for about 1 month before serving. *Makes 1 large cake or 2 smaller cakes.*

GOLDEN FRUIT CAKE

$5^3/_4$ cups sifted all-purpose flour

1 tsp. baking powder

$^1/_2$ tsp. salt

$^1/_4$ tsp. mace

$^1/_4$ tsp. ground nutmeg

3 cups light seedless raisins, washed and dried

2 cups cut-up candied pineapple

$1^1/_2$ cups red and green candied or well-drained maraschino cherries, halved

1 cup coarsely chopped pecans

1 cup shredded coconut

2 cups softened butter

$2^1/_4$ cups berry or fine granulated sugar

9 eggs

1 Tbsp. grated lemon rind

$^1/_4$ cup lemon juice

Line deep 8-inch square cake pan and deep 6-inch square cake pan with 2 layers of foil. Preheat oven to 300°F. Sift flour, baking powder, salt, mace and nutmeg together. Add prepared fruit, nuts and coconut; toss lightly until all are coated with flour.

Cream butter; gradually beat in sugar. Add eggs one at a time, beating well after each addition. Mix in lemon rind and juice. Add floured fruit in several batches, mixing well after each addition. Turn batter into prepared pans; spread evenly. Bake for 2 to $2^1/_4$ hours. Allow cakes to mellow for 2 to 3 weeks before serving. *Makes 2 cakes.*

UNBAKED CHRISTMAS CAKE

Evelyn Caldwell, known to many as "Penny Wise," told me she received over 1,000 letters asking for this recipe after we presented it on Woodward's cooking show.

3 cups shelled whole Brazil nuts
1 lb. graham wafers, finely ground (use amount needed to obtain desired consistency)
1 lb. seedless raisins
1/4 cup dates
1 cup diced candied fruit and peel
1 jar (6 oz.) cherries, drained
1 lb. marshmallows, cut into quarters
3/4 cup orange juice
1 Tbsp. grated orange rind
1/4 tsp. ground nutmeg
1/8 tsp. ground ginger
1/4 tsp. ground cinnamon
1/4 tsp. ground cloves
1/8 tsp. allspice
1 tsp. vanilla extract

Line 9 x 5 x 3-inch loaf pan with 2 strips of foil that extend about 3 inches above sides of pan. Place nuts in large mixing bowl; add graham wafer crumbs, raisins, dates, candied fruit and peel, and cherries.

In top of double boiler, combine marshmallows, orange juice, orange rind, nutmeg, ginger, cinnamon, cloves, allspice and vanilla. Stir until marshmallows are melted. Add to fruit mixture, blending thoroughly. Turn into pan; pack down. Wrap well and refrigerate. To serve, cut in slices with a cooled, sharp, thin-bladed knife. I serve my cake in little paper cups as it is really like a sweet confection. *Makes 1 loaf.*

Note: We have left the recipe exactly as Evie gave it to me. I know if I changed one item she would come back and get me!

Media party for the opening of Salmon House on the Hill. Back row from the left: Muriel Wilson, *Victoria Colonist;* Ethel Post, *Vancouver Province;* Mona Brun, Woodward's and BCTV; Maureen Martin (my daughter); Margaret Murphy, Vancouver School Board; Jean Cannem, hostess, BCTV "Morning Show" and the "Jean Cannem Show"; Eileen Norman, a.k.a. Edith Adams, *Vancouver Sun.* Front: Alex McGillivry, *Vancouver Sun;* Evelyn Caldwell, a.k.a. Penny Wise, *Vancouver Sun,* directing the photographers; Jack Ferry and Liz Fitzsimmons of Jack Ferry & Associates.

CLEVER JUDY FROSTING

One of my favourite frostings. I have a hard time saving enough for the cake what with all my tasting!

3 1/2 squares unsweetened chocolate
3 cups sifted icing sugar
4 1/2 Tbsp. hot water
1 egg
1/2 cup softened butter or margarine
1 1/2 tsp. vanilla extract

Melt chocolate in bowl over hot water. Remove from heat. Beat in sugar and water with electric mixer. Beat in egg, then butter or margarine and vanilla. Place bowl in larger pan of ice water and beat until frosting is of spreading consistency. *Frosts top and sides of 2-layer 9-inch cake.*

BROILED FROSTING

1/4 cup softened butter or margarine
1/2 cup brown sugar, lightly packed
3 Tbsp. evaporated milk or cream
1/2 cup coconut or coarsely chopped nuts

Combine all ingredients. Spread mixture over warm 8- or 9-inch square cake. Place about 6 inches from heat and broil for 2 or 3 minutes, or until the topping bubbles and browns. *Frosts one 8- or 9-inch cake.*

SNOWY WHITE FROSTING

1 1/2 cups sugar
1/2 cup water
3 egg whites
1/8 tsp. cream of tartar
pinch salt
1 tsp. vanilla extract

In small saucepan, combine sugar and water. Cook over medium heat, stirring until sugar is dissolved. Cover and bring to a boil. Remove cover and cook mixture until soft ball stage (236° to 238°F on candy thermometer). Beat egg whites, cream of tartar and salt in large mixing bowl until moist, stiff peaks form.

Pour hot syrup over egg whites in thin stream. Beat constantly with mixer at high speed until frosting holds stiff peaks. Mix in vanilla. Tint frosting with food colouring if desired. *Makes enough to frost and fill 8- or 9-inch double layer cake.*

BLENDER FROSTING

1 cup sugar
3 squares unsweetened chocolate
3/4 cup evaporated milk
pinch salt
1/4 tsp. peppermint extract (optional)

Put sugar in blender, cover and blend at high speed for about 1 minute. Cut chocolate into small pieces; add to blender along with remaining ingredients. Blend at high speed for about 3 minutes or until thick; scrape sides with rubber spatula if necessary. Chill frosted cake for firmer frosting, if desired. *Makes enough to cover tops of two 8-inch layers.*

FLUFFY FROSTING

2 egg whites
1/4 tsp. cream of tartar
2 Tbsp. light corn syrup
2 1/2 Tbsp. water
1 1/2 tsp. vanilla extract
1/2 tsp. lemon extract
3 1/2 cups icing sugar, sifted

Mix egg whites and cream of tartar in medium-size bowl; beat until firm peaks form. Set aside. Combine corn syrup, water, vanilla and lemon extract. Add alternately with icing sugar to egg white mixture, beating well after each addition. Beat until frosting is creamy-stiff and easy to spread. *Makes enough to frost top and sides of one 9-inch triple-layer cake.*

CREAM CHEESE FROSTING

4 oz. cream cheese
1 Tbsp. milk (approximately)
2 1/2 cups sifted icing sugar (approximately)
1/2 tsp. vanilla extract

Thoroughly blend cream cheese and milk; gradually beat in icing sugar. Add vanilla. (Add a small amount of extra milk or icing sugar, if necessary, until frosting is of good spreading consistency.) *Makes enough frosting for top and sides of 8- or 9-inch square cake.*

Note: Double the recipe to frost and fill 8- or 9-inch layer cake.

Variations
• Chocolate Cream Frosting: Add 1 square melted unsweetened chocolate and pinch salt.
• Almond Frosting: Omit vanilla and add 1/2 tsp. almond flavouring.
• Orange Cream Frosting: Omit milk and vanilla. Add 1 Tbsp. orange juice and 1/2 tsp. grated orange rind.

cookies, bars and squares

mona says . . .

- To keep cookies soft, store in tightly covered container with a slice of fresh bread or an apple wedge. Keep crisp cookies in a jar with a loosely fitting lid. To freeze cookies, wrap well and place in a sturdy container, overwrap with more plastic wrap, seal, label and freeze. Thaw in the unopened container.

- When decorating cookies, etc., with small amounts of chocolate, place chocolate in a custard cup and stand in a pan of simmering water. (Do not allow any water into the cup.)

- For a decorative touch on squares or unfrosted cakes, place a paper doily with an open design over top, and sprinkle with sifted icing sugar. Lift doily straight up to remove, leaving icing sugar design.

- Some of the recipes in this section are fairly time consuming but the extra time and effort bring rewards.

This Christmas catalogue dates from 1972.

SUGAR COOKIES

²/₃ cup shortening

³/₄ cup sugar

1 tsp. vanilla extract

1 egg

4 tsp. milk

2 cups sifted all-purpose flour

1¹/₂ tsp. baking powder

¹/₄ tsp. salt

Cream shortening, sugar and vanilla thoroughly. Add egg and beat until light and fluffy. Stir in milk. Sift flour, baking powder and salt together; blend into creamed mixture. Divide dough in half; chill for 1 hour.

Preheat oven to 375°F. Roll out half of dough (keep other half chilled) on lightly floured surface to ¹/₈-inch thickness; cut with cookie cutters in desired shapes. Bake on greased cookie sheet for 6 to 8 minutes. Cool slightly, then remove from pan and cool on rack. *Makes about 2 dozen.*

The Woodward's bear as Zoro.

Variations

• **To Decorate:** Before baking, sprinkle cookies with candy sprinkles, crushed hard peppermint stick candy, gumdrops (whole or sliced), coloured sugar.

• **To Frost:** Cool cookies before frosting. Make icing by adding enough light cream to sifted icing sugar to make spreading consistency. If various colours are desired, divide icing into portions and tint with food colouring. Pipe on different coloured designs with a decorating tube or add colourful candies.

BASIC DROP COOKIES

3¹/₂ cups all-purpose flour

1 tsp. baking powder

1 tsp. baking soda

¹/₂ tsp. salt

2 cups brown sugar, packed

1 cup butter or margarine

2 eggs

1 tsp. vanilla extract

¹/₂ cup sour milk (to sour milk, mix with 2 tsp. lemon juice or vinegar)

Preheat oven to 375°F. Mix together flour, baking powder, baking soda and salt. Cream sugar, butter or margarine, eggs and vanilla. Add flour mixture alternately with sour milk to creamed mixture. Mix well. Drop by teaspoonfuls onto greased baking sheets. Bake for 12 to 15 minutes. *Makes 7 to 8 dozen, depending on the size.*

Variations

• **Chocolate Nut Drops:** Add 1 cup chocolate pieces and ¹/₂ cup chopped walnuts.

• **Almond Date Drops:** Add 1 cup cut-up dates and ¹/₂ cup chopped almonds. Substitute 1 tsp. almond flavouring for vanilla. Before baking, sprinkle cookies with a mixture of 1 Tbsp. grated orange rind, 2 Tbsp. sugar and ¹/₄ tsp. ground cinnamon.

- **Hermits:** Add 2 tsp. ground cinnamon and 1 tsp. ground nutmeg to the flour mixture. Add 1 cup cut-up dates, 1 cup raisins and 1 cup chopped nuts.
- **Cherry Coconut Drops:** Add 1 cup coconut and 1 cup cut-up maraschino cherries (drained). Drop dough by teaspoonfuls into crushed corn flakes and toss lightly to coat. Shape into balls and top with half a maraschino cherry.

GINGERBREAD COOKIES

Christmas is a great time to bake this recipe with the younger members of your family.

1 cup shortening
1 cup sugar
1 egg
1 cup molasses
2 Tbsp. vinegar
5 cups sifted all-purpose flour
1 1/2 tsp. baking soda
1/2 tsp. salt
2 to 3 tsp. ground ginger
1 tsp. ground cinnamon
1 tsp. ground cloves

Cream shortening and sugar thoroughly. Stir in egg, molasses and vinegar; beat well. Sift together flour, baking soda, salt, ginger, cinnamon and cloves; stir into molasses mixture. Chill for about 3 hours.

Preheat oven to 375°F. Roll dough to 1/8-inch thickness on lightly floured surface. Cut into desired shapes. Place 1 inch apart on greased cookie sheet. Bake for 5 to 6 minutes. Cool slightly on pan, then remove to rack and cool. *Makes about 5 dozen 4-inch cookies.*

Variation

- For gingerbread boys that will stand up, bake cookies with "built-in" skewers. Place wooden skewers on cookie sheet; arrange cut-out dough on top with skewer 1/3 up back of cookies. Bake and cool thoroughly. To decorate, use icing sugar frosting in decorating tube.

BASIC REFRIGERATOR COOKIES

This recipe has stood the test of time.

2/3 cup butter or margarine
1 cup light brown sugar
1 egg
1 tsp. vanilla extract
2 cups sifted all-purpose flour
1/4 tsp. salt
1/2 tsp. baking soda

Cream butter or margarine; then gradually add sugar, beating well. Add egg and vanilla; mix well. Mix flour, salt and baking soda; stir into butter mixture. Shape finished dough into logs about 2 inches in diameter. Cover with waxed paper; chill until firm (about 1 to 2 hours). Preheat oven to 350°F. Slice logs thinly and place cookies on ungreased cookie sheet. Bake for 8 to 10 minutes. *Makes about 5 dozen.*

Variations

- **Nut and Fruit:** Add 2 Tbsp. red and green chopped maraschino cherries (well drained) and 2 Tbsp. chopped nuts to dough.
- **Chocolate:** Blend 1 square unsweetened chocolate, melted and cooled, into butter mixture. For Chocolate Nut Variation, mix 4 Tbsp. chopped nuts into dough.
- **Black and White:** Prepare plain chocolate dough. Top each cookie with miniature marshmallow for last 3 minutes of baking time.
- **Turtles:** Prepare plain chocolate dough; chill. Cut rolls into thin slices. Between 2 slices, place whole walnut or pecan for head, and 4 pieces chopped walnut or pecan for legs.
- **Orange:** Omit vanilla and add 1 1/2 Tbsp. grated orange rind to butter mixture.
- **Lemony Coconut:** Omit vanilla and add 1/2 tsp. lemon extract to butter mixture. Mix 2 Tbsp. shredded coconut into dough.
- **Almond:** Omit vanilla and add 1/2 tsp. almond extract into butter mixture. Top each cookie with blanched almond half before baking.
- **Sandies:** Follow basic recipe for plain cookies. While baked cookies are still warm, dredge with coloured berry sugar.

FRUITCAKE COOKIES

1 1/4 cups sifted all-purpose flour (sift before
     measuring)
1/2 tsp. baking soda
1/2 tsp. salt
1/2 tsp. ground cinnamon
1/2 cup butter or margarine
3/4 cup sugar
1 egg
2 1/2 cups pitted dates, coarsely chopped
1/2 cup candied orange peel, cut
1/2 cup candied lemon peel, cut
1/2 cup glacé cherries, chopped
3/4 cup walnuts

Preheat over to 375°F. Sift flour, baking soda, salt and cinnamon together. In large bowl, beat butter or margarine, sugar and egg until light and fluffy. Stir in flour mixture until well combined. Add fruits and nuts; mix well. Drop by level tablespoonfuls, 2 inches apart, on ungreased cookie sheet. Bake for 8 to 10 minutes or until lightly browned. Cool on pan for 1 minute, then remove to wire rack or waxed paper to cool. *Makes about 4 dozen.*

Christmas baking at the Bruns, 1989. Left to right: Pam, my daughter-in-law; Jennifer, my granddaughter; yours truly; my grandsons Kent and James. I think a family who cooks together stays together—these times provide many happy memories.

RAISIN DROPS

1 cup light or dark raisins
1/2 cup shortening
1 cup sugar
2 eggs
1/4 cup milk
1 2/3 cups quick-cooking rolled oats
1 1/2 cups sifted all-purpose flour
1 tsp. baking soda
1/2 tsp. salt
1 tsp. ground cinnamon

Preheat oven to 350°F. Rinse raisins in boiling water; drain. Cream shortening and sugar. Add eggs and milk; beat well. Stir in rolled oats and raisins. Add flour, baking soda, salt and cinnamon; stir well. Drop by teaspoonfuls onto greased cookie sheet. Bake for 15 to 18 minutes. *Makes 3 1/2 dozen.*

ORANGE DROP COOKIES

2 cups all-purpose flour
2 tsp. baking powder
1 tsp. salt
1 cup butter or shortening
1 cup sugar
2 eggs, well beaten
1/4 cup orange juice
1 Tbsp. grated orange rind
2 cups wheat bran cereal

Preheat oven to 350°F. Mix together flour, baking powder and salt. Cream butter or shortening. Gradually blend in sugar, creaming well after each addition. Thoroughly mix in eggs. Alternately add flour and orange juice, mixing well after each addition. Add orange rind and cereal; mix thoroughly. Drop by rounded tablespoonfuls onto greased baking sheets. Bake for about 13 minutes or until lightly browned. *Makes about 4 dozen.*

REFRIGERATOR OATMEAL COOKIES

Great for packed lunches.

1 cup shortening
1 cup brown sugar
1 cup granulated sugar
2 eggs
1 tsp. vanilla extract
1 1/2 cups sifted all-purpose flour
1 tsp. salt
1 tsp. baking soda
3 cups quick-cooking oatmeal
1/2 cup chopped walnuts

Thoroughly cream shortening and sugars. Add eggs and vanilla; beat well. Sift flour, salt and baking soda together; combine with creamed mixture. Add oatmeal and walnuts. Mix thoroughly. Form dough into logs 1 to 1 1/2 inches in diameter. Wrap well in waxed paper and chill thoroughly.

Preheat oven to 350°F. Cut logs into slices approximately 1/4 inch thick. Bake on ungreased cookie sheet for approximately 10 minutes or until lightly browned. *Makes about 5 dozen.*

ALEX'S FAVOURITE OATMEAL COOKIES

My six-year-old great-grandson, Alex Gustafson, loves these.

2/3 cup butter
1 cup brown sugar
1 egg
1 tsp. vanilla extract
1/2 tsp. baking powder
1/2 tsp. baking soda
1 cup all-purpose flour
1 tsp. ground cinnamon
1 1/2 cups rolled oats
1/2 cup shredded coconut
1 cup dried cranberries
3/4 cup white chocolate chips
1 cup semi-sweet chocolate chips

Preheat oven to 350°F. Cream butter and sugar together. Add egg and vanilla, mixing until well blended.

In separate small bowl, mix baking powder, baking soda, flour and cinnamon. Add to butter mixture; beat until blended. Add oats, coconut, cranberries and both chocolate chips; stir well.

Drop by rounded tablespoonfuls onto greased or non-stick cookie sheets. Bake for 10 to 13 minutes, depending on desired crispness. Store in airtight container. *Makes about 40 cookies.*

SUNFLOWER SEED COOKIES

1 cup margarine or butter
1 cup brown sugar, firmly packed
1 cup granulated sugar
2 eggs
1 tsp. vanilla extract
1 1/2 cups all-purpose flour (unsifted)
3/4 tsp. salt
1 tsp. baking soda
3 cups quick-cooking rolled oats
1 cup sunflower seeds

Cream margarine or butter, brown sugar and granulated sugar thoroughly. Add eggs and vanilla; beat to blend well. Add flour, salt, baking soda and rolled oats; mix well. Gently mix in sunflower seeds. Roll into logs about 1 1/2 inches in diameter. Wrap in plastic wrap and chill thoroughly. (Dough can be kept in refrigerator for several days before baking.)

Preheat oven to 350°F. Cut logs into 1/4-inch slices; place on ungreased cookie sheet. Bake for 10 minutes or until lightly browned. Cool on wire racks. Store in air-tight containers. *Makes about 9 dozen.*

PEANUT WHIRLS

1/2 cup shortening

1/2 cup peanut butter

1 cup sugar

1 egg

1 tsp. vanilla extract

1 1/4 cups sifted all-purpose flour

1/2 tsp. baking soda

1/2 tsp. salt

2 Tbsp. milk

1 cup semi-sweet chocolate chips

Cream shortening, peanut butter and sugar together. Add egg and vanilla; beat well. Sift flour, baking soda and salt together; add to peanut butter mixture, alternating with milk. Turn onto lightly floured surface. Roll into rectangle 1/4 inch thick. Melt chocolate pieces over hot water and cool slightly. Spread onto rolled cookie dough. Roll dough up jelly-roll fashion. Wrap well and chill for 1/2 hour. Spray baking sheet very lightly with vegetable cooking spray if you wish. Preheat oven to 350°F. Cut dough into 1/4-inch slices. Place on baking sheet about 2 inches apart. Bake for about 10 minutes. *Makes about 3 dozen.*

MELTING MOMENTS

1 cup butter

1/2 cup sifted icing sugar

1 tsp. lemon extract

2 cups sifted all-purpose flour

1/4 tsp. salt

1 recipe Lemon Filling

Preheat oven to 400°F. Cream butter to thickness of mayonnaise; add sugar gradually, creaming constantly. Add lemon extract, flour and salt and blend well. Using a level teaspoon measure, shape into balls and flatten slightly. Place on ungreased cookie sheet 1 inch apart. Bake for 8 to 10 minutes or until very lightly browned. Sandwich together with lemon filling. *Makes about 5 dozen double cookies.*

Lemon Filling

1 egg, slightly beaten

grated rind of 1 lemon

2/3 cup sugar

3 Tbsp. lemon juice

1 1/2 Tbsp. softened butter

Blend all ingredients in top of double boiler. Cook over hot water, stirring constantly, until thick. Chill until firm.

CHERRY ROUNDS

1/2 cup butter or margarine

1/4 cup brown sugar

1 egg yolk

1/2 tsp. vanilla extract

1/4 tsp. salt

1 1/4 cups sifted all-purpose flour

1 egg white, slightly beaten

3/4 cup finely chopped walnuts

1/3 cup cherry preserves

Cream butter or margarine, sugar, egg yolk, vanilla and salt until light and fluffy. Stir in flour. Chill approximately 30 minutes.

Preheat oven to 350°F. Shape dough into 1-inch balls; dip in egg white and roll in walnuts. Place 2 1/2 inches apart on greased cookie sheet; press

A vintage ad for kitchen appliances.

centres with thumb. Fill centres with small amount of cherry preserves (approximately $\frac{1}{2}$ tsp. in each). Bake for 12 to 15 minutes or until done. Cool slightly. Remove from pan and cool on racks. *Makes about 3 dozen.*

Note: For attractive tea-table cookies, press centres of cookies before baking, but do not fill with preserves until serving time.

COCO-MINT SANDWICHES

FOR THE COOKIES:
$\frac{3}{4}$ cup margarine or butter
1 cup sugar
1 egg
$\frac{1}{2}$ tsp. vanilla extract
2 cups sifted all-purpose flour
$\frac{3}{4}$ cup cocoa
1 tsp. baking powder
$\frac{1}{2}$ tsp. baking soda
$\frac{1}{2}$ tsp. salt
$\frac{1}{4}$ cup milk

Cream margarine or butter and sugar until fluffy. Add egg and vanilla; beat well. Sift flour, cocoa, baking powder, baking soda and salt together. Add to creamed mixture alternately with milk, mixing well. Shape dough into two 10 x $1\frac{1}{2}$-inch logs. Wrap well and chill for several hours or overnight.

Preheat oven to 325°F. Cut logs into $\frac{1}{8}$-inch slices. Bake on ungreased cookie sheet for 10 minutes. Remove from cookie sheet at once and cool on racks.

FOR THE MINT FILLING:
3 Tbsp. margarine or butter
$1\frac{1}{2}$ cups sifted icing sugar
1 Tbsp. milk
2 or 3 drops green food colouring
1 or 2 drops peppermint oil or $\frac{1}{2}$ tsp. peppermint extract

Combine all ingredients until smooth and creamy. Sandwich cookies together with mint filling. *Makes $3\frac{1}{2}$ dozen.*

FRAN'S COOKIES

My sister-in-law's favourite. She used this recipe a lot—she had six children!

1 cup butter or margarine
2 cups granulated sugar
1 cup brown sugar
1 Tbsp. vanilla extract
2 eggs
2 cups all-purpose flour
2 tsp. baking powder
1 heaping tsp. baking soda
$\frac{1}{4}$ tsp. salt
1 cup chopped walnuts
2 cups quick-cooking oats
2 cups coconut
2 cups cornflakes cereal

Preheat oven to 350°F. In large bowl, cream butter or margarine with both sugars. Add vanilla and eggs. Sift flour, baking powder, baking soda and salt in medium bowl. Add flour mixture to butter mixture and combine thoroughly. Add walnuts, oats and coconut, mixing well. Mix in cereal, taking care not to crumble flakes more than necessary. Drop dough from a teaspoon onto greased cookie sheet and bake for 12 to 15 minutes. Remove cookies from oven and cool on sheet for 1 minute, no longer, then remove to rack. This cookie freezes very well. *Makes 9 to 11 dozen.*

WHIPPED SHORTBREAD

1 lb. butter
1 cup icing sugar
3 cups sifted cake flour
$\frac{1}{2}$ cup cornstarch
1 tsp. vanilla extract

Preheat oven to 350°F. Using electric mixer, cream butter until very light and fluffy. Continue beating while adding sugar, flour and cornstarch. Beat until all ingredients are well combined. Beat in vanilla. Drop shortbread by spoonfuls on cookie sheet. Bake for approximately 12 minutes. *Makes 4 to 5 dozen.*

POMEROY'S SHORTBREAD

Mrs. Pomeroy was a favourite customer with the "Bea Wright" staff.

1 lb. butter
1 cup brown sugar
1 egg yolk
5 cups all-purpose flour

Preheat oven to 325°F. Cream butter and sugar; add egg yolk and stir well. Add flour, a small amount at a time, until dough is the consistency of putty. Roll out $1/2$ to $3/4$ inch thick. Prick with fork and cut into desired shapes. Bake for about 30 minutes or until firm and golden brown. *Makes approximately 6 dozen medium pieces.*

SCOTTISH SHORTBREAD

2 cups all-purpose flour
1 cup butter
$1/2$ cup sugar
pinch salt

Preheat oven to 350°F. Mix all ingredients in bowl, then knead very well. Roll out $1/3$ to $1/2$ inch thick (depending on how thick you like your shortbread) and cut shapes as desired. Bake on ungreased brown paper on cookie sheet for 20 to 25 minutes. The more this dough is worked the better it is. *Makes 3 dozen.*

CHOCOLATE TRUFFLES

6 squares semi-sweet chocolate
$1/4$ cup sifted icing sugar
3 Tbsp. butter or margarine
3 egg yolks, slightly beaten
1 Tbsp. rum or brandy
finely grated semi-sweet chocolate
finely chopped nuts
coconut

In top of double boiler, melt chocolate squares over hot, not boiling, water; add icing sugar and butter or margarine. Remove from heat. Stir small amount of hot mixture into beaten egg yolks; add warmed yolks to hot mixture, stirring well. Blend in rum or brandy. Chill, without stirring, for 1 to 2 hours. Shape into 1-inch balls. Roll $1/3$ of the balls in finely grated chocolate, $1/3$ in finely chopped nuts, and $1/3$ in coconut. *Makes about 2 dozen.*

OATMEAL TRUFFLES

1 cup quick-cooking rolled oats
3 Tbsp. cocoa
1 egg, well beaten
$2 1/2$ cups sifted icing sugar
1 tsp. instant coffee
$1/4$ tsp. vanilla extract
1 to 3 tsp. water
sifted icing sugar
cocoa
corn syrup
coconut

In large bowl, combine oats, the 3 Tbsp. cocoa, egg, $2 1/2$ cups icing sugar, coffee and vanilla. Work all ingredients together until mixture is a stiff, smooth paste. Add water as necessary to bind. (The amount of water required depends on the size of egg used. Mixture should be a stiff, smooth consistency, not sticky. Omit water if desired consistency is obtained without it.) In small bowl, combine a small amount of sifted icing sugar and cocoa. Roll oatmeal mixture with hands, dusting palms with sugar and cocoa mixture. Set truffles aside and allow to set for 2 hours. Brush truffles with corn syrup and roll in coconut. (If desired, tinted coconut can be used for an attractive effect.) *Makes $2 1/2$ dozen.*

RUM BALLS

2 cups fine graham cracker crumbs
2 Tbsp. cocoa
1 cup sifted icing sugar
$1/8$ tsp. salt
1 cup finely chopped walnuts
$1 1/2$ Tbsp. honey
$1/4$ cup rum or brandy
sifted icing sugar

In large bowl, combine graham cracker crumbs, cocoa, icing sugar, salt and walnuts. Mix until well distributed. In small bowl, combine honey and rum or brandy; add to graham crumb mixture. Stir with spoon and knead with hands until well combined. Coat hands with icing sugar and roll mixture into little balls. Roll balls in sifted icing sugar. Store in airtight container such as a tin box for at least 12 hours to ripen. *Makes about 40 rum balls.*

Note: If mixture seems too dry, add a little extra rum or brandy until mixture is desired consistency.

BUTTERSCOTCH BROWNIES

$1/2$ cup butter or margarine
1 cup brown sugar, firmly packed
1 egg, beaten
$3/4$ cup sifted all-purpose flour
$1/4$ tsp. salt
1 tsp. baking powder
1 Tbsp. milk
$1/2$ cup chopped pecans or walnuts
1 tsp. vanilla extract
butter icing (of your choice)
1 square semi-sweet chocolate

Preheat oven to 350°F. Butter 8-inch square pan. Melt butter or margarine with sugar in heavy skillet over low heat; stir until mixture is smooth. Transfer to mixing bowl and cool. Beat in egg. Sift flour, salt and baking powder together; add to sugar-egg mixture. Blend in milk, nuts and vanilla. Pour into pre-

pared pan. Bake for 25 minutes or until firm on top. Cool in pan; remove and cool completely.

Prepare a butter icing and spread over cake. Melt chocolate over hot water. (Thin with butter, if necessary.) Drizzle in parallel lines about 1 inch apart over entire cake. Draw a knife crosswise through the chocolate lines to give a ripple effect. Cut into squares. *Makes 16 squares.*

LEMON SQUARES
This recipe won a prize in a CBC radio contest.

FOR THE BASE:
2 cups sifted all-purpose flour
1 cup butter
$1/2$ cup icing sugar

Preheat oven to 350°F. Mix all ingredients and pack into bottom of greased 13 x 9-inch pan. Bake for 20 minutes.

FOR THE TOPPING:
4 eggs
2 cups granulated sugar
6 Tbsp. lemon juice
1 tsp. grated lemon rind
$1/4$ cup all-purpose flour
$1/4$ tsp. baking powder
$1/4$ tsp. salt
icing sugar

Beat eggs slightly; add granulated sugar, lemon juice and lemon rind. Sift together flour, baking powder and salt. Mix with egg-lemon mixture and beat only until smooth.

Pour filling over base as soon as it is removed from the oven. Return to oven and continue baking for approximately 25 minutes. Sift extra icing sugar over top while cake is still warm. Cut into squares when cool. *Makes 24 squares.*

NANAIMO BARS

Care parcels were sent from Britain to the coal miners in Nanaimo—hence the name. That's one of the legends.

1/2 cup margarine or butter
1/4 cup granulated sugar
1 egg
1 tsp. vanilla extract
5 Tbsp. cocoa
2 cups graham wafer crumbs
1 cup coconut
1/2 cup chopped nuts
1/4 cup butter
3 Tbsp. canned milk
2 Tbsp. vanilla custard or instant pudding powder
  (Bird's brand)
2 cups sifted icing sugar
4 squares semi-sweet chocolate
1 Tbsp. butter

Combine 1/2 cup margarine or butter, granulated sugar, egg, vanilla and cocoa in top of double boiler. Cook over boiling water, stirring until mixture resembles a custard. Combine crumbs, coconut and nuts. Add to custard mixture, blending well. Spread in 9-inch square pan, pressing down firmly. Refrigerate.

Cream the 1/4 cup butter, milk, custard powder and icing sugar.

Spread over mixture in pan. Allow to stand 15 minutes. Melt chocolate in top of double boiler over hot water. Add butter and blend well. Spread over custard layer. Refrigerate. *Makes 16 squares.*

BUTTER TART BARS

FOR THE BASE:
3/4 cup sifted all-purpose flour
1/4 cup brown sugar
1/3 cup butter

Preheat oven to 350°F. Combine ingredients until crumbly; press into bottom of ungreased 8-inch pan. Bake for 12 to 15 minutes.

FOR THE TOPPING:
1 cup seedless raisins
2 eggs
1/2 cup granulated sugar
1/2 cup dark corn syrup
1/8 tsp. salt
1 tsp. vanilla extract
1/4 cup all-purpose flour

Rinse and drain raisins; place in bowl. Beat in eggs; gradually beat in sugar. Add corn syrup, salt, vanilla and flour. Mix well and pour over baked base.

Return to oven and bake for 25 to 30 minutes, until topping is golden. Cool; cut into bars. (This topping makes an excellent filling for butter tarts.) *Makes 16 to 20 bars.*

UNBAKED O'HENRY CAKE SQUARES

whole graham wafers (enough to line pan and
  top squares)
1 cup brown sugar
1/2 cup milk
1/2 cup butter
1 cup crushed graham wafers
1 cup chopped walnuts
1 cup coconut
1 tsp. vanilla extract
1 recipe of your favourite butter icing

Lightly grease 8- or 9-inch square pan; line bottom with whole graham wafers. Boil sugar, milk and butter in saucepan for 1 minute. Remove from heat and immediately add crushed wafers, walnuts, coconut and vanilla. Mix thoroughly. Place mixture over wafers in pan and top with whole wafers. Spread with butter icing immediately. Chill in refrigerator before cutting. *Makes 16 to 20 squares.*

SURPRISE BARS

FOR THE BASE:
1 cup all-purpose flour
$^1/_2$ cup butter
$^1/_4$ cup icing sugar

Preheat oven to 350°F. Mix ingredients until crumbly. Press into bottom of ungreased 8-inch square pan. Bake for 10 to 15 minutes or until lightly golden.

FOR THE TOPPING:
2 eggs
1 cup brown sugar
1 tsp. vanilla extract
1 tsp. baking powder
2 Tbsp. all-purpose flour
$^1/_2$ tsp. salt
$^1/_2$ cup coconut
1 cup walnuts

Beat eggs until light. Add sugar and vanilla. Add baking powder, flour and salt. Stir to combine ingredients thoroughly. Stir in coconut and walnuts. Spread over baked base. Return to oven and bake for 25 minutes or until done. *Makes 16 to 20 bars.*

DOLLIE BARS

1 cup graham wafer crumbs
$^1/_4$ cup butter or margarine, melted
1 cup chocolate chips
1 cup chopped walnuts or pecans
1 cup fine coconut
$^1/_3$ cup chopped maraschino cherries
$1^2/_3$ cups sweetened condensed milk

Preheat oven to 350°F. Mix graham wafer crumbs and butter together and press mixture into greased 8 x 8-inch pan. Sprinkle chocolate chips in a layer over top, then walnuts or pecans, then coconut and last, cherries. Pour condensed milk over all. Spread lightly. Bake for approximately 30 minutes. Cool and cut into bars or fingers. *Makes 16 to 20 bars.*

DANISH APPLE BARS

$2^1/_2$ cups all-purpose flour
1 tsp. salt
1 cup shortening
1 egg yolk plus enough milk to measure $^2/_3$ cup
1 cup crushed cornflakes cereal
4 apples, peeled and cored
1 cup granulated sugar
1 tsp. ground cinnamon
1 egg white
1 cup icing sugar
1 Tbsp. water
$^1/_2$ tsp. vanilla extract

Preheat oven to 400°F. Grease a 12 x 17-inch jelly roll pan or cookie sheet with sides. Sift flour and salt. Cut in shortening until mixture is crumbly. Slowly add egg-milk mixture to flour mixture. Lightly stir to moisten. Divide in half. Roll one half into rectangle to fit baking sheet. Place on sheet and sprinkle with crushed cereal. Slice apples thinly and arrange over crumbs. Sprinkle with granulated sugar and cinnamon. Roll remaining dough to fit pan and place over apples. Pinch edges closed all around. Beat egg white until stiff and brush over top crust. Bake for 35 to 40 minutes.

Combine icing sugar, water and vanilla to make a light glaze. When pastry is baked and still warm, drizzle glaze over top. Serve either warm or cold. *Makes 36 bars.*

PARTY SQUARES

42 chocolate Oreo cookies
2 cups whipping cream
1 cup pastel mints
2 cups miniature pastel marshmallows

Crush cookies; spread $^1/_2$ on bottom of 8-inch square pan. Whip cream; add mints and marshmallows. Pour over cookie crumbs. Top with remaining crushed cookies. Place in refrigerator for 2 days. *Makes 12 to 16 bars.*

SESAME TOFFEE BARS

1/4 cup sesame seeds

1 cup margarine or butter

1 cup brown sugar, packed

1 egg, beaten

1 tsp. vanilla extract

2 cups sifted all-purpose flour

1/4 tsp. ground cinnamon

1/4 tsp. allspice

1/8 tsp. ground nutmeg

1/2 cup chopped nuts

1 3/4 cups semi-sweet chocolate chips

Preheat oven to 350°F. Toast sesame seeds for 10 to 15 minutes, or until golden brown. Set aside. Cream margarine or butter with sugar; add egg and vanilla, mixing well. Sift flour with cinnamon, allspice and nutmeg. Blend into creamed mixture. Stir in nuts. Spread to a 13 x 15-inch rectangle that is 1/4 inch thick on a greased cookie sheet. Bake for 20 minutes.

Melt chocolate chips in small pan over boiling water. When slab is baked, remove from oven; spread melted chocolate over top while still hot and sprinkle with sesame seeds. Cut into bars while warm. *Makes approximately 4 dozen bars.*

RICE KRISPIE BARS

This is an old-timer but it's still as popular as ever!

1/4 cup butter or margarine

40 regular white marshmallows or 4 cups white miniature marshmallows, approximately

1/2 tsp. vanilla extract

5 cups Rice Krispies, approximately

Melt butter or margarine in large saucepan. Add marshmallows; cook, stirring constantly, over low heat until marshmallows melt. Remove from heat. Add vanilla. Stir in Rice Krispies. Press warm mixture into well-buttered 13 x 9 x 2-inch pan. Cut into squares when cool. *Makes about 24 squares.*

Note: Mixture is more easily pressed into pan with buttered spatula or knife, or place waxed paper on surface and press with hands.

Variations

- **Snowballs:** Shape warm mixture into balls and roll in shredded coconut. Try making a face with raisins, candies, nuts or icing (coconut for hair).
- **Chocolate Frosted Rolls:** Shape warm mixture into 2 rolls about 12 inches long by 1 1/2 inches in diameter. Allow to set. Drizzle with melted semi-sweet chocolate pieces, allow to set, then slice.
- **Sandwich Wafers:** Press very thin layer of warm mixture into buttered pans. Cool. To serve, cut into 3-inch squares. Slice ice cream in 3-inch squares and place wafers on either side of ice cream. Serve immediately.
- **Tart Shells:** Press warm mixture in a thin layer into buttered muffin cups to form a tart shape. Allow to set. Remove tart shells from muffin cups and fill with vanilla ice cream, cream filling or well-drained fresh, canned or frozen (thawed) fruit. Drizzle with sundae sauce. Top with a swirl of whipped cream and garnish with nuts or glacé cherries.

MARSHMALLOW FUDGE SQUARES

3 squares unsweetened chocolate, melted

1 3/4 cups sweetened condensed milk

2 cups fine graham cracker crumbs

1/2 cup chopped walnuts

1/2 tsp. vanilla extract

pinch salt

18 large marshmallows, halved

1 square semi-sweet chocolate

1 tsp. butter or margarine

Preheat oven to 325°F. Melt unsweetened chocolate in top of double boiler. Add condensed milk, graham cracker crumbs, walnuts, vanilla and salt. Stir to combine thoroughly. Spread mixture into greased 8-inch square pan. Bake for 25 minutes. Immediately after removing from oven, cover with halved marshmallows, cut side down. Cool. In top of double boiler, melt semi-sweet chocolate and butter or margarine. Drizzle chocolate over marshmallows. Cool. When completely cold, cut into small squares. *Makes approximately 30 small squares.*

pastries and desserts

mona says . . .

- Use a pastry blender for cutting shortening into flour. The particles formed will flatten during the rolling out and thus provide the tenderness and flakiness characteristic of good pastry. Do not use a fork or spoon: they "cream" or blend rather than cut.

- Use cold water to keep the shortening from melting.

- Add just enough water to moisten the flour. If dough is sticky, you have added too much flour during the rolling, which will make the pastry tough.

- Handle pastry dough as little as possible. Re-rolling and over-handling also toughens pastry.

- Grate peel before cutting fruit and store the peel in the freezer. Canned or frozen juice may be used with peel when your recipe calls for both juice and rind. No waste!

- Keep chocolate cool and dry. If it becomes warm the cocoa butter rises to the surface, melts, and forms a greyish-white film when cooled. This film does not affect the flavour but does affect the appearance when the chocolate is meant to be used for garnish. Restore the colour by melting the chocolate. Chocolate stored in the refrigerator should be tightly wrapped in a container so as not to absorb odours. Do not store cocoa in your refrigerator, but do keep it in a tightly covered container in a cool place.

- You can use several methods to melt chocolate, but use as little heat as possible. Unsweetened, semi-sweet and sweet chocolate may be melted over hot (not boiling) water. Or place it in a greased pie plate in a warm oven until melted. Watch it carefully. Don't forget about it! Another simple method is to place chocolate in a double boiler over water, cover, heat water till bubbles form, then turn off the heat. Let stand until chocolate softens; stir until smooth. Cooking steps can be doubled up: melt chocolate with shortening, butter or margarine, or with hot liquids.

- Easy microwave melting: Microwave on medium power for 2 minutes. Remove and stir until melted. Time will increase slightly with number of squares.

- Garnish with chocolate to give a professional look to many dessert recipes.

  - To grate chocolate, thoroughly chill grater and chocolate in the refrigerator. Cool your hands under cold water and dry them. Using an up and down motion, grate chocolate as quickly as possible and handle it as little as possible.

- To make chocolate curls, warm chocolate slightly at room temperature. For little curls, use a vegetable peeler to shave thin strips from narrow side of chocolate. For large curls, use a knife or vegetable peeler to scrape chocolate from the long side. Use a toothpick to pick up curls (otherwise they shatter) and chill until firm before arranging on food.

BASIC PASTRY

2 cups all-purpose flour
1 tsp. salt
2/3 cup chilled shortening
approximately 6 Tbsp. cold water

Sift flour; measure. Add salt and sift again. Using a pastry blender, thoroughly cut in half the shortening until mixture resembles coarse cornmeal. Cut in remaining shortening coarsely, until particles are about the size of peas. Sprinkle water, 1 Tbsp. at a time, over small portions of mixture; press particles together as they absorb the water (use a fork); do not stir. Push aside pieces of dough as formed; sprinkle remaining water over dry portions. Use only enough water to bind pastry together. Press together lightly with fingers or wrap dough in waxed paper and press together gently. Handle dough as little as possible for the most tender and flaky results. Chill dough before rolling. *Makes one 9-inch 2-crust pie.*

SOUR CREAM PASTRY

1 1/2 cups unsifted all-purpose flour
2/3 cup corn oil or margarine
1/2 cup sour cream

Place flour in medium mixing bowl; cut in oil or margarine with a pastry blender until particles are fine. Stir in sour cream to form a dough. Wrap in plastic wrap and chill thoroughly (at least 2 hours). *Makes enough pastry for a double-crust pie.*

BASIC CRUMB CRUST

1 1/2 cups crushed cornflake cereal or graham
    cracker crumbs
1/3 cup sugar
1/3 to 1/2 cup melted butter or margarine

Combine cereal or graham cracker crumbs with sugar; blend in melted butter or margarine. Press firmly into 8- to 9-inch pie plate. Chill for 1 hour or bake in preheated 350°F oven for about 8 minutes (the baked crust is firmer). *Makes 1 crumb crust.*

BERRY PIE

1 recipe Basic Pastry
4 cups fresh raspberries or blueberries
1 Tbsp. lemon juice
1/4 cup all-purpose flour
1 cup sugar
1/4 tsp. ground cinnamon
1/8 tsp. ground nutmeg
1 1/2 Tbsp. butter
1 egg yolk
1 Tbsp. water
sweetened whipped cream or vanilla ice cream
    (optional)

Line 9-inch pie plate with half the pastry, trimming edge even with outside of pie plate. Refrigerate pie shell and remaining half of pastry. Wash berries; drain thoroughly. Place berries in large bowl; sprinkle with lemon juice. In separate bowl, combine flour, sugar, cinnamon and nutmeg. Toss mixture gently with berries until well distributed.

Preheat oven to 400°F. Turn berries into pastry-lined pie plate, mounding in centre. Dot with butter. Roll out remaining pastry. Make several slits near centre for steam vents. Place pastry over filling. Fold edge of top crust under bottom crust; press together to seal and crimp pastry attractively. In small bowl, beat egg yolk with water. Brush mixture over top crust. Place pie on baking sheet to catch any juice. Bake for 45 to 50 minutes or until done. Cool on wire rack for at least 45 minutes before serving. Serve warm with whipped cream or ice cream, if desired. *Serves 8.*

PUMPKIN PIE

This brings back mouth-watering memories of the pumpkin pie served in the Cambie Room at Woodward's Oakridge.

1 1/2 cups canned or cooked and mashed pumpkin
3/4 cup sugar
1 tsp. ground cinnamon
1/2 to 3/4 tsp. ground ginger
1/4 to 1/2 tsp. ground nutmeg
1/4 to 1/2 tsp. ground cloves
1/2 tsp. salt
3 eggs, slightly beaten
1 1/4 cups fresh milk
2/3 cup evaporated milk
1 9-inch unbaked pastry shell (have edges
    crimped high)
sweetened whipped cream and walnut or pecan
    halves, for garnish (optional)

Preheat oven to 400°F. In large bowl, thoroughly combine pumpkin, sugar, cinnamon, ginger, nutmeg, cloves and salt. Blend in eggs, milk and evaporated milk. Pour filling into unbaked pastry shell. Bake for approximately 50 minutes or until knife inserted halfway between centre and edge comes out clean. Cool thoroughly before serving. If desired, garnish with whipped cream and walnut or pecan halves. *Makes one 9-inch pie.*

TO FREEZE PUMPKIN
Peel pumpkin and cut into 1-inch cubes. Steam until soft. Mash. Cool by placing pumpkin in bowl of ice water. Stir often to speed cooling. Pack into cartons, label and freeze.

APPLE COTTAGE PIE

2 cups peeled, cored and sliced apples
    (about 3 medium)
2 Tbsp. water
pinch salt
1 cup sugar
1/2 tsp. ground cinnamon
1/4 tsp. ground nutmeg
2 eggs
1/4 tsp. salt
1/2 cup light cream
3/4 cup milk
1 cup creamed cottage cheese, sieved
1 tsp. vanilla extract
1 9-inch unbaked pastry shell, chilled

Cook apple slices with water and salt in a covered saucepan until tender (apples should be quite dry but still retain shape). Remove from heat and stir in 1/2 cup of the sugar, cinnamon and nutmeg; set aside.

Beat eggs and 1/4 tsp. salt slightly. Heat cream and milk together until a film appears on the surface. Slowly pour into eggs, beating vigorously. Add cottage cheese, remaining 1/2 cup sugar and vanilla.

Preheat oven to 450°F. Spoon cooked apple slices into pastry shell. Pour cottage cheese mixture over top. Bake for 15 minutes, then lower oven temperature to 325°F and bake for 30 minutes longer or until knife inserted in centre comes out clean. Serve at room temperature. *Serves 6.*

OLD-FASHIONED APPLE PIE

1 recipe Basic Pastry (page 162)
³⁄₄ to 1 cup sugar
1 to 2 Tbsp. all-purpose flour
³⁄₄ tsp. ground cinnamon, or to taste
¹⁄₈ tsp. salt
4 to 5 cups peeled, cored and sliced apples
1 Tbsp. lemon juice
2 Tbsp. butter

Preheat oven to 425°F. Divide pastry in half and roll out bottom crust of pastry; fit into 9-inch pie plate. Trim edge even with outside of pie plate rim. Combine sugar, flour, cinnamon and salt. Spread half the mixture over pastry in pie plate. Place apple slices over top. Sprinkle remainder of sugar mixture over apples. Sprinkle lemon juice over all; dot with butter. Roll out remaining pastry. Make several slits near middle for steam vents. Place pastry over filling and trim to 1 inch larger than top. Fold edge of top crust under bottom crust. Crimp to seal. Bake on lower rack for 30 to 40 minutes or until done (place pie plate on cookie sheet to catch any juice spills).

If crust gets too brown, cover lightly with a tent of foil. *Makes one 9-inch pie.*

APPLE TORTE

FOR THE CRUST:

1 ¹⁄₄ cups all-purpose flour
1 egg yolk
1 Tbsp. sugar
grated rind of 1 large lemon
¹⁄₂ cup softened butter

Sift flour into large bowl. Make well in middle. Place egg yolk, sugar, lemon rind and butter in well. Stir with fork until all ingredients are well blended and dough is smooth. Pat dough in bottom and up sides of 9-inch flan pan or plate. Chill for 2 hours.

FOR THE FILLING:

6 cups peeled, cored and sliced apples
¹⁄₂ cup sugar
¹⁄₂ tsp. ground nutmeg
¹⁄₂ cup whipping cream
1 egg yolk
¹⁄₂ cup blanched almonds, slivered
extra whipping cream, whipped (optional)

Preheat oven to 350°F. Place apple slices in attractive fashion over pastry. Sprinkle with sugar and nutmeg. Bake for 15 minutes. Remove from oven. Beat whipping cream, egg yolk and almonds slightly to combine; cover apples with mixture. Return torte to oven and bake for 20 to 25 minutes longer or until golden brown. Garnish with whipped cream, if desired. *Serves 8.*

GYPSY APPLE PIZZA

A great favourite with Judith Mathews who wrote the very popular column "Living" for the Richmond Review—*a delightful lady and a true friend.*

pastry of your choice
7 cups tart unpeeled apples (about 7 medium apples) cored and cut into slices a little less than ¹⁄₂ inch thick
¹⁄₂ cup sugar
1 tsp. ground cinnamon
¹⁄₄ tsp. ground nutmeg
³⁄₄ cup all-purpose flour
¹⁄₂ cup sugar
¹⁄₂ cup butter or margarine
slightly sweetened whipped cream or vanilla ice cream (optional)

Cut a 15-inch circle from an 18-inch wide piece of aluminum foil. Roll pastry on foil to fit circle. Trim edge with pastry wheel. Place foil and pastry on large baking sheet with edges. Leaving a ³⁄₄-inch border at outside of pastry, overlap apple slices, making 2 circles.

Combine ¹⁄₂ cup sugar, cinnamon and nutmeg. Sprinkle evenly over apples. In bowl, combine flour and remaining $\frac{1}{2}$ cup sugar. Cut in butter or margarine until mixture resembles coarse crumbs. Sprinkle mixture evenly over top. Turn up the $\frac{3}{4}$-inch edge of pastry and foil. Flute edges. Bake for approximately 20 to 25 minutes or until crust is golden and apples are tender.

Serve warm with slightly sweetened whipped cream or vanilla ice cream, if desired. This is also tasty served cold, or it may be reheated. *Serves 8.*

Note: For an attractive garnish, place a small whole apple and a few green leaves in centre of cooked apple pizza.

PEACH PARFAIT TORTE

1 cup sifted all-purpose flour
$\frac{1}{4}$ cup sugar
6 Tbsp. butter or margarine
1 egg yolk
1 package (3 oz.) strawberry jelly powder
$1\frac{1}{2}$ cups hot water
1 cup vanilla ice cream, softened
1 can (14 oz.) cling peach slices, well drained
whipping cream, whipped (optional)

Preheat oven to 375°F. Sift flour and sugar together in medium bowl; cut in butter or margarine with pastry blender until mixture is crumbly. Stir in egg yolk; mix thoroughly with a fork until pastry holds together and leaves sides of bowl clean. Press into bottom and 1 inch up side of 8-inch springform pan. Bake for 20 minutes or until golden. Place on wire rack and cool completely in pan.

Dissolve jelly powder in hot water in medium bowl. Remove $\frac{1}{2}$ cup and set aside.

Cool remaining jelly slightly. Stir in ice cream, 1 Tbsp. at a time. The mixture will start to thicken. Pour into cooked shell; chill for 45 minutes or until firm. Chill reserved $\frac{1}{2}$ cup jelly mixture for 5 minutes, until about the consistency of unbeaten egg white. Arrange peach slices in attractive pattern on top of filling in shell; spoon the $\frac{1}{2}$ cup jelly over and around peaches.

Chill for several hours, until firm. When ready to serve, loosen pastry around edge of pan with knife; release spring and carefully lift off side of pan; place torte, still on metal base, on serving plate. Cut into thin wedges with a sharp thin-bladed knife. If desired, decorate around base and on top with whipped cream. *Serves 8.*

STRAWBERRY GLAZE PIE

A favourite with everyone. More memories of Woodward's restaurants.

1 package (1 Tbsp.) plain gelatin
$\frac{1}{4}$ cup cold water
4 cups sliced fresh strawberries or raspberries
1 cup water
1 cup sugar
1 8-inch baked pie shell
whipped cream, for garnish

Soak gelatin in $\frac{1}{4}$ cup cold water. Cook 1 cup berries in 1 cup water until soft. Strain. Add sugar and gelatin to hot liquid. Stir until dissolved. Chill until consistency of egg white. Fold in remaining 3 cups berries. Pour into baked pastry shell. Chill until firm. Serve with whipped cream. *Serves 5 to 6.*

COCONUT LEMON TARTS

2 eggs
1 cup sugar
juice and rind of 1 lemon
$2\frac{1}{2}$ cups coconut
$\frac{1}{4}$ cup melted butter
12 large tart shells, unbaked

Preheat oven to 375°F. Beat eggs until light and fluffy. Fold in sugar. Add lemon juice and rind. Fold in coconut. Stir in butter, combining all ingredients well. Fill tart shells $\frac{2}{3}$ full. Bake for 25 minutes. Chill and serve cold. These tarts freeze well. *Makes 12 tarts.*

SOUR CREAM CHERRY PIE

1 1/2 cups fine graham cracker crumbs

1/4 cup sifted icing sugar

6 Tbsp. melted butter

1/2 tsp. ground cinnamon

3 eggs

3/4 cup sugar

3/4 cup sour cream

2 cups fresh tart cherries, pitted

1/2 tsp. vanilla extract

Combine crumbs, icing sugar, butter and cinnamon. Pat into 9-inch pie plate, reserving a quarter of the crumbs for topping. (An easy way to form crust is to distribute crumb mixture evenly in pie plate, then press another pie plate of same size into crumbs; trim any excess at top edge.) Chill pie shell thoroughly.

Preheat oven to 325°F. Beat eggs well, add sugar, sour cream, cherries and vanilla. Combine well. Pour mixture into chilled pie shell. Sprinkle with reserved crumbs. Bake for 1 hour or until cherry custard is firm. Serve pie very hot or very well chilled. *Serves 6.*

MARGARITA PIE

Another favourite recipe from our cooking course in Mexico—a real winner!

FOR THE CRUST:

3/4 cup pretzel crumbs

1/3 cup butter or margarine, melted

3 Tbsp. brown sugar

Thoroughly combine all ingredients in a bowl. Press mixture over the bottom and up the sides of a greased 9-inch pie plate. Chill crust.

FOR THE FILLING:

1/2 cup lemon juice

1 package unflavoured gelatin

4 eggs, separated

1 cup sugar

1/4 tsp. salt

1 tsp. grated lemon rind

1/3 cup tequila

3 Tbsp. orange-flavoured liqueur

whipped cream, for topping

lime twists, for garnish

Sprinkle lemon juice with gelatin and let stand. Beat egg yolks in top of double boiler. Blend in 1/2 cup of the sugar; add salt and lemon rind. Add softened gelatin and cook over boiling water, stirring constantly, until mixture is slightly thickened.

Transfer to bowl and blend in tequila and liqueur. Chill until mixture is cold but not thickened any further. Beat egg whites until foamy. Gradually beat in remaining 1/2 cup sugar until whites hold soft peaks. Pour cooled mixture slowly on egg whites, about 1/3 at a time, folding in carefully after each addition. Let stand in refrigerator until mixture mounds in a spoon. Swirl into prepared crust and chill until set.

To serve, whip cream (sweeten if desired). Spread on top of pie in thin layer. Garnish around edge of pie with whipping cream rosettes and lime twists. *Serves 6.*

BLENDER INSTANT PIE

Remember the blender instant pie craze? Why not try it again?

4 eggs

1 cup milk

1 cup buttermilk

1/2 cup sugar

1/2 cup buttermilk baking mix (such as Bisquick)

1/4 tsp. ground nutmeg

Preheat oven to 375°F. Place all ingredients in blender. Blend thoroughly. Pour into 9-inch greased pie plate. Bake for 50 minutes or until done. Baking mix will form crust on bottom. *Serves 6.*

BLODWEN'S GREEN TOMATO MINCEMEAT

This is from Blodwen Jones, a Welsh girl who was my soul-mate through high school and for many, many years after (actually, we were always in hot water).

6 cups peeled, cored and chopped apples (tart variety is best)
6 cups chopped green tomatoes
4 cups brown sugar
1 1/2 cups vinegar
3 cups raisins
1 Tbsp. ground cinnamon
1 tsp. ground cloves
3/4 tsp. allspice
3/4 tsp. mace
3/4 tsp. pepper
2 tsp. salt
3/4 cup butter

In large deep kettle, bring all ingredients except butter slowly to boiling point. Simmer for 3 hours. Stir in butter. Pour mixture into 6 sterilized 1-pint jars. Seal according to manufacturer's directions. Label and date. *Makes six pints.*

Note: If desired, 1 Tbsp. brandy or rum can be stirred into each jar before sealing. Once opened, keep mincemeat in refrigerator.

DANISH PUFF PASTRY

A good recipe for Easter and spring entertaining.

1 cup butter
2 cups all-purpose flour
2 Tbsp. cold water
1 cup water
1 tsp. almond extract
3 eggs
1 recipe Icing Sugar Glaze

Preheat oven to 350°F. Cut 1/2 cup of the butter into 1 cup of the flour. Sprinkle with the 2 Tbsp. cold water. Mix with fork and gather into ball. Divide into 2 equal portions. Form dough into two 12 x 3-inch strips. Place on ungreased baking sheet. Bring the 1 cup water to a boil and add remaining 1/2 cup butter; stir to melt. Add almond extract. Remove from heat. Stirring vigorously, add remaining 1 cup flour. Continue stirring until smooth. Beat in eggs, one at a time. Continue stirring until batter leaves sides of pan. Spread mixture evenly over dough strips. Bake for 1 hour or until top is crisp and nicely browned. Drizzle glaze over hot, baked puffs. Cut into sections while still warm. Serve warm. *Serves 10 to 12.*

Icing Sugar Glaze

2 cups icing sugar, sifted
1/2 tsp. almond extract
3 Tbsp. water (approximately)
toasted slivered almonds

In small bowl, stir icing sugar, almond extract and water until smooth. Beat well. Stir in almonds.

LEMON OMELET SOUFFLÉ

6 eggs, separated
6 Tbsp. sugar
3 Tbsp. lemon juice
1 tsp. grated lemon rind
1 1/2 tsp. fine granulated sugar

Preheat oven to 375°F. Beat egg yolks until light and lemon-coloured. Beat in the 6 Tbsp. sugar, 1 Tbsp. at a time. Add lemon juice and rind. Beat egg whites until firm. Gently fold into yolk mixture.

Heat a heavy ovenproof 7- to 8-inch skillet, then butter it well. Sprinkle with 1 tsp. of the fine granulated sugar. Pour the soufflé mixture into the skillet and bake for about 15 minutes. Sprinkle with remaining 1/2 tsp. fine granulated sugar and serve at once. *Serves 4.*

CRÊPES "SUZANNE"

This is my granddaughter's favourite treat. A lot of work but very impressive and tasty.

FOR THE ORANGE BUTTER:

3/4 cup butter
1/2 cup sugar
1/4 cup orange-flavoured liqueur
freshly grated orange rind to taste

Using a mixer, cream butter and sugar until light and fluffy. Add liqueur and orange rind. Beat until well blended. Set aside.

FOR THE BATTER:

1 cup unsifted all-purpose flour
1/4 cup butter or margarine, melted and cooled
2 eggs
2 egg yolks
1 1/2 cups milk

In bowl combine flour, butter or margarine, eggs, egg yolks and 1/2 cup of the milk. Beat until smooth. Beat in remaining milk until well blended. Refrigerate, covered, for at least 30 minutes.

FOR THE ORANGE SAUCE:

1/2 cup butter
3/4 cup sugar
1 to 2 Tbsp. shredded orange rind
2/3 cup orange juice
2 oranges, peeled and sectioned
1/2 cup orange-flavoured liqueur

Melt butter in large skillet. Stir in sugar, orange rind and orange juice. Cook over low heat, stirring frequently, until rind is translucent, about 20 minutes. Add orange sections and liqueur. Keep warm.

TO FINISH THE CRÊPES:

3 Tbsp. orange-flavoured liqueur

Heat 8-inch skillet until drop of water sizzles and rolls off. For each crêpe, brush skillet lightly with butter. Pour in about 2 Tbsp. of batter, rotating pan quickly to spread batter completely over bottom of skillet. Cook until lightly browned. Turn and brown other side. Turn out onto wire rack.

Spread each crêpe with orange butter, dividing evenly between crêpes. Fold each in half and then in half again. When all are folded, place in a chafing dish with the orange sauce. Cook over low heat until heated through.

To serve, gently heat liqueur in a small saucepan, just until vapour rises. Ignite with a match and pour over crêpes. Serve flaming. *Serves 6 to 8.*

My granddaughter, Suzanne Martin, cooking with me on a show. Later on in the show we traded places and she made Crêpes "Suzanne." It was a tremendous favourite with the audience.

LEMON CAKE PUDDING

3 Tbsp. butter or margarine
1 cup sugar
4 eggs, separated
3 Tbsp. all-purpose flour
1/4 tsp. salt
6 Tbsp. freshly squeezed lemon juice
1 cup milk
1 tsp. freshly grated lemon rind

Preheat oven to 325°F. Cream butter or margarine and sugar. Beat egg yolks well, add to creamed mixture and mix well. Stir in flour, salt and lemon juice. Blend in milk and lemon rind. Beat egg whites until stiff but not dry; fold into batter. Pour mixture into a buttered 1½-quart casserole. Place casserole in a shallow pan of hot water about 1 inch deep. Bake for 50 to 60 minutes. Serve hot or cold. *Serves 4.*

APPLE DUMPLINGS WITH BROWN SUGAR SAUCE

1 recipe Basic Pastry (page 162)
6 medium apples, peeled and cored
brown sugar, as needed
ground cinnamon, to taste
ground nutmeg, to taste
6 tsp. butter
1 recipe Brown Sugar Sauce

Preheat oven to 375°F. Roll prepared pastry dough into a 12 x 16-inch rectangle, ⅛ inch thick. Cut into 6 squares. Place one apple on each square. Fill centre of apples with brown sugar, then sprinkle each with additional brown sugar, cinnamon and nutmeg. Dot with butter.

Gently gather corners of pastry square to centre and pinch edges together. Place dumplings on ungreased baking sheet. Bake for 25 to 40 minutes, or until apples are tender and pastry is golden. Serve warm with hot Brown Sugar Sauce. *Serves 6.*

Brown Sugar Sauce
½ cup brown sugar, packed
1 Tbsp. cornstarch
⅛ tsp. salt
1 cup warm water
1 Tbsp. butter
1 tsp. vanilla extract

In small saucepan, combine sugar, cornstarch and salt. Stir in warm water gradually. Cook over medium heat, stirring constantly, until thickened and clear, about 3 to 5 minutes. Remove from heat; stir in butter and vanilla. *Makes about 1 cup.*

APPLE OAT CRISP

4 cups sliced apples
2 to 3 tsp. lemon juice
⅓ cup all-purpose flour
1 cup rolled oats
½ cup brown sugar
1 tsp. ground cinnamon
⅓ cup melted butter

Preheat oven to 375°F. Grease 1½-quart baking dish. Arrange apple slices in the dish and sprinkle with lemon juice. Combine flour, oats, sugar and cinnamon. Add melted butter, mixing until crumbly. Sprinkle crumbs over apples. Bake for about 30 minutes or until apples are tender. If apples are tart, add a little sugar to them just before sprinkling with the topping. *Serves 4 to 6.*

SOUR CREAM RHUBARB CRUMBLE

5 cups fresh rhubarb cut into 1-inch pieces
¾ to 1 cup granulated sugar
2 Tbsp. quick-cooking tapioca
½ cup all-purpose flour
¼ tsp. salt
1 tsp. ground cinnamon
½ cup rolled oats
¾ cup brown sugar, lightly packed
⅓ cup softened butter
1 cup sour cream
2 Tbsp. icing sugar
⅛ tsp. ground cinnamon

Preheat oven to 375°F. Butter broad, shallow baking dish. Place rhubarb in dish; sprinkle with granulated sugar and tapioca; mix lightly. Combine flour, salt, the 1 tsp. cinnamon, rolled oats and brown sugar. Mix in butter until crumbly. Sprinkle crumb mixture over fruit. Bake for 40 to 50 minutes.

Combine sour cream, icing sugar and the ⅛ tsp. cinnamon, mixing well. Chill thoroughly.

Serve crumble warm with sour cream topping. *Serves 6.*

BROWNIE PUDDING

1 cup sifted all-purpose flour
3/4 cup granulated sugar
2 tsp. baking powder
2 Tbsp. cocoa
1/2 tsp. salt
1/2 cup milk
2 Tbsp. oil
1 tsp. vanilla extract
1 cup chopped walnuts
3/4 cup brown sugar
1/4 cup cocoa
1 3/4 cups hot water

Preheat oven to 350°F. Grease 8-inch square pan. Sift flour, granulated sugar, baking powder, the 2 Tbsp. cocoa and salt together. Stir in milk, oil and vanilla. Mix until smooth. Stir in walnuts. Pour batter into pan. In small bowl, stir together brown sugar and the 1/4 cup cocoa. Sprinkle mixture evenly over batter. Pour hot water over batter. Do not stir. Bake for approximately 45 minutes. Serve warm. Delicious with vanilla ice cream or sweetened whipped cream. *Serves 6 to 8.*

STEAMED WALNUT POTATO PUDDING

1 cup sugar
1 cup ground suet (or butter)
1 cup sifted all-purpose flour
1 tsp. salt
1 tsp. baking powder
1 tsp. ground nutmeg
1 tsp. allspice
1 cup finely chopped apple
1 cup grated carrot
1 cup grated potatoe
1 cup walnuts, coarsely chopped
1 recipe Hard Sauce

When Woodward's began importing Australian goods, the food products arrived by air freight. This cake—in the shape of Australia—arrived via Qantas to celebrate the occasion.

Combine sugar and suet or butter. Sift flour, salt, baking powder, nutmeg and allspice together. Add to sugar mixture. Add apple, carrot, potato and walnuts; blend thoroughly. Pour into well-greased and floured 1½-quart mould. Cover tightly with lid or aluminum foil. Steam for 2 hours in tightly covered container. Let stand for 5 minutes before unmoulding. Serve with lemon, brandy or plain hard sauce. *Serves 6 to 8.*

Hard Sauce

⅓ cup butter
1 cup icing, brown or granulated sugar
few grains salt
1 tsp. vanilla extract or other flavouring

Cream butter thoroughly. Sift sugar and gradually add to butter until mixture is very smooth; add salt and flavouring. *Makes ½ cup.*

Variations

- **Brandy or Wine Sauce:** Add 1 tsp. brandy or 1 to 3 Tbsp. sherry.
- **Lemon Sauce:** Add 1 tsp. lemon juice and 1 Tbsp. grated lemon rind.
- **Orange Sauce:** Add 2 Tbsp. orange juice and 2 Tbsp. grated orange rind.
- **Rich Hard Sauce:** Beat in 1 egg or ¼ cup whipping cream.
- **Spicy Hard Sauce:** Add ½ tsp. ground cinnamon, ¼ tsp. ground cloves and ½ tsp. lemon juice.

SHERRY JELLY

1 package (3 oz.) lemon jelly powder
⅔ cup boiling water
juice of 1 orange
juice of 1 lemon
1 cup sherry
sweetened whipped cream (optional)

Dissolve jelly powder in boiling water. Add fruit juices and sherry. Pour into 4 individual moulds and chill until firm. To serve, unmould. Top with whipping cream, if desired. *Serves 4.*

Note: For a special treat, top with sliced fruits in season, such as raspberries, strawberries or peaches.

SHERRY CHOCOLATE SAUCE

½ cup light corn syrup
4 squares semi-sweet chocolate
⅛ tsp. salt
2 Tbsp. butter
¼ cup sherry

Combine corn syrup and chocolate. Heat gently, stirring constantly, until chocolate is melted and mixture is blended. Remove from heat and stir in salt, butter and sherry. Cool to lukewarm. Serve over ice cream or pudding. *Makes approximately 1¼ cups.*

SUNDAE DESSERT IDEAS

To brighten an ice cream dessert, try one of these toppers.

- **Chocolate Chow:** Over low heat, stirring constantly, melt together 1 package (6 oz.) semi-sweet chocolate pieces and ¾ cup whipping cream. When completely melted, add 1 tsp. vanilla and 2 Tbsp. chopped walnuts. Serve warm.
- **Flaming Strawberry Sauce:** Melt ½ cup red currant jelly. Stir in scant 2 cups frozen sliced strawberries, thawed. Heat until mixture comes to a boil. Pour ¼ cup brandy into centre of fruit and heat undisturbed. Light, and serve flaming.
- **Parfait Sauce:** Combine 1 Tbsp. each sugar and cornstarch; add scant 2 cups frozen raspberries, thawed. Cook, stirring constantly, until mixture boils and is thickened and clear. Serve warm.
- **Maple Nut Sauce:** Boil 1 cup maple syrup and 2 Tbsp. butter for 5 minutes. Cool; stir in ¼ cup light cream and 3 Tbsp. slivered almonds.
- **Quick Citrus Sauce:** Combine ¾ cup sugar, 4½ tsp. cornstarch, ½ cup water and ¾ cup frozen lemonade, limeade or orange juice concentrate, thawed. Cook, stirring constantly, until mixture boils and is thickened and clear. Cool.

liquid refreshments
you've always wanted to make

mona says . . .

- To dress up fruit cocktails and drinks, frost the rims of the glasses. Dip them in lightly beaten egg whites, then in extremely fine sugar. Let rims dry before using the glasses.
- To build up a supply of ice cubes for entertaining, freeze water or juice in ice cube trays until hard and very dry. Remove to a heavy-weight, large, plastic bag and store in freezer.
- You can very easily make attractive ice cubes for drinks, or ice rings or blocks for punch bowls. Half-fill an ice cube tray, a 9 x 5 x 3-inch loaf pan or a ring mould with plain or pastel-tinted water. Partially freeze. Add maraschino cherries, citrus slices and pineapple chunks in a decorative design. Freeze to anchor fruit. Fill with ice water and freeze until firm. Float cubes in drinks, and blocks or rings in punch bowl.

The Woodward's bear saves summer with easy recipes.

CAFÉ BRULOT

1/2 cup instant coffee granules
4 cups boiling water
3 sticks cinnamon
1 Tbsp. whole cloves
1/4 to 1/3 cup sugar
1/2 cup brandy
rind from 1 orange and 1 lemon, cut into strips

Dissolve coffee in boiling water. Add cinnamon sticks and cloves; cover and let stand for 15 minutes. Strain and reheat. Meanwhile, combine sugar, brandy and fruit rind in chafing dish. Heat; then flame the brandy mixture. Slowly add coffee. When flame is extinguished, ladle into demitasse cups. *Makes 9 (4-oz.) servings.*

COFFEE CARIOCA

2 oranges, peeled
1/2 cup instant coffee granules
1/4 cup sugar
4 cups boiling water
1/4 cup rum
sweetened whipped cream
grated orange rind, shaved chocolate or ground
  cinnamon, for garnish (optional)

Remove white membrane from oranges, cut into 1/4-inch slices and remove seeds. Place in large heat-proof bowl with coffee and sugar. Stir in boiling water; let stand for 30 minutes. Strain coffee into saucepan. Heat almost to boiling. Remove from heat and stir in rum. Serve in demitasse cups topped with whipped cream. If desired, garnish with grated orange rind, shaved chocolate or cinnamon. *Makes 9 (4-oz.) servings.*

To advertise their Supreme Coffee, Woodward's added coffee essence to newspaper ink and printed advertisements that smelled like coffee.

HOT SPICED WASSAIL

This is a great recipe for holiday open house entertaining.

1 6-inch stick cinnamon, broken into pieces
16 whole cloves
1 tsp. whole allspice
3 medium oranges
whole cloves
6 cups apple juice or cider
2 cups cranberry juice cocktail
1/4 cup sugar
1 tsp. aromatic bitters
1 cup rum, or to taste
fresh orange slices, for garnish

Wrap broken cinnamon pieces, 16 cloves and allspice in piece of cheesecloth. Tie and set aside. Stud oranges with cloves. In large saucepan, combine juice or cider, cranberry cocktail, sugar and aromatic bitters. Add spice bag and oranges; simmer, covered, for 10 minutes. Add rum and heat through. Remove spice bag and oranges. Pour into warm serving bowl and float studded oranges and fresh orange slices on top. *Makes 9 (8-oz.) servings.*

MEXICALI HOT CHOCOLATE

1 quart milk
3 squares semi-sweet chocolate
1 tsp. ground cinnamon
2 eggs
6 sticks cinnamon

In a large saucepan, heat milk just to scalding. Blend in chocolate and cinnamon, stirring until chocolate melts. Beat until smooth. In a small bowl, beat eggs. Slowly beat in about 1 cup of the chocolate mixture, then add warmed eggs to remaining chocolate mixture in pan and beat well. Heat slowly, stirring constantly, for 1 minute. Beat again until frothy. Ladle into heated glasses or mugs. Add a cinnamon stick to each glass for a stirrer. Serve warm. *Makes 6 (6-oz.) servings.*

QUICK EGGNOG PUNCH

1 quart eggnog
2 cups softened vanilla ice cream
2 cups lemon-lime carbonated beverage, chilled
pinch ground cinnamon and/or ground nutmeg
(optional)

Combine eggnog and ice cream in punch bowl. Stir to combine. Slowly add lemon-lime beverage. If desired, sprinkle top lightly with cinnamon and/or nutmeg. *Makes about 16 (4-oz.) servings.*

HAPPY LEMON PUNCH

2 cups strong hot tea
1 1/2 to 2 cups sugar
1/2 cup grenadine
2 cups freshly squeezed lemon juice, chilled
2 cups unsweetened pineapple juice, chilled
lemon and orange slices, for garnish

Combine tea and sugar, stirring until sugar has dissolved. Chill thoroughly. Add grenadine and chilled juices. Pour over block of ice in punch bowl. Garnish with lemon and orange slices. *Makes 14 punch cup servings.*

Variations

- **Sparkling Punch (non-alcoholic):** Add 3 1/2 cups chilled lemon-lime soft drink. Stir gently. *Makes 2 3/4 quarts.*
- **Champagne Punch:** Add one bottle chilled champagne and 1 cup chilled vodka. Stir gently. *Makes 3 quarts.*

SPICED SNOWBALL DRINK

A great favourite with children.

1 cup water
3/4 to 1 cup semi-sweet chocolate chips
1/4 cup sugar
pinch salt
2 cups milk
1 cup light cream
1/4 tsp. ground cinnamon, or to taste
1/8 tsp. ground nutmeg, or to taste
1 tsp. vanilla extract
sweetened whipped cream and chocolate curls, for garnish (optional)

In large heavy saucepan, bring water to boil. Add chocolate, sugar and salt; stir constantly, just until chocolate has melted and mixture is smooth. Add milk, cream, cinnamon and nutmeg. Stir constantly and bring just to a boil. Remove from heat. Add vanilla. Just before serving, beat until foamy. Serve warm. Top with whipped cream "snowball" and garnish with chocolate curls, if desired. *Makes 6 (5-oz.) servings.*

CRANBERRY FIZZ

1 can (14 oz.) jellied cranberry sauce
1/4 cup lemon juice
3/4 cup orange juice
ice cubes
3 1/2 cups well-chilled ginger ale
orange slices and maraschino cherries, for garnish

In large bowl, beat cranberry sauce until smooth; stir in juices. Place ice cubes in 2-quart punch bowl or juice pitcher. Pour cranberry mixture over ice cubes. Carefully pour ginger ale down side of bowl or pitcher; mix with up and down motion. Float orange slices and maraschino cherries on top. *Serves 12 to 15.*

FRUIT PUNCH WREATH

FOR THE WREATH:

3 cups water
1 medium orange
1 lemon
1 cup water

Pour 3 cups water into $5\frac{1}{2}$- to 6-cup ring mould. Freeze for approximately 1 hour or until top is solid. Slice orange and lemon. Remove seeds and cut slices in half. Arrange in attractive petal fashion on ice ring. Pour 1 cup water over fruits and freeze until solid.

FOR THE FRUIT PUNCH:

6 cups red fruit punch (Hawaiian tropical punch, etc.)
$1\frac{1}{2}$ cups frozen orange juice concentrate, just thawed
2 to $2\frac{1}{4}$ cups water
maraschino cherries with stems, for garnish (optional)

Pour fruit punch, orange juice concentrate and water into punch bowl. Stir to combine thoroughly.

Unmould ice wreath by placing quickly in a dish of warm water—just long enough to loosen. Add ice mould to punch, fruit side up. Garnish with maraschino cherries, if desired. *Makes about 18 (4-oz.) servings.*

Variation: 1 to 2 cups of vodka can be added to punch, if desired.

MELON PUNCH BOWL

Try this idea for a stunning "punch bowl" at your next patio party. Select a large watermelon; stand it on end and cut a very thin slice off the bottom to make it stand upright easily and securely. Cut top third off watermelon. Use a cup as a guide to trace scallops around top outside edge of melon. Carve scalloped edge, following pattern. (Or use a saw-tooth pattern rather than scallop pattern.) Scoop out fruit for later use. Chill melon "punch bowl."

DOUBLE STRAWBERRY SODA

2 scoops strawberry ice cream
2 tsp. strawberry jam
lemon-lime carbonated beverage, as needed

Place ice cream in bottom of large glass. Drizzle strawberry jam over top. Fill to top of glass with lemon-lime carbonated beverage; stir well with long spoon. *Serves 1.*

MINTY CHOCOLATE SODA

$\frac{2}{3}$ cup milk
1 Tbsp. chocolate syrup
dash peppermint extract
2 scoops vanilla ice cream
ginger ale or lemon-lime carbonated beverage,
    as needed
whipped cream
chocolate syrup

Combine milk, chocolate syrup and peppermint extract in tall glass; stir well. Add ice cream. Fill to top of glass with ginger ale or lemon-lime carbonated beverage; stir well. Top with swirl of whipped cream and a drizzle of chocolate syrup.

BERRY MILK

2 cups fresh strawberries or raspberries, or sliced
    fresh fruit of your choice
$\frac{1}{4}$ cup sugar
$1\frac{1}{2}$ cups milk

Combine all ingredients in blender; blend for 30 seconds. *Serves 2.*

Variation: Add 2 cups vanilla ice cream.

sandwiches for all occasions

mona says . . .

- When making a quantity of sandwiches, always prepare the filling first. Refrigerate prepared fillings until you have sliced the bread for spreading. The only exceptions are processed cheese, butter and margarine, which should all be at room temperature or well creamed.
- Use edible garnishes: they not only look attractive but also taste delicious. Here are some ideas.
  - Cucumber Twists: Wash cucumber but do not peel it; slice thinly. Make a cut from edge to centre of each slice and twist into a bow shape. For added appeal, sprinkle with paprika and/or chopped fresh parsley.
  - Pickle Fans: Choose small to medium cucumber pickles. Make several thin lengthwise cuts from top to approximately 1/4 inch from bottom. Spread slices to form a fan.
  - Tomato Twists: Prepare as for cucumber twists.
  - Carrot Curls: Peel carrot; cut long thin shavings with vegetable peeler. Roll up, fasten with tooth picks and chill in ice water. Drain; remove toothpicks.

- To keep party sandwiches fresh and moist until serving time, arrange them in a shallow pan lined with damp paper towels, then cover with a clean towel or plastic wrap and refrigerate.

Freezing Sandwiches

- Spread a thin layer of butter or margarine on both slices of bread, covering from crust to crust. Do not use mayonnaise, salad dressing or jelly as a spread: they make the sandwiches soggy.
- Moisten filling with as little mayonnaise as possible. Sandwich binders that freeze well are fruit juices, such as lemon, orange or pineapple; applesauce; and sour cream. Cheddar cheese, cream cheese, sliced and ground meats, canned tuna, salmon, cooked egg yolks (do not use egg whites; they toughen when frozen) and peanut butter are suitable fillings.
- Do not use salad greens, green pepper or carrots; they lose their crispness when frozen.
- Wrap each sandwich individually in freezer paper, aluminum foil or plastic wrap.
- Frozen sandwiches thaw in three hours.

MONTE CRISTO AU GRATIN SANDWICHES

6 slices bread, lightly buttered on one side

9 slices turkey or ham, or a combination of both

1 large tomato, cut into 6 slices

salt and pepper to taste

3 Tbsp. chopped green onions

3 eggs, slightly beaten

3 Tbsp. water

2 Tbsp. salad oil (or as needed)

1 1/2 cups shredded Swiss cheese

1/2 cup milk

1/2 cup mayonnaise

1/8 tsp. garlic salt

1/8 tsp. dry mustard

1/8 tsp. ground nutmeg

Lay out bread slices. For each sandwich use 3 slices of meat, 2 slices tomato seasoned with salt and pepper and 1 Tbsp. chopped green onion. Beat eggs with water. Dip sandwiches in egg mixture (skewer with toothpicks for handling ease, if desired). Fry both sides in oil until golden. Place in baking dish. Mix cheese, milk, mayonnaise, garlic salt, mustard and nutmeg in saucepan. Heat, stirring constantly, until mixture thickens and cheese melts. Pour over sandwiches and broil 6 inches from heat for 3 to 5 minutes, until bubbly. A delicious way to use up leftover turkey or ham. *Makes 3 hearty sandwiches.*

CHICKEN DINNER SANDWICHES

1 lb. chicken breasts

4 slices bacon

2 English muffins, split, toasted and buttered

1 medium onion, cut into 4 thin slices

1 large tomato, cut into 4 thick slices

1/2 cup shredded Cheddar cheese

Simmer chicken in small amount of boiling salted water until meat is no longer pink in centre, about 15 minutes. Discard skin and bones; slice meat. Meanwhile, cut bacon slices in half crosswise and partially fry to remove most of the fat; bacon should still be limp. Set aside. Distribute chicken evenly over 4 toasted muffin halves; top each with 1 onion slice and 1 tomato slice. Distribute cheese evenly over each and top each with 2 pieces of bacon. Broil about 4 inches from heat until cheese is bubbly and bacon is crisp, about 3 to 5 minutes.

Serve with a fresh raw vegetable salad tray, such as carrot, celery, and red or green pepper strips, and condiments, such as pickles and olives. *Serves 2 (2 open sandwiches each) or 4 (savouries).*

GRILLED CRAB SANDWICHES

1 can (7 1/2 oz.) crabmeat, well drained and flaked

1 tsp. lemon juice

1/2 cup shredded sharp cheese

1/4 cup chopped celery

2 Tbsp. drained sweet-pickle relish

2 Tbsp. chopped green onions

1 hard-cooked egg, chopped

approximately 3 Tbsp. salad dressing or mayonnaise
   (to desired consistency)

1/2 tsp. prepared horseradish

10 slices bread, buttered generously on one side

5 tomato slices

salt and pepper to taste

Place crabmeat in bowl and sprinkle with lemon juice. Add cheese, celery, relish, green onions and egg. Stir in mayonnaise and horseradish. Spread mixture on unbuttered sides of 5 slices of bread. Top with tomato slices; season with salt and pepper. Top each with bread slice, buttered side up. Cook in griddle, sandwich grill or skillet until sandwiches are golden brown and filling is piping hot. To serve, cut sandwiches in half. *Makes 5 sandwiches.*

TURKEY DAGWOOD SANDWICHES

8 slices rye bread, buttered on one side

1 cup shredded lettuce

4 large slices cooked turkey (or several smaller slices)

salt and pepper to taste

12 slices crisp-cooked, drained bacon

1 avocado, peeled, pitted and cut into 8 wedges

$1/4$ cup mayonnaise

$1/4$ cup sour cream

$1/3$ cup crumbled blue cheese

1 large tomato, cut into 8 wedges

2 hard-cooked eggs, quartered

finely chopped green onions, for garnish

Cut 4 slices of bread in half. For each sandwich, arrange 1 whole slice bread with $1/2$ slice on either side. Cover bread with shredded lettuce; top with turkey. Season with salt and pepper. Top each with 3 slices bacon and 2 avocado wedges. In bowl, combine mayonnaise, sour cream and blue cheese. Drizzle mixture over sandwiches. Top each with 2 tomato wedges and 2 hard-cooked egg quarters. Garnish with finely chopped green onions. Serve with knife and fork. *Makes 4 hearty open-faced sandwiches.*

FANCY SANDWICH VARIATIONS

• Pinwheels: Cut off all crusts, except bottom, from unsliced loaf of white bread. (Retaining bottom crust makes cutting easier.) Turn loaf on its side; cut lengthwise into slices about $1/2$ inch thick To keep bread slices from cracking as they are rolled, flatten first with a rolling pin. Work with only a few slices at a time to keep them from drying out. Spread fillings of choice to bread edges. (If filling is spread to the edge of the bread, it's less likely to dry out—an old Danish trick.) Across one narrow end, place 2 or 3 stuffed olives, or 1 slivered dill pickle or 2 small gherkins, or 2 Vienna sausages, if desired. Starting at that end, roll bread tightly but carefully in jelly-roll fashion. Wrap rolls separately and refrigerate. To serve, cut rolls into $1/2$-inch slices. If desired, broil slices to serve hot.

• Ribbon Sandwiches: Cut and trim bread as for pinwheels. Use 5 bread slices for each stack; fill with variety of any easily spread filling and press gently but firmly together. Dark and light slices of bread can be alternated but they must be the same size. Wrap and refrigerate until filling is firm. To serve, cut each stack into bars or squares.

ZIPPY SARDINE SANDWICHES

8 slices white bread

tartar sauce

1 medium cucumber, scored and thinly sliced

2 cans (4 oz. each) tiny sardines in oil, drained

$1/4$ cup sour cream

2 Tbsp. ketchup

Spread bread with tartar sauce. On 4 slices, arrange a layer of cucumber, double layer of sardines and another layer of cucumbers. Blend sour cream and ketchup together. Spread a generous tablespoonful over filling for each sandwich. Cover with remaining bread slices. *Makes 4 sandwiches.*

CORNED BEEF ON PUMPERNICKEL

2 cups coleslaw

2 tsp. caraway seeds

$1 1/2$ cups canned corned beef, chilled

2 small tomatoes

12 slices light pumpernickel, buttered on one side

Drain coleslaw well. Blend with caraway seeds in small bowl. Cut corned beef into 12 slices. Cut each tomato into 6 thin slices. For each sandwich, layer corned beef, tomato slices and coleslaw; top with remaining bread. Cut each sandwich diagonally in half. *Makes 6 sandwiches.*

CREAM CHEESE VARIATIONS

Divide 1 package (8 oz.) cream cheese into thirds. To one third, add 3 or 4 small gherkins, finely chopped. To second third, add 2 ripe olives, chopped and 1 Tbsp. chopped pimiento. To remaining third, add 2 Tbsp. grated carrot and 1 Tbsp. chopped walnuts.

HAM-CELERY TRIANGLES

2 cups finely diced cooked ham
1/2 cup finely diced celery
1 tsp. grated onion
1/3 cup mayonnaise or salad dressing
1 tsp. prepared mustard
12 thin slices white bread (buttered, if desired)

Mix together ham, celery, onion, mayonnaise or salad dressing and mustard. Spread 6 slices of bread with mixture. Top with remaining 6 slices. Cut each sandwich diagonally into quarters. *Makes 6 sandwiches.*

BREAD SPREADS

These hefty sandwich fillings are great for variety in the lunch box or midnight snacks.

CHEESE-PIMIENTO-OLIVE FILLING
2 cups coarsely shredded sharp Cheddar cheese
1/2 cup mayonnaise
1 Tbsp. minced onion
1 tsp. Worcestershire sauce
3 Tbsp. chopped pimiento
1/2 cup chopped black olives

Allow shredded cheese to stand at room temperature for 20 minutes; add mayonnaise and beat until smooth. Mix in remaining ingredients. Will keep for 2 weeks in covered container in refrigerator. *Makes approximately 2 cups.*

SPICY CORNED BEEF FILLING

1 1/2 cups canned corned beef
1/4 cup sweet-pickle relish
3/4 cup chopped celery
1 Tbsp. chopped fresh parsley
1 tsp. onion powder
1/8 tsp. garlic salt
pepper to taste
1/3 cup mayonnaise

Place corned beef in medium bowl and break up with fork. Add remaining ingredients and mix well. Store, covered, in refrigerator for up to 1 week. *Makes approximately 2 1/2 cups.*

The mascot bear as a jaunty sailor.

SAVOURY HAM FILLING

1 can (7$\frac{1}{2}$ oz.) tomato sauce
$\frac{1}{3}$ cup devilled ham
1 package (8 oz.) cream cheese
$\frac{1}{4}$ cup finely chopped celery
1 Tbsp. chopped fresh parsley
$\frac{1}{4}$ cup chopped pimiento-stuffed olives
pepper to taste

Mix all ingredients together. Store, covered, in refrigerator for up to 5 or 6 days. *Makes approximately 2 cups.*

SALMON SALAD FILLING

2 cans (7$\frac{1}{2}$ oz. each) salmon, drained and flaked
2 tsp. lemon juice
$\frac{1}{2}$ cup mayonnaise
1 tsp. prepared mustard
$\frac{1}{4}$ tsp. dill weed
$\frac{1}{8}$ tsp. ground nutmeg
$\frac{1}{2}$ cup finely chopped celery
2 hard-cooked eggs, peeled and chopped
freshly ground black pepper to taste

In medium bowl, combine all ingredients and blend well. Cover. Chill thoroughly. *Makes 2$\frac{1}{2}$ cups (enough filling for 10 to 12 sandwiches).*

BLENDER MUSHROOM BUTTER

$\frac{1}{2}$ lb. fresh mushrooms
1 Tbsp. finely chopped onion
$\frac{1}{4}$ cup butter
$\frac{1}{2}$ cup softened butter
$\frac{1}{4}$ tsp. salt, or to taste
pinch black pepper
3 Tbsp. dry sherry or brandy

Wash mushrooms; dry thoroughly. Slice. Sauté mushrooms and onion in $\frac{1}{4}$ cup butter over low heat, until just golden (do not overcook). Remove from heat; allow to cool. Place mixture in blender; add $\frac{1}{2}$ cup softened butter, salt, pepper and sherry or brandy. Blend until smooth. Refrigerate in a covered container. Before using, allow to soften to easy spreading consistency. Use in making canapés and fancy sandwiches. *Makes 1$\frac{1}{2}$ cups.*

index

mona says . . .